THE HUMANIST COMEDY

Also by Alexander Welsh

The Hero of the Waverley Novels
The City of Dickens
Reflections on the Hero as Quixote
George Eliot and Blackmail
From Copyright to Copperfield
Strong Representations
Freud's Wishful Dream Book
Hamlet in His Modern Guises
Dickens Redressed
What Is Honor?

Alexander Welsh

The Humanist Comedy

Yale UNIVERSITY PRESS

NEW HAVEN AND LONDON

Published with assistance from the foundation established in memory of Henry Weldon Barnes of the Class of 1882, Yale College.

Yale University Press books may be purchased in quantity for educational, business, or promotional use. For information, please e-mail sales.press@yale.edu (U.S. office) or sales@yaleup.co.uk (U.K. office).

Set in Scala type by IDS Infotech Ltd., Chandigarh, India.
Printed in the United States of America.

Library of Congress Cataloging-in-Publication Data

Welsh, Alexander.
  The humanist comedy / Alexander Welsh.
    pages cm
  Includes bibliographical references and index.
  ISBN 978-0-300-19751-8 (pbk.)
  1. Humor in literature. 2. Literature—History and criticism—Theory, etc. 3. Humanism in literature. I. Title.
  PN56.H83W45 2014
  808.87—dc23

                                                                  2013035993

A catalogue record for this book is available from the British Library.

This paper meets the requirements of ANSI/NISO Z39.48–1992 (Permanence of Paper).

10 9 8 7 6 5 4 3 2 1

Years ago, bent upon the kingdom of heaven, I parted from home, from parents, a sister, relations, and—what was more difficult—sumptuous meals. Yet making my way toward Jerusalem like a soldier, I could not leave behind the library I had put together with so much devotion and hard work in Rome. And so, miserable me, I would fast—and read Cicero. After many nights at vigil, after heartrending tears brought on by memory of past sins—I would read Plautus.

—*St. Jerome, Epistulae*

SCENES FROM THE COMEDY

Prologue   1

ACT ONE: Laughter at the Gods in Classical Times   9
   1. Old Comedy in Aristophanes' Hands   16
   2. Lucretius on the Unholy Nature of Things   32
   3. Laughter Overheard by Cicero   41
   4. Lucian Laughing Outright   55

ACT TWO: Humanist Games in Christian Times   65
   1. Erasmus's Praise of Folly   70
   2. Montaigne's *Que sais-je?*   88
   3. Hobbes's Braving of the Dark   98
   4. Spinoza's Deification of the Whole Lot   108
   5. Bayle's Send-up of a Comet   123
   6. Hume's Jesting with Natural Religion   139
   7. Whose *Aberglaube?*   155

ACT THREE: Laughter at the Passing Generations   169
   1. New Comedy in the Hands of Plautus and Shakespeare   177
   2. Unfailing Impersonations by Molière   200
   3. Adaptation of the Tragicomedy by Novelists   216
   4. Jesus vs. God in Saramago's Novel   230

Notes   249
Index   261

THE HUMANIST COMEDY

PROLOGUE

This book addresses neither the *Divine Comedy* nor the *Human Comedy* but something in between hereby nominated the Humanist Comedy. Its authors were not Dante or Balzac but formidable construers of Western thought and literature in their own right, and they could raise a laugh when they needed to. A few were professional entertainers, the others just eager to put down nonsense of any kind. All took advantage of comedy's give-and-take and good humor to create, and then to occupy, a contested space between the human and the divine. Their opponents cried sacrilege because the humanists were making away with the religious grounds of their faith—or likely threatening their social standing, political niche, or means of making a living. The humanists of the modern era typically immersed themselves in classical learning, both because they were astounded by the rediscovered writings of the ancient Greeks and Romans and because classical culture proved there could be alternatives to the Judeo-Christian tradition and its sacred texts. Humanists called themselves so because they rejoiced in human talents, most particularly the use of reason; but in advancing philosophy and science they had to contend against received ideas, many of which had become religious dogma. That is why eventually, by the twentieth century, in some quarters Humanism had become a polite name for atheism. How close early modern humanism with a small *h* came to atheism is a valid question, but not one to be decided here. All the humanist comedy required was room for play between human capabilities and divine powers.

In his short but capacious book *Homo Ludens,* Johan Huizinga argued that game playing goes all the way back to prehistoric times. Even animals can be seen to engage in play, and customarily youngsters put in more time at it than grownups do. Play contributes importantly to learning both mechanical and social skills. Sporting contests teach competition but also the setting forth of rules. The lively experimentation that play and make-believe afford can lead to knowledge. Huizinga charted the play element at work behind warfare and law making, the recourse to make-believe not only in myth and poetry but in philosophy and art. He understood the advance of civilization as tending to dampen and restrict the play element, but that has not usually been the case. In so-called wisdom literature of ancient times, for that matter, foolishness regularly appeared to conspire with wisdom.

The *ludi,* or games, featured in the present book enabled resistance to the religious beliefs of the surrounding civilization. The players counted on the freedom generally ceded to comedy—and to clowning, which seems to go even farther back in time—in order to make leeway for skeptical or contrarian thinking. A play of ideas is constructive and inviting. People do find it easier to negotiate serious differences with a smile. Behind the grimacing, humanist comedians prayed in their hearts for tolerance; and in minds where humanism caught on it tended to increase religious tolerance. The comedy reckoned with here is by no means confined to the *commedia erudita* of quattrocento Italy, written in Latin primarily for reading, and sometimes referred to as humanist comedy. Rather, the present comedy has been multifaceted, in effect a collaborative product of differing talented minds over a couple of millennia of historical time. Dante, after all, was not the one who characterized his *Commedia* as divine. In truth his poem of one hundred cantos was enormously popular; a generation or two after his death its interpretation became the object of learned discourse that continues to this day; and "Divine" has come to be understood as a compliment to the poet as well as designation of the subject matter. Balzac did not initially set out to compose anything like his *Comédie humaine;* that was the collective name he gave to the revision and rearrangement of his vast production of prose fiction. The humanist comedy to be surveyed here was the work of many hands, ancient and modern. Moreover, certain of the scripts rehearsed in the present book are generally considered to be downright philosophical, not comical. The idea is to appreciate their authors' contentions, disputes, and misgivings as comedy for a change. Laughter can offend, but it also breaks the tension, affords relief when people are genuinely uncertain. The scenes from this comedy presented here are selective but arranged in chronological order, except that in the last act the story begins over again in classical times with New Comedy.

In act one, two Old Comedies by Aristophanes and a couple of dialogues by his admirer Lucian five centuries later frame major philosophical and didactic works by Lucretius and Cicero. The word *humanist* is not usually applied to classical texts as such, yet not a few Greek and Roman classics deserve to be thought of as humanist because they celebrate, if only in sport, one or more human causes against the divine. Think of Homer's *Odyssey*, even, as the singular triumph of one man against all the odds, a number of the gods, and one or two semidivine creatures content to make love with him for eternity. And what else did *humanism* stand for in the Renaissance if not to distinguish human capacities from divine? The players in act two of our comedy learned more from Cicero and Lucretius than from Old Comedy or the delightful dialogues of Lucian, but that did not stop Erasmus or his friend Sir Thomas More from translating some of the dialogues from Lucian's Greek into the far more accessible Latin of their own time.

The players of act two flourished—if that's the word when lives and careers were sometimes at risk—in Renaissance and Reformation times, in the Enlightenment and post-Enlightenment. They are represented here by Desiderius Erasmus, Michel de Montaigne, Thomas Hobbes, Baruch Spinoza, Pierre Bayle, David Hume, and Matthew Arnold. Historians in any number of fields would agree that these were humanists, often recognized as such in their time. But were they humorists? Surely Erasmus writing in Latin and Hume in English designed to entertain as well as to instruct, and Arnold could scarcely restrain himself from satirizing contemporary Barbarians and Philistines—his words for the aristocracy and bourgeoisie. The others here perform more soberly on the whole but also get carried away by the pleasures of argument. They too indulge in satire and reductio ad absurdum, and who doesn't enjoy such sport? Sometimes even those who are made fools of enjoy it, or pretend to. At other times the tentativeness of an amusing debater wins an opponent over, since the speaker need not mean to offend. Montaigne and Bayle, Hobbes and Spinoza certainly entertain readers attuned to their high spirits. Their reputations as philosophers or expositors of religion have varied over time and according to opinion, but they also deserve to be appreciated as humanist comedians.

There is a second comedic theme to rehearse here. Humanists frequently conjectured that the lowly purpose of imagining gods above was to fill the heavens with beings who went right on living instead of dying a natural death. In both classical and Christian sects religion was closely linked to belief in life after death. As Harold Bloom quips in *The American Religion*, "Clearly we possess religion, if we want to, precisely to obscure the truth of our perishing." This subtext of many religious propositions is all too human and traceable to the nagging consciousness of mortality. People do not quite like to admit this, unless with a smile. Thus ancient Greeks referred to the gods collectively as the immortals, and outstanding mortals of both genders were sometimes thought to become gods hereafter. One way or another, especially with the rise of Christianity, believers invested in *both* divinity and personal immortality. Our humanist comedians chiefly, though not exclusively, fenced with concepts of divinity, since many took for granted their own and others' lives coming to an end.

How should mortality, the finitude of each privileged member of the species *Homo sapiens*, be a subject for comedy? Well, it rapidly did become such. By the end of Aristophanes' lifetime, a style—or better, the plot—of New Comedy was overtaking that of Old Comedy in Attica; and subsequently New Comedy flourished in Roman theater, still later in modern theater and the rise of the novel. Most of the surviving ancient texts, indeed, are translations or imitations of the original by the Roman playwrights Terence and Plautus. Both the characters and actions of New Comedy have more of a sameness than the several plays of Aristophanes alone. They present young lovers who are typically opposed by one or more elders, assisted by clever slaves owned by the parent, and happily or grudgingly given in marriage by the end. Cowardly braggarts, pimps, and parasites are common butts of this comedy; but almost always the *senex*, or old fellow, takes a fall and changes his mind. Thus the happy marriage plot anticipates the passing of that older generation. The actions and dialogue make light of deaths on their way; the promise of marriage and future generations distracts from individual mortality. Just as in a humanist comedy laughter serves to bridge, explore, and ease the tensions between belief and unbelief in the deity, so in New Comedy—familiar, predictable, comedy for stage or page—laughter renders tolerable the losses involved.

The love plot of New Comedy implicitly conceded the passing of at least two generations, the younger as well as the older. For the young couple in love look forward to living together and having children to care for, children who will survive them in turn. Birth, copulation, and death are in truth the crude facts behind a marriage plot, something that the sequence of Shakespeare's extraordinary comedies wittily drove home. The inventors of New Comedy also played fast and loose with individual identities by means of fanciful disguise and impersonation, as if to enlarge on the possibilities of a single lifetime. This tradition flourished in commedia dell'arte and seventeenth-century comedy on the Continent as well as in London theater. Because of the years it takes humans to grow up, come of age, and become responsible (or irresponsible) parents of children to follow, some changes of identity or role playing are inevitable in real life. The theme at the heart of New Comedy is the passing of generations. Eventually novelists in both Europe and the Americas took up the story, with happy endings for the younger principals, inevitable passing on for the oldsters, tragicomedy for all concerned.

Act three of the present show, featuring Plautus and Shakespeare, Machiavelli and Molière, and key novelists such as Scott, Hugo, and Dickens, puts belief in divinity aside for an overview of this so-called New Comedy—perennial New Comedy, almost as old as Old Comedy in classical times and destined to continue after the rise of the novel as well as in modern theater and film. What this comedy and the humanist comedy have in common is their essentially secular outlook on the world and experience of humanity. Thereby this act concludes with a postmodern novel by José Saramago, *The Gospel According to Jesus Christ*, that is at once tragicomic and another humanist workout. As Huizinga argued, make-believe and play help us to understand ourselves, to learn, and to cope, and that certainly applies to Saramago's achievement.

On most of the authors represented in this book there exists a huge critical and historical secondary literature. It would take another lifetime to assimilate all that has been written about any one of them, and I doubt if enough lifetimes are coming my way to finish that job satisfactorily. The sparse endnotes therefore serve to identify the translations or editions quoted and the references in parentheses, to record my conscious indebtedness to others, and occasionally to recommend secondary reading that strikes me as particularly compelling. The argument for positive uses of impersonation comes from my article "State-of-the-Art Impersonations for Comedy and Everyday," *Social Research* 75 (2008), and I am grateful to the editor, Arien Mack, for permission to include that here. Anyone contemplating the reflection of classical texts in the mirror of later times is indebted to the Loeb Classical Library and especially to the updating of that collection under the general editorship of Jeffrey Henderson.

Needless to say, for a book with the scope of this one it is impossible to count the number of editors and colleagues, teachers and students who have contributed over the years to the author's understanding in one way or another. One result of a long career in university life is the privilege of being first the younger and then the older contemporary of very many productive scholars. I have to thank the National Humanities Center for a Josephus Daniels Fellowship that provided the chance to engage in daily conversation among forty scholars from several generations and many specialties, while reading comedies and theories of the same by the book: a very enjoyable experience with not a few laughs. Nearer at hand, I am especially grateful to Ruth Bernard Yeazell and David Quint for reading and criticizing the first draft of the present comedy; also to Douglas Cairns over in Edinburgh, for signaling a tentative go-ahead for act one. I wish to thank the two anonymous readers for Yale University Press for their positive endorsement of my second draft and additional suggestions. Eric Brandt and Susan Laity kindly managed the acquisition and subsequent go-round at the press; Lawrence Kenney skillfully performed the copyediting.

One does not study and restudy the art, literature, philosophy, or religious writings of earlier times merely in order to grasp what happened in the past, or the so-called facts of history. Those written and other remains unfold a history of human desires, desire in the sense of appetite and sexual drive to be sure, but also of seeking to understand right and wrong, belief and unbelief. The history of human expectations and misgivings, meditation and entertainments, informs our present-day understanding of thinking and behavior both local and global. We are extraordinarily lucky to have recovered an acquaintance with ancient Greek and Roman story in addition to the dominant Abrahamic faiths of our medieval and modern forebears. How else would what I am christening the Humanist Comedy ever have gotten under way were it not for bemused laughter at the gods resounding from long ago? On with the show.

ACT ONE

Laughter at the Gods in Classical Times

The gods, the givers of good things, stand there in the forecourt,
And among the blessed immortals uncontrollable laughter
Went up as they saw the handiwork of subtle Hephaistos.
—Demodokos, in Homer's *Odyssey,* trans. Richmond Lattimore

First Slave. Say, do you really believe in the gods?
Second Slave. Sure.
First Slave. What's your evidence?
Second Slave. Because I'm godforsaken. Isn't that enough?
—Aristophanes, *Knights,* trans. Jeffrey Henderson

In a famous story, the laughter *of* the gods resounds in the *Odyssey*. The blind minstrel Demodocus, a stand-in for Homer himself we may be sure, chooses to sing of the affair of Ares and Aphrodite. The two gods are brazenly taking their pleasure together in her crippled husband's marriage bed, but Hephaestus has only pretended to be away. He has exercised his divine powers to create an unbreakable net of steel with which to ensnare the lovers in the very act of adulterous betrayal. He risks exposing his own cuckolding but cannot stop himself now. This is a vengeful practical joke, which purposes to expose the lovers and to demonstrate the power of craftsmanship over the warlike powers of his rival. Hephaestus's angry triumph attracts other gods to the scene. The goddesses modestly hold back, but no doubt enjoy the joke in their own way. Hermes and Apollo bemusedly exchange asides confessing envy of Ares locked together with Aphrodite in this way, and the laughter of the male gods continues. In the words of Stephen Halliwell, for most ancient Greeks "a deity incapable of laughter was the exception not the rule."[1] There is evidence even in the *Iliad* that the Olympian gods were capable of laughing, but this instance in book 8 of the *Odyssey* is the best known and pretty well demonstrates that Homer's audience could join in the laughter. After all, Demodocus the singer of tales has been asked to entertain the Phaeacians and their guest, the homeward bound Odysseus, and this is what he comes up with. Homer goes about entertaining wider audiences with the story and most likely wrote down the verses for still others to read. And with which gods in the story do human listeners and readers identify, if not the laughers?

The gods of the ancient Greeks readily lend themselves to easy exchanges and close identifications with humankind. Except in an underworld or when rapidly traveling through the air, they operate on the same plane as human beings. Their manifestations in Homeric epic tend to be theatrical. In this very episode, as so often in the *Odyssey*, Athena is present disguised as a man, assisting her favorite, Odysseus, and looking out for his chances. She *is* the Phaeacian who marks the winning distance of the hero's discus throw, and she enhances his physical appearance as needed, here and elsewhere. It is understandable that Odysseus and others frequently compare humans to gods. He compliments a rival Phaeacian athlete's physique as that of a god, for example, but then calls the man stupid to his face. Such comparisons arise naturally because the

Olympians are so obviously anthropomorphic. Some will insist that all gods are anthropomorphic in one degree or other, but, characteristically, in Homer they are simply "the immortals." Unlike us they never die; and they often travel about the world with magical speed and power. Yet in most respects they behave just like humans. Note that *immortals* defines their being entirely with respect to mortals. They disguise themselves as mortals and often have children by mortals; and occasionally in Greek story a human of either sex will become a god. In truth Homer's gods never seem to know any more about themselves than Homer knows. It can hardly be surprising that mortals sometimes laugh at as well as with the gods.

The god Hermes has rich associations with comedy, and rites would be devoted to him in Athens as the god of commerce, no less. This easy mingling of human and divine business manifests itself early in one of the finer so-called Homeric hymns. The authors of the hymns are unknown, but the hymn to Hermes tells of the god's childhood. His mother was the nymph Maia, who is frequently visited by Zeus in the cave where she lives while Hera is asleep in heaven, "and neither immortal gods nor mortal humans knew." The immortal child of this affair is certainly precocious. On the day he is born he sneaks out of the cave, spots a tortoise, and fashions a lyre out of its shell; rustles fifty of Apollo's cattle and herds them backward so that their hoofprints will confuse anyone attempting to track them; invents the use of fire-sticks for kindling a fire and roasts a couple of heifers; and slips back into the cave before dawn the next day. Maia scolds her child, though resignedly and therefore not very seriously. He not only comes right back at her but lays out his life plans. Here is Michael Crudden's translation of what Hermes has to say to his mother:

> I shall enter whatever craft is best, so keeping us both
> In clover for ever: the two of us will not endure
> Staying here in this place, the only immortals deprived of gifts
> And prayers, as you are bidding. Better that all one's days
> Be spent conversing among the immortals with riches, wealth,
> And plenty of booty, than sitting at home in a murky cave.
> As for honour, I too shall enter that rite which Apollo enjoys.
> If my father will not allow me, then I shall try—it is in
> My power—to be the leader of thieves. (9, 166–76)[2]

The second day in the life of this ambitious youth is already under way, and the story in the hymn occupies only two days. Apollo swiftly catches up with the thief, and they speak at one another in the Homeric manner of dialogue; indeed, the full-grown god and the infant pretty well come to an understanding as they climb to Olympus to put the case before Zeus himself. "Loud was the laughter of Zeus when he saw the roguish child / Denying about the cattle in fine and skilful speech" (389–90), but he rules that the cattle must be returned. Apollo and Hermes start off together for this purpose, and on the way Hermes demonstrates the use of the tortoise-shell lyre and sings of the birth of the gods. Apollo is so charmed that he exclaims such a lyre might be worth fifty heifers. The two are in fact reconciled and exchange gifts as the hymn comes to a close: "In this way the lord Apollo showed love for Maia's son / With friendship of every sort, and the son of Kronos bestowed / Favour upon him besides. With all mortals and immortals both / He [Hermes] has dealings; seldom though does he help, but unceasingly cheats / Throughout the gloomy night the tribes of mortal men" (574–78).

"Mortals and immortals both" can serve as a refrain of the hymn to Hermes. Though neither gods nor humans witness his conceiving, both will be taken in by the trickster. "A vast vexation for mortal men and immortal gods" (161), his mother predicts when the infant is only two days old; and already Apollo testifies before Zeus that "never have I, at least, seen any who'd be his match, / Of gods or those men who swindle mortals over the earth" (339–40). As it happens, there is only one human actor in this story as told in the hymn. While walking backward in craftily designed sandals and herding backward the cattle of Apollo, Hermes is seen by "an old man who toiled at a vineyard where flowers bloomed" (87), and the baby god warns the old man not to tell of what he has seen or heard, if he knows what's good for him. Apollo encounters the same man even as he commences his search for the cattle and hears him say, "I cannot swear to it, sir, / But I thought that I saw a child, and this child, whoever he was, / Was following fine-horned heifers, although a mere infant babe" (208–10). This seems a very small part to play, but the sole witness to the theft is mortal. He tells of what he has seen despite Hermes' warning and bestows an element of reality on these goings-on. At the same time, the old man needn't have been there at all because in the next moment Apollo, famously adept at augury, "was watching a long-winged bird, / And suddenly knew that the thief was the son of Kronos' son Zeus" (214–15). So the author of the hymn wanted, it seems, to have at least one human eyewitness; and Apollo himself, despite his powers of divination, continues to employ human detective means in following the thief's tracks—"a mighty marvel is this that I see with my eyes!" (219). When he subsequently enters Maia's cave, he checks out the storerooms full of her possessions in order to be sure with whom he is dealing, as if this were the home of a ruler like Menelaus in the *Odyssey* rather than the cave of a mountain nymph.

The most human thing about the hymn's version of events is the amusement of the gods, their readiness to take young Hermes' behavior as a joke, trusting to signs that he means to entertain as well as get his own way. The egregiousness of his avowals—"Father Zeus, to you of course I'll tell the truth, / For I am honest, and don't know how to tell a lie" (368–69)—sets them laughing. Gods are supposed to be immortal, but in this yarn their age difference counts. One-day-olds do not ordinarily make their own musical instruments and carry out elaborate schemes to steal their families' cattle, but should an infant gesture toward something valuable, the appreciative smiles of the big gods will very likely motivate the youngster's repeating of the gesture. The expectations narrated in the *Hymn to Hermes* are comedic, not serious. Moral behavior, it would seem, weighs heavily even on gods, so it is a relief to make light of it. And they do make light of it. As soon as Apollo catches up with Hermes and accuses him of stealing the cattle, Hermes protests how that could be: "I was born / Just yesterday. . . . Yet by my father's head I'll swear, if you wish, a great oath: / I neither declare myself to be guilty, nor have I seen / Anyone else who stole your cattle, whatever it is / These 'cattle' may be" (272–77). It need not take a god as smart as Apollo to realize that Hermes hasn't sworn a thing, nor has he strictly told a lie with these words; besides, there is a "gleam" in his eye, and Apollo replies with "gentle laughter" (278, 281).

"Criminal though he is, Hermes has the devotion and admiration of the author of the *Hymn*," Norman O. Brown contended in his book devoted to myths about the god. "Nowhere is moral disapproval expressed." Well, yes and no: comedy has it both ways. The theft would not be funny if it were not wrong as well as winked at; Zeus would not heartily laugh at Hermes' lies if he were not about to put him straight.

"How are we to explain this tolerant and admiring attitude toward theft?" Brown asks. Well, for one thing, because this theft is very cleverly carried out, especially for a one-day-old. But sometime in the sixth century BC, no doubt adopting earlier stories told about the birth of Hermes, whoever composed this delightful hymn adopted the license of comedy. At the end of his book Brown himself put the answer to his question this way: "The subject—the conflict between Hermes and Apollo—has real religious and ethical significance; but to enlist the sympathies of the audience on the side of Hermes the poet appeals chiefly to their sense of humor." And thus "the *Hymn* comes as close to the Aristophanic manner as is possible in the 'Homeric' style."[3]

One reason for interpreting such texts as humanist comedy is that Greek and Latin literature often championed humanity over against divinity. The poets imagine a rivalry with the gods and then come out for the underdogs. The principals in so-called Old Comedy may be little better than clowns, yet the unfolding action and dialogue invite the audience to identify with them. Aristophanes notoriously mocked gods and philosophers both, turned the beliefs of his time topsy-turvy, yet the Athenians did not censure his blasphemy and were much more taken up with his political satire. The authors treated in the second act of the present book—Erasmus, Montaigne, Hobbes, Spinoza, Bayle, Hume, and Arnold—stand out from the broader Christian culture as humanists. They were in their time and are known today as humanists. And the frequency with which they cite and quote from Lucretius, Cicero, and Lucian testifies to the liberating effect of classical precedents.

Merely to take note of this liberating effect calls attention to a split in Western thought that widened with the rise of Christianity. Some classical philosophy, notably that originating with Plato and Aristotle, could be absorbed by and literally contribute to subsequent Christian theology. But it is easy to see how monotheism, as compared to polytheism, raises the stakes of freely producing plays or writing stories about the deity. As for laughter, it is inconceivable to laugh at—or in company with—the God of Abraham. Essentially the reasons for this were spelled out by Erich Auerbach in the first chapter of *Mimesis*, where he compared the representation of this world by Homer to that of the Elohist in Genesis 22. Whereas Homeric epic foregrounds all the action and dialogue, divine or human, the biblical narrative of Abraham and Isaac sets forth a "claim of absolute authority," and we are not told where God's voice originates because "the two speakers," divine and human, "are not on the same level."[4]

No doubt that is why later humanists were pleased to tap the vein of humor in the classical modes of narrating and staging roles for the gods. Otherwise it was hard to challenge or even question an awesome voice coming from on high. The humanists' listeners or readers similarly have their feet on the ground, prepared to tolerate, not to say enjoy, the comedy for its penchant to say certain things and yet not to say them, at least not to insist.

1. OLD COMEDY IN ARISTOPHANES' HANDS

If it were not for Aristophanes we would have little understanding of what so-called Old Comedy was like. We know a good deal of the wider background, the flourishing of comedy in Attica in the fifth century BC. There were two well-attended festivals a year with competition for the best performances. Anyone was welcome in the large outdoor theater. Spectators did have to pay, though at least by the fourth century subsidies were available for poor people. The competition was more of a secular than a sacred event. We know the names of playwrights and producers and a great many comedies, not least the first-, second-, and third-prize winners. We know of at least forty plays by Aristophanes, but the texts of only eleven have survived intact. With the exception of Menander's *Dyskolos*, the comedies of his contemporaries survive only in fragments.

In any society, performance onstage is in itself liberating. Playing a part is not the same thing as being that person; writing and producing a play are not the same thing as plotting and carrying out actions in the home or marketplace, in heaven or the political sphere. Also, the actors and chorus in Attic theater wore masks and costumes not to be seen on the street. Comedy redoubled this freedom, since laughter can liberate onstage or off. The spoken language thought appropriate to comedy, including vulgarity and obscenity, was not proper to public life. Aristophanes brilliantly exploited this theatrical opportunity to increase the fun and to get away with it. Unlike the practice of New Comedy in the following century, actors impersonated living celebrities of the day onstage, often by name. Aristophanes pilloried the politician Cleon in play after play, brought on Euripides whenever he pleased to differ with the tragedian, and remorselessly satirized Socrates in *Clouds*.

The long drawn-out Peloponnesian wars between Athens and Sparta (431–404 BC) dominated the political consciousness of the audience during the height of Aristophanes' writing and producing of comedies. Notoriously, it is very hard for *man*kind, at any rate, to oppose a war, no matter how destructive, once it is under way. But Aristophanes, a conservative politically, came out in his plays for peace. In his first surviving comedy, *Acharnians*, which won first prize in 425, the hero from the countryside, Dicaeopolis (the name means something like good advice for the city), manages to negotiate a private peace with the Spartans for himself and his family. In *Peace*, awarded second prize in 421, the hero Trygaeus fails to reach Zeus and persuade him to stop the war, but deals with Hermes and manages to rescue the statue of Peace from the cave where War has put her away: again, the fertile life of country folk is the alternative posed to warfare. *Lysistrata*, perhaps the best known of Aristophanes' comedies today, was produced in 411, after the overwhelming defeat of Athens in the battle of Syracuse. Famously, the heroine leads a strike of warriors' wives on the home front while others occupy the Acropolis, all with the purpose of bringing the war to an end.

One has to assume that the reason his plays survive intact, from among the many prize-winning experiments of Old Comedy, is the variety and imaginative stretch of the surprises Aristophanes held in store for his original audiences and his readers over time. Recognizable traits of human nature mix with unbelievable feats of entrepreneurship, such as Trygaeus's flying off into the heavens on the back of a dung beetle, a fairy tale acted out before our eyes with the help of stage machinery. Perhaps the hardest thing to grasp is the character of such protagonists, not a few pushing the limits of ethical behavior or played by actors who might be stuntmen. Lysistrata was unique: men and women still can and do identify with her today, but Aristophanes, who makes her his protagonist, was not exactly a feminist. Dicaeopolis, Trygaeus, the Sausage Seller in *Knights*, Cario in *Wealth*, possibly Lovecleon in *Wasps*, but certainly Strepsiades in *Clouds* and Peisetaerus in *Birds*—the two plays that concern us most here because of their representation of the gods—seem to be all of a type. Cedric Whitman suggested they could be traced back in folklore to the character of the god Hermes.[5]

Aristophanes produced *Clouds* in 423 BC, and it took third prize, but that text has not survived. Instead we have a revision, still unfinished half a dozen years later but valuable in itself and instructive to compare with *Birds*. The Clouds of the title are a chorus of female deities, but the traditional gods are still around to swear by and to fall back on at the end. Philosophy that boasts of possessing a scientific view of the world and the complacently amoral use of rhetoric for winning cases at law bear the brunt of Aristophanes' satire. It is the latter possibility that attracts Strepsiades, the all-too-human hero of *Clouds*, who has no money at hand to pay his debts when just now at the end of the month his creditors are bound to show up. Strepsiades, an old man and a father, scarcely resembles Hermes. He is neither as smart nor as ambitious as that god even when a child—not even as smart as his own lackadaisical son Phidippides, whose craze for horses and chariot racing has undoubtedly contributed to the family's money troubles. Strepsiades shares Hermes' deviousness, however, and in a monologue at the end of the play confessing his disillusionment with Clouds, the old man prays to the god and (apparently) receives his answer. These same lines (1476–92) warrant inferring that the stage setting for *Clouds* included a statue of Hermes outside the door to Strepsiades' house and that perhaps he should be imagined as belonging to an Athenian cult of Hermes.

In the prologue, shared with Phidippides, once that young man has been woken, Strepsiades sets forth his idea. At the Thinkery down the street, conducted by Socrates, they teach one how to win arguments whether right or wrong. His son should forget about horses and register at the Thinkery. Here's the father, in Jeffrey Henderson's translation: "I'm told they have both Arguments there, the Better, whatever that may be, and the Worse. And one of these Arguments, the Worse, I'm told, can plead the unjust side of a case and win. So, if you learn this Unjust Argument for me, then I wouldn't have to pay anyone even a penny of these debts that I now owe on your account." Phidippides will have nothing to do with it and goes back into the house. So his father decides he will have to try to learn this stuff himself, though "how is an old man like me, forgetful and dense, to learn the hairsplitting of precise arguments?" (112–18, 129–30).[6]

It goes without saying that Strepsiades is a clown, to be laughed at but not to astound; a mortal, hence vulnerable Hermes from the outback. He has his moments of inspiration, to be sure, and is rather endearing. Note that he understands perfectly well the ethics of the matter, that it is wrong not to pay his debts. He wants to have it both ways, as clowns so often do; consistency would not be nearly as entertaining.[7] Strepsiades' son has already made him look more than a little foolish. This combination of savvy and naiveté enables him to pound on the door of the Thinkery, however, and then hold up his end in a series of comic routines with the pupil who appears. Pupil: "And look, this is a map of the entire world. See? That's Athens right here." Strepsiades: "What do you mean? I don't believe it; I don't see any juries in session" (206–8). The language of their exchanges coarsens, but similar laugh lines shape the dialogue of *Clouds* from beginning to end.

By now Socrates in person has appeared in a basket above the stage, like a deus ex machina. Strepsiades calls to him:

> SOCRATES. Why do you summon me, o creature of a day?
> STREPSIADES. Well, first of all tell me, please, what you're up to.
> SOCRATES. I tread the air and scrutinize the sun.
> STREPSIADES. So you look down on the gods from a basket?
>   Why not do it from the ground, if that's what you're doing?
> SOCRATES. Why, for accurate discoveries about meteorological
>   phenomena I had to suspend my mind, to commingle my
>   rarefied thought with its kindred air. (223–30)

Socrates henceforth remains the principal butt of the comedy—not a Socrates we would recognize from Plato's dialogues but nonetheless the contemporary of Aristophanes and known for his eccentricity and open way of life. What seems highly unlikely is his dedication to the scientific or naturalist way of thinking, possibly linked with early stoicism, which Aristophanes satirizes in *Clouds*. Not that one could wish the business away, for it lies at the heart—or mind, one should say—of this comedy. Socrates prays to female gods such as Air and Empyrean in addition to the Clouds and is the only principal character wholly persuaded that Zeus does not exist: "What do you mean, Zeus? Do stop driveling. Zeus doesn't even exist!" The beauty of clouds, for the empiricist, is that one sees with one's own eyes what they can do: "Now then: where have you ever yet seen rain without Clouds?" (367, 370). By the time this Socrates' researches are completed Athenians should have no longer any need for those personified Olympian gods. Teaching a Strepsiades might easily turn a classroom into a nightmare and leave no time for research. The clamorous give-and-take between the two also reduces Socrates to a clown.

After enough such clowning the chorus advises Strepsiades to put his grown-up son to school instead. So the father drags the son out of the house, and these two go at it again. Strepsiades has now learned to swear by gods like Fog and Whirl, and when Phidippides just as casually swears by Zeus that triggers a parental outburst: "What stupidity, believing in Zeus at your age!" (818–19). All the more reason for putting him to school. Socrates declares, however, that the Arguments themselves will instruct Phidippides, and out of the Thinkery emerge Better Argument and Worse Argument—in what sort of masks and costume one can only imagine. They too do not teach anything within the audience's hearing but keep calling each other names until the chorus leader asks them to state their positions, so that the young man may choose. It becomes increasingly evident that Better Argument is moralistic and very old-fashioned. Worse Argument is all for wine, women, and doing what comes naturally. When Better protests that Phidippides will then need some way to escape being punished for adultery and that sort of thing, Worse challenges him to agree that whoever wins on this point wins the debate. He then forces Better to concede that almost all—prosecutors, tragedians, politicians, and the majority of the spectators, at whom they both start to point—are "wide-arsed." Better has to agree that Worse has the better argument. Worse Argument gets to teach Phidippides.

Predictably the new philosophy taught in the Thinkery makes faster headway with Phidippides than his father. When Strepsiades inquires about his son's progress, Socrates reports that the new pupil has completed the course, and "you can beat whatever lawsuit you like." Strepsiades is ecstatic and can see immediately that his son has "that innocent look when you're guilty, even of a serious crime . . . that Athenian expression all over you" (1151, 1174–76). Phidippides now speaks with a professional confidence, with logic that takes itself for granted. Accordingly, his father's self-confidence expands once again, though not necessarily his logic. The expected creditors arrive one after the other, and he merely—and rudely—tells them off. Not to say that Strepsiades the clown is not having a great day: "So tell me," he demands of the second creditor, "do you think that Zeus rains new water every time, or that the sun draws up from below the very same water again?" The creditor replies that he couldn't care less. "Then how can you justifiably ask for your money back, knowing nothing of meteorology?" (1278–84).

Alas, Strepsiades appeals to this Cloudlike reasoning just before the turning point in the action. In this comedy the role of the chorus is rather like that in a good many tragedies of the same period, belatedly shifting its commentary a little as it comprehends what is happening. The Clouds—goddesses indeed—begin to moralize about people who do not pay their debts and predict that Strepsiades may be sorry he sent his son to the Thinkery for his education. A moment later Strepsiades comes rushing out of his house calling for help, followed by Phidippides, who has been beating him. (It turns out the quarrel started when the son made insulting remarks about Aeschylus and then started reciting lines from Euripides, but that's neither here nor there.) In *Clouds* Aristophanes scripts his clown's recognition lines this way: "By god I truly have had you taught to speak against what's right, my boy, if you can carry this proposal, that it's right and good for a father to be beaten by his sons" (1338–41).

The Clouds have never exactly opposed the traditional gods. Early on, in the parabasis, the chorus has even invited Zeus and Poseidon to join in the song and dance (563–74). The exodus of the comedy does restore authority, of a sort, to the gods. It makes great theater, but the message is tricky because it assumes Strepsiades' penitence and singles out Hermes. Yet Hermes is one of the Olympian Twelve, after all, and Strepsiades has been chastened by the mere thought as well as the blows of sons beating fathers. "I must have been insane when I rejected the gods for Socrates. Well, Hermes old friend, don't be angry with me or bring me some disaster, but forgive me for taking leave of my senses because of their idle talk. You be my counsellor: should I slap them with an indictment and pursue them in court? . . . [a pause] That's good advice: I shouldn't cobble up lawsuits but rather burn down the idle talkers' house as quick as I can" (1476–85). Even if we were privileged to witness the performance of this scene and could see the actor bending his ear and listening to an image of Hermes, we would still have to take Strepsiades' word for what Hermes told him. But he promptly grabs a torch and sets fire to the Thinkery, an action not incompatible with the spirit of Hermes himself. Socrates and two pupils escape unhurt, and Strepsiades pursues them as they flee offstage.

What then should we conclude about the treatment of the gods in *Clouds?* Trust Hermes? Conceivably the moral is delivered by Strepsiades' very last words, shouted at the fleeing thinkers: "Chase them! Hit them! Stone them! They've got it coming many times over, but most of all for wronging the gods" (1508–9). But that would be like trusting Strepsiades. That last phrase illustrates what *sanctimony* has come to mean over time: pure hypocrisy, since what has really turned Strepsiades around is Socrates' teaching that it's fine for grown sons to beat their fathers. The latent purpose of crying wrong to the gods here is the extremely common one of rallying humankind around the cause. Most invoking of the gods in *Clouds* is for more naked human purposes, and satirized accordingly. Worse Argument instances Zeus's mistreatment of *his* father in order to strike down Better Argument's belief that justice exists in heaven. Minutes later he holds up Zeus's womanizing as a model for Phidippides and a precedent to cite should the young man find himself in trouble. Throughout the play Aristophanes makes fun of swearing by such-and-such god simply by having Socrates' hangers-on every so often swear by a new god. Above all are the Clouds, new gods eager to play their part. The chorus leader speaks for them (and more than this once for Aristophanes himself): "Of all the gods we do the most good for your city, but we are the only deities to whom you make no offerings or libations, the very ones who watch over you!" (577–79). This is all good fun but takes the whole idea of immortals looking out for the interests of mortals very lightly. Here she speaks again later:

> We want to announce what the judges stand to gain if they do the right thing and give this Chorus their support. One, if you want to plow your fields in season, we'll rain on you first and everyone else later. Two, we'll guard your crops and vines against attack either by drought or too much drenching. But any mortal who would slight our honor as goddesses should bear in mind what punishments he'll suffer from us: he'll get no wine or anything else from his land, for when his olives and vines start to sprout, we'll let fly at them so hard that they'll be sheared off. And if we spot him making bricks, we'll start raining and pulverize his roof tiles with a salvo of hailstones. And when he or any of his relatives or friends has a wedding, we'll rain all

night long, so that maybe he'll wish he'd wound up in Egypt
instead of miscasting his vote. (1115–30)[8]

She means and does not mean to bribe and threaten the judges of this
festival's competition, right? It's all a joke. But in order to bring this off,
the parody of how Athenians imagine their relation to the gods has to be
part of the joke.

In *Birds* Aristophanes resorted to the same dramatic stratagem as in
Clouds, inventing new gods and having them serve as the chorus, with
wonderful effect. Birds do happen to be more animated, more colorful
and vociferous than clouds. *Birds* has a larger cast, yet at the same time a
more unified plot. In this comedy the Birds unmistakably rival the
Olympian gods, who have on their side three speaking roles, as contrasted
with Hermes' silent role in *Clouds*. The Birds stage a revolution, motivated and led by the human protagonist, one Peisetaerus. He is another
clown, to be sure, but more imaginative than Strepsiades and rewarded
with a triumphant exodus. The action in *Birds* is extravagantly
marvelous—surreal—yet determinedly diachronic. There is even a
creation story, but also allusion to contemporary events and naming of
historical individuals. The author's characteristic wordplay is in top gear.
Birds won second prize in 423, but for all these reasons truly deserves first
prize among the eleven extant plays of Aristophanes. With help from
birdlife, humanity comes out ahead in this one. The comedy leaves spectators and readers bemused, pondering whether gods may not need
humanity more than humanity needs the gods.

There need be no reason to hark back to ancient Greece or to frequent
a theater in order to marvel at birds. Birds command human attention
virtually anywhere, even if the concern is strictly practical like harvesting
their guano or keeping them out of jet engines. Birds are alive and
breathing but mortal and in many ways akin to human beings. They
possess a knowledge of the seasons and calculate times for migration so
accurately that they have a reputation for augury, to say nothing of the
capacity to navigate. Many are monogamous and care for their young as a
pair. The young are not as precocious as Hermes but certainly grow up
much faster than human infants. Birds construct nests, a key part of their
habitat, from a variety of materials. They are capable of preening and
bathing and are astonishingly good at song and communication at a

distance. Many birds swim and even dive after fish. Some feed on live vermin and others prefer roadkill, or eat the very same grains that humans do. The bird kingdom, one might say, displays an impressive division of labor. So varied are their species, shape, color, and lifestyle that bird watching among our own species is a popular pastime to this day.

And birds fly. That's the enviable part of it. No wonder wings appear attached to human figures in so many paintings, statues, pageants, and productions like that of Aristophanes' drama. Birds have inspired centuries of human attempts to fly, and even now that far more advanced flying machines have been engineered, sports like hang-gliding pay tribute to the original inspiration. It is also entirely possible that the gods owe their way of getting about to bird watching. Here is an abbreviated sampling of how the leader of the chorus in *Birds* expatiates on the matter to the spectators, once our man Peisetaerus has persuaded him that birds can found a city in the sky to rival Olympus:

> Now then, ye men by nature just faintly alive . . . wingless ephemerals, suffering mortals, dreamlike people: pay attention to us, the immortals, the everlasting, the ethereal, the ageless, whose counsels are imperishable. . . . In the beginning were Chaos and Night and black Erebus and broad Tartarus. . . . There was no race of immortal gods before Eros commingled everything; then as this commingled with that, Sky came to be, and Ocean and Earth, and the whole imperishable race of blessed gods. Thus we're far older than all the blessed gods. . . . And mortals get all their greatest blessings from us birds. To start with, we reveal the seasons of spring, winter, and autumn. It's time to sow when the crane whoops off to Africa . . . then it's the kite's turn to appear and reveal another season, when it's time to shear the sheep's spring wool. . . . And we're your Ammon, your Delphi, your Dodona, your Phoebus Apollo, for you don't embark on any course without first consulting the birds—about business, about acquiring a livelihood, about a man's getting married. . . . Well then, if you treat us as gods you'll have the benefit of prophets, muses, breezes, seasons. (685–736)

Thus it can be said that humans already regard birds as gods of a sort, and the next move is for birds to capitalize on this belief.

The prologue to *Birds* is shared by Peisetaerus and his sidekick Euelpides, who come on toting a crow and a jackdaw they have purchased with the idea that these birds will help them locate Tereus, "the hoopoe who once was human and turned into a bird" (15–16) after marrying Procne and raping her sister Philomela. (The women in this famous myth were transformed to a nightingale and a swallow, respectively.) Ostensibly the two men are simply looking for a good place to settle down, but they are on the road, like tramps, and have left unspecified troubles behind. Why consult Tereus? Partly because Peisetaerus can identify with Tereus's unruly ways, or because if he could become a bird he would escape his creditors altogether, or because he already has some vague idea of exploiting the bird kingdom for his own ends. But he is not very serious; it's a clown act again. When the two approach Tereus's place, a slave bird with a menacing beak stops them in their tracks. Slave: "You two are dead!" Peisetaerus: "But we're not mortals!" Slave: "Well, what are you?" Peisetaerus: "Me? I'm a yellowbelly, a Libyan bird." And so on. But clearly Tereus, once a human, knows the birds and can serve as a go-between. When our clowns meet up with him, the comic routine carries on. What's it like to be a bird? Tereus: "It wears quite nicely. To begin with, you must get by without a purse." Euelpides: "You've removed much of life's fraudulence right there" (64–65, 156–58).

After a little more of this, Peisetaerus hits on his idea. If birds stopped flying off in different directions and founded their own city, their power would increase immeasurably: "And then you'll rule over humans as you do over locusts; and as for the gods, you'll destroy them by Melian famine" (185–86). He alludes to what the Athenians notoriously did to the people of the island of Melos in 416. This is dark humor, to be sure, but the plan excites Tereus, who with soaring avian lyrics summons the birds: that is, the chorus of twenty-four singers, who now enter one after another, each representing a different species. A flamingo, a mede, another hoopoe, gobbler, partridge, francolin, wigeon, halcyon, snippet, owl, and so on: each wears a different mask and outfit. This could be a colorful fashion parade if it were not for the initial animosity of the chorus. Given the way humans customarily mistreat birds—killing, roasting them, stealing their eggs—the chorus thinks Tereus has betrayed them by bringing them into the presence of Peisetaerus and Euelpides.

Peisetaerus rises to the occasion with a burst of diplomatic and rhetorical genius. He puts aside the history of human exploitation and concentrates instead on the birds' relation to the gods. Birds were here first. He is sorry for them, for they were once kings: "Yes you, kings of all that exists—starting with yours truly and including Zeus himself—and born a long time before Cronus, and the Titans, and even Earth" (467–69). There is an uncanny plausibility to all this even today, for the fossil record suggests there were flying creatures long before humans came to walk upright; and how did gods learn the use of wings unless from observing birds? Rhetorically, Peisetaerus is extremely shrewd. He begins to outline his case for a revolution in the skies; and just as human revolutionaries have often been persuaded in historical times, the purpose is to restore the original order of things, not to invent one anew. As this clown embarks on a series of debating points to ease the chorus's doubts, comedy plays over the slipperiness that logic can be prone to. For example, "the most impressive proof of all is that Zeus, the current king, stands there with an eagle on his head as an emblem of his royalty, as does his daughter with an owl, and Apollo, being a servant, with a hawk" (514–16). Not proof perhaps, but a sign? Euelpides, for his part, cannot be said to help much with his entertaining asides and distractions but keeps the tone of the whole from becoming too sacrilegious.

At this point Peisetaerus does revert to human hunting, trapping, and dieting on birds and delivers a particularly grisly account of such matters in order to show he is on their side. That kind of thing didn't happen, he remarks, when the birds were in charge. This gambit pays off, and the birds ask him what they should do. The answer is to come together and construct a city of birds in the sky and to fortify it, to wall off the heavens from the earth. Peisetaerus's ultimate purpose, however, would seem to be winning a surrogate war against Zeus:

> And when that's up and ready, reclaim your rulership from
> Zeus; and if he refuses, and isn't willing, and doesn't give up at
> once, declare a holy war against him, and deny the gods the
> right to travel through your territory with erections, the way they
> used to descend for adultery with their Alcmenes and Alopes
> and Semeles. And if they do trespass, then clap a seal on their
> boners, so they can't fuck those women anymore. And I urge

you to dispatch another bird as a herald to mankind,
announcing that, the birds being sovereign, they must
henceforth sacrifice to the birds, and only afterwards to the
gods. (554–69)

On the one hand, Peisetaerus reminds the birds of some of the ways they
can plague humans, should they not go along with the new order. On the
other, he points out to them all the favors birds can do for humanity, if
they accept birds as their Zeus, Earth, Poseidon, and so forth. Birds can be
especially helpful in controlling insect populations that interfere with
agriculture. "But," the leader of the chorus questions, "how will we give
them wealth? Because that's a strong passion of theirs" (592). Peisetaerus
can only come up with augury on this one. Birds are good at augury and
thus can help with risk taking and futures trading. After this the chorus is
persuaded to accept the persuader's advice.

Whether in deference to archaic hospitality codes or by a nice touch
of Aristophanes' humor, Tereus has waited until now to ask the two men
to introduce themselves and to invite them in to lunch. He assures them
he has a certain root they can chew on and thereby grow wings, and cour-
teously accedes to Peisetaerus's request that his wife, Procne, sing the
nightingale's song. While the human and formerly human characters are
lunching, the chorus leader and chorus perform the parabasis; when the
two adventurers return to the stage they are sporting wings, and
Peisetaerus is very much in control. The birds will need a name for their
city, he points out. With a classic rhetorical maneuver he facetiously
suggests Sparta as the name, so that they are bound to accept his next
suggestion as their own: Cloudcuckooland. Because the walls of
Cloudcuckooland still have to be built, he sends Euelpides flying off,
ostensibly to help with that.

As in other Aristophanes scripts, the action has become completely
unreal, taken itself right out of this world. Yet we identify with Peisetaerus,
largely because there is no other character with whom to identify. He has
emerged as the person in charge. Curiously, it helps that we can also look
down on him, for secretly we are all a bit clownish, coarse, and crass as
compared to the manners imposed on us from above almost before we
can walk and talk. The surreal surroundings, like the cartoon drawings in
a book for children, license a combativeness generally disapproved of in a

domestic space. No sooner has his protagonist reached this degree of ascendancy than Aristophanes typically brings on a series of less able clowns, would-be self-aggrandizers seeking a part of the action. Typically this kind of character, the *alazon*, or impostor, makes his appearance onstage without any introduction.[9] One after another such impostors rouse the sarcasm and combativeness of the lead clown before he drives them off. They deserve to be so treated and thereby reaffirm the audience's identification with the protagonist and main action. In *Birds* the successive impostors are a priest, a poet, an oracle collector, Meton the astronomer and geometer, a so-called inspector, and a decree seller. Subsequently, as if Peisetaerus still had not taken enough exercise, the play introduces a father beater, a composer of dithyrambs, and an informer, each of them looking for wings, which have now become all the rage.

After the decree seller runs away, Peisetaerus goes off to sacrifice a goat brought in by the first of the six impostors; and Aristophanes treats the audience to a second parabasis in which the chorus of Birds now boasts of its own divinity as follows: "To me, the omniscient / and omnipotent, shall all mortals / now sacrifice with pious prayers. / For I keep watch over all the earth, / and keep safe the blooming crops / by slaying the brood of all species / of critters, who with omnivorous jaws / devour all that in soil sprouts from the pod / and the fruit of the trees where they perch; / and I slay those who spoil fragrant gardens / with defilements most offensive; / and upon creepers and biters every one / from the force of my wing / comes murderous destruction" (1059–71). Accordingly, the chorus leader warns humankind not to mistreat birds or keep them in cages and, after the antistrophe, addresses directly the judges of this play much the way the female leader did in *Clouds*. He hints broadly what favors Birds can do for the judges in particular, then closes with a reminder of how bird shit sometimes drops on people from the sky.

At this point a messenger comes in to report to Peisetaerus that the wall around the city in the sky has been completed. The messenger is full of admiration for the masonry and carpentry of the birds who built it and the sheer numbers of the workforce: "The din of their pecking was just like a shipyard! And now all those gateways are gated and bolted and surrounded by guards, patrolled by bell ringers." But hardly has he finished when a second messenger has arrived, exclaiming that "one of . . . Zeus' gods has . . . flown through the gates into our airspace" (1157–60, 1172). This proves to be Iris, one of the Olympians who have traditionally borne wings. Peisetaerus treats her the way he has treated the impostors, only more so. He ridicules Iris, insults her, pretends to be surprised that no top cock among his birds has not raped her, and threatens to rape her himself. She is frankly confused that he doesn't understand who the gods are and that she is one of them. So he tells her to her face, "Birds are gods to humans now, and to them must humans sacrifice, not, by Zeus, to Zeus!"

> PEISETAERUS. And as for you, if you annoy me one bit, I'll deal
>   with the servant girl first, Iris herself, spread her legs and
>   screw her, and she'll be amazed how an old hulk like me
>   can stay aloft for three rammings!
> IRIS. Blast you, mister, you and your foul language!
> PEISETAERUS. Buzz off now, and make it quick! Shoo, shoo!
> IRIS. I swear my father will put a stop to your insolence!
> PEISETAERUS. Good grief, fly somewhere else why don't you,
>   and inflame some younger man. (1236–37, 1253–61)

Even as this encounter takes place the wider action of *Birds* is unfolding fast. The herald whom Peisetaerus has sent to humankind returns with the news that people are going bird-crazy, imitating birds and giving themselves bird names. Flatteringly enough, they are said to be full of praise for Peisetaerus and look up to him as some sort of guru; though he is but a clown (if lately equipped with wings), not a god.

Birds does not conclude the way *Clouds* does, with the chorus moralizing and Strepsiades at least pretending to penitent piety. New actors enter upon the drama, actors with name recognition that promises a future for Peisetaerus. First, Prometheus slips in, carefully muffled up so that Zeus won't see him, but Peisetaerus recognizes him as soon as he sees his face. Prometheus has come to tell him that ambassadors are on their way from Olympus. Prometheus: "Zeus is finished!" Peisetaerus: "And approximately when was he finished?" Prometheus: "From the very moment you colonized the air. Now not a single human sacrifices to the gods any more, and since then not a whiff of thigh bones has wafted up to us" (1514–18). Prometheus wishes to prepare him and to advise him not to reach a settlement "unless Zeus returns his scepter to the birds and gives you Princess for your bride." Princess is a beautiful maiden who at present is a sort of executive assistant to Zeus. Prometheus: "That's why I came here, to let you in on this. I've always been a friend to humanity." Peisetaerus: "Yes, if it weren't for you we wouldn't have barbecues." Prometheus: "And I hate all the gods, as you know" (1535–36, 1544–47). Sure enough, moments later the embassy arrives, consisting of Poseidon, Heracles, and an unnamed god of the Triballians, savage allies of the Athenians.

Poseidon ranks as their leader; Heracles may have been appointed for the human connection on his mother's side; the Triballian god has apparently come along just for Aristophanes to make fun of. Peisetaerus pretends hardly to notice or to have time for the gods, as he goes about ominously cooking "some birds who've been convicted of attempted rebellion against the bird democracy" (1583–85). This is not so funny. Aristophanes' humor suddenly changes course, since this is typically how revolutionary leaders thin out their followers in order to stay in power. Whatever the case, the smell of the meat brings Heracles over to Peisetaerus's side immediately. It is already clear that Poseidon's mission is to negotiate a settlement with the birds rather than fight them, but it won't do to have Heracles surrendering their position in advance. The dialogue that follows mocks divine rule as rule with all-too-human interests and litigation over estates. Anxious to put Heracles back in his place, Poseidon carelessly argues as if (a) Zeus were mortal, and (b) his power little differed from that inherent in an extremely large but finite human estate. He and Peisetaerus go at Heracles like a pair of lawyers:

> POSEIDON. What, you chump? Don't you realize that you've
>   been getting duped all along? What's more, you're harming
>   yourself. Look, if Zeus surrenders his rule to these birds,
>   you'll be left a pauper when he dies, because you now stand
>   to get the whole estate that he leaves behind at his death.
> PEISETAERUS. Good grief, how he's trying to fast-talk you! Come
>   aside here, I want a word with you. Your uncle's out to cheat
>   you, poor fellow. Of your father's estate you don't get a single
>   penny; that's the law. You see, you're a bastard, illegitimate.
> HERACLES. Me, a bastard? What are you talking about?

PEISETAERUS. That's exactly what you are, your mother being an
   alien. Why else do you think that Athena as a daughter
   could be called The Heiress, if she had legitimate brothers?
   (1641–54)

One has to hand it to Peisetaerus: he applies to Greek myth the kind of
shrewd analysis—or strictly speaking, analogy, since he cannot know
exactly what laws of inheritance apply on Olympus—that later, self-
confessed humanists will apply to holy scripture. All three members of
the embassy agree to the proviso that Zeus return the scepter to the birds.
Poseidon votes no to allowing Peisetaerus to marry the girl Princess, but
he is outvoted on this by the other two. There can be no doubt who comes
out top dog: the birds he has prepared "have been cut up just in time for
my wedding!" (1688–89). Who will ever pay Peisetaerus's debts, however?
We are never told.

   Aristophanes' *Peace* places Trygaeus and Hermes on more or less
equal terms and enacts a jolly show in a good cause. But Hermes is
Hermes, with a reputation and latitude of behavior congenial to the
mortal hero's, whereas *Birds* pits Peisetaerus against Poseidon. Once
again a man and a god exchange words on more or less equal terms, but
Poseidon has little reputation for a sense of humor and is far more prone
to violence than Hermes; and he walks off the loser, from an embassy that
one would never dream of being subject to a vote. Zeus has directed him
to reach a settlement, but not on the terms Prometheus has spitefully
(he hates the gods) urged on Peisetaerus. The clown, the human match
for the gods, triumphs. That it is also a victory for the birds is almost
forgotten. In the herald's words introducing the exodus, "You triple-
blessed winged race of birds: welcome your ruler to his prosperous palace
. . . as he comes bringing a lady of beauty surpassing description, and
brandishing the thunderbolt, winged missile of Zeus." The Princess is
mute, but the chorus sings of her youth and beauty also and compares
their wedding to that of "Olympian Hera / and the mighty lord of the
lofty / throne of the gods" (1707–14, 1731–35). It has been quite a day for
Peisetaerus, who first came across as an itinerant tramp. His sidekick
Euelpides has not been heard from since he was told to go off and help
with the fortification of Cloudcuckooland—and a good thing, since his
witticisms would hardly be in place here.

Conceivably this castle in the sky could all come crashing down the next day. Peisetaerus's erections, so to speak, are performed under comic license. A more permanent institution of this comedy could well be its kingdom of the birds, a synecdoche for the astonishing plant and animal kingdoms as a whole. Unlike the immortal beings on Olympus, who after this seem more fragile, the evidence available to humanity tells of a continuing process of growth and decay, birth, reproduction, and death. That's where the teachings of Epicurus would be relevant, but insufficient written texts of his philosophy survive. Happily Lucretius expounded the Epicurean creed in his great poem *De rerum natura*.

2. LUCRETIUS ON THE UNHOLY NATURE OF THINGS

Lucretius was a contemporary of Cicero. His skill in rendering narrative and argument in Latin hexameters was closely studied by Virgil and Ovid. His long didactic poem *De rerum natura*, or *On the Nature of Things*, dropped from sight in the dark ages and was rediscovered by Italian humanists of the quattrocento. His inspired account of Epicurean philosophy attracted enthusiastic readers and translators in the Renaissance and Enlightenment, to say nothing of the Romantics. Nature, in Lucretius's view, came along before gods, who had nothing to do with the creation of the universe. On the contrary, it is a fair inference from *On the Nature of Things* that humankind invented the gods in order to explain what was manifestly happening all around. Storms and wild beasts could be terrifying enough without some such explanation, though on the whole Lucretius's poem emanates appreciation of nature. Moreover, in modern times both evolutionary biology and particle physics have come round to something like ancient Epicurean views of the universe.[10]

De rerum natura seems a far stretch from Old Comedy, yet Lucretius knew Greek extremely well, associated Athens with Epicurus (ca. 341–269 BC), and held a number of views in common with Aristophanes. Both sought after peace rather than war, valued a conservative country life, and despised political power and ambitions. Possibly they were even temperamentally alike—but the style of their written contributions was as different as can be. One scripted comic dialogue and satire, the other an inspired and persistently argued didactic poem of 7,415 lines. Aristophanes' method is a send-up; everything can be seen in at least two ways and left at that. Lucretius's is a put-down; this is the nature of things, the way things are.

Aristophanes' *Birds* concluded with more than one marvelous touch. Think of that young and beautiful Princess who, as Prometheus informs us, is in charge of Zeus's thunderbolt among other things. Mysteriously but satisfyingly the thunderbolt comes with her when she descends from Olympus to marry Peisetaerus as agreed. This says something about thunderbolts as Zeus's weapon of choice: perhaps they should not be taken so seriously. But now listen to Lucretius on thunderbolts: "This is to understand the true nature of the fiery thunderbolt, and to see by what power it plays its part; not by unrolling the scrolls of Tyrrhenian charms, vainly to search for signs of the hidden purpose of the gods" (6.379–82).[11] And then he goes out of his way to argue the point. Bypassing the question of what evidence believers, or his readers, may have that thunderbolts *are* divinely and purposefully targeted against specific human offenders, Lucretius points to overwhelming evidence that they are nothing of the kind.

Just trust your experience of thunder and lightning and think about it. If the gods possess this destructive weapon, why don't they teach humans a lesson by striking down the guilty instead of taking off so many innocent people with their storms? Why waste thunderbolts by aiming most of them at high mountains, the desert, and the sea? If Jupiter is trying to tell us something, why doesn't he show himself hurling his weapons? Or conversely, why make such a thundering racket that we know to take cover before the lightning strikes? Why strike so many places at the same time? Why, as sometimes happens, destroy shrines dedicated by humanity to the gods? Lucretius's consideration of thunderbolts plays out amid a wider discourse on atmospheric change: the weather, not wholly predictable by science to this day. The materialist and atomistic Epicurean philosophy teaches that the causes of all such phenomena are embedded in nature, even if we cannot fully trace them.

Certain of these arguments were current in Athens even before Epicurus arrived on the scene, for in *Clouds* they are attributed to Socrates, the character Aristophanes used as a catchall for the new science. Strepsiades and Socrates get to arguing about thunder and clouds. Strepsiades takes the easy line that Zeus moves the clouds about. Socrates the schoolmaster responds, "Didn't you hear me? I repeat: when the clouds are full of water and run into one another, they crash because of their density." His bad pupil still doesn't believe him, so Socrates elaborates with a homely analogy to the farts the old man lets off after gorging himself with soup. That satisfies Strepsiades with regard to thunder, but not how the fiery lightning could materialize if not from Zeus's hands: "It's quite obvious that Zeus hurls it against perjurers." Socrates: "How's that, you moron redolent of the Cronia, you mooncalf! If he really strikes perjurers, then why hasn't he burned up Simon or Cleonymus or Theorus, since they're paramount perjurers? On the other hand, he strikes his own temple, and Sunium headland of Athens, and the great oaks. What's his point? An oak tree certainly doesn't perjure itself!" (*Clouds*, 383, 398–402).

Aristophanes thus deployed Socrates for sidelong hits at favorite targets of his satire. All three points that he scores about Zeus's poor aim anticipate the Epicurean arguments relayed some three hundred years later by Lucretius. As often, the laughter invited by Aristophanes' lines darts in so many directions that it never quite settles down. Compare the sarcasm and drive of Lucretius's implied dialogue in that brief excursus from his account of the nature of things: "Why again do [the gods] aim at deserts and waste their labour? Or are they then practising their arms and strengthening their muscles? And why do they suffer the Father's bolt to be blunted against the earth? Why does he himself allow this, instead of saving it for his enemies? Why again does Jupiter never cast a bolt on the earth and sound his thunder, when the heaven is clear on all sides? Does he wait until clouds have come up, to descend into them himself, that he may be near by to direct from them the blow of his bolt?" (6.396–403). The thrust of such rhetorical questions is totally dismissive—the answer is, For no reason, nothing at all. And Lucretius keeps the rhetorical questions streaming past the reader. He invents reasons that his reader has not even thought of, such as the gods' target practice or physical fitness needs, and rhetorically dismisses these also. This is a little like saying outright, You fool—moron or mooncalf.

If Lucretius does not quite laugh at the gods in *De rerum natura*, in places he certainly laughs rather scornfully at those who believe in the gods. One of his most serious purposes is to persuade his readers never to *fear* the gods, because of the uncalled-for emotional stress and the sometimes badly mistaken actions that follow. His method is rational argument, most famously in his argument against the immortality of the soul. Not only is the soul, or mind, just as mortal as the body, but if people would accept and practice the Epicurean creed they would on this account never fear death. Reason assures one that all awareness of life, the very memory of being alive, growing older, and dying, dies with one: no laughing matter, but nothing to be afraid of either. Reasoning itself, nevertheless, can be enjoyable, and a note of triumph can usually be felt, if not always sounded, in winning an argument. Not only that, but *ratio* also translates as a *law* of nature. So human reason must be able to cope and to understand nature.

Lucretius formally professes to believe in the gods as well as the laws of nature. But those gods are simply out of this world. They are immortal, and nothing in the universe—in nature—is immortal or everlasting. Typically Lucretius gestures toward the gods in the proem to individual books of his long poem. Book 1 opens with a prayer to Venus, since erotic desire is an obvious means for nature to renew itself. As the beloved of Mars, she can also help restore peace by distracting him, and Lucretius goes out of his way to fix this image of the god and goddess: "For you [Venus] alone can delight mortals with quiet peace, since Mars mighty in battle rules the savage works of war, who often casts himself upon your lap wholly vanquished by the ever-living wound of love, and thus looking upward . . . his breath hangs upon your lips." Tell him, please, that the Romans want peace. The lovely prayer is then subsumed by the poet's imagination of the dwelling place of the gods: "For the very nature of divinity must necessarily enjoy immortal life in the deepest peace, far removed and separated from our affairs; for . . . needing us not at all, it is neither propitiated with services nor touched by wrath" (1.31–49). This passage is often thought to have inspired Botticelli's wonderful painting of Venus and Mars.

The conditions imposed on the gods here become a constant refrain in *De rerum natura*. In the proem to the last book—not a prayer, unless to Epicurus himself—the poet scolds humanity a bit in case we still haven't gotten the point. The gods do not need our services and certainly do not wish to harm us. One may do oneself harm, however, by believing that such is their lookout, since then "you will not be able to approach their shrines with placid heart, you will not have the strength to receive with tranquil peace of spirit the images which are carried to men's minds from their holy bodies, declaring what the divine shapes are" (6.76–78). There can be no practical need even to contemplate the gods, only the imaginary tour of a peaceful never-never land where they achieve nirvana. In book 3, after another nod to divine Epicurus, the poet peers into the void: "Before me appear the gods in their majesty, and their peaceful abodes, which no winds ever shake nor clouds besprinkle with rain, which no snow congealed by the bitter frost mars with its white fall, but the air ever cloudless encompasses them and laughs with its light spread wide abroad" (3.18–22). In book 5 he reassures us that an abode of the gods cannot exist in this world (5.146–47). In sum, it is very much as if the gods of old now live in a retirement community somewhere far away, a place with strictly imaginary visiting privileges for mortals.

Since "nature is seen to be free at once and rid of proud masters, herself doing all by herself of her own accord, without the help of the gods" (2.1090–92), it follows that Epicureanism frees humanity as well— except from nature, that is, of which we are very much a part. Even the rather intimate knowledge of how men and women and other species of domestic animal and plant life are born from "seed," grow to maturity and reproduce, and inevitably die and decay helped shape Lucretius's understanding of evolution much as it did Darwin's. Epicureans were shrewd observers and did well not to turn away from what they saw. Animal life clearly evolved by fits and starts, and sometimes whole species perished. Similarly, primitive humans suffered from famine and lack of shelter, sheer ignorance of natural poisons, and their own subjection to carnivores—though such losses were not as terrible, he remarks, as the self-inflicted casualties of war or drowning at sea (5.999–1001). But Darwin was never looking for a fight, whereas Lucretius, aside from the question of how representative an Epicurean he may have been, seems to have had it in for unthinking worship of the gods and to have found what is generally called creationism these days faintly ridiculous. The word *religio* never appears in a favorable light in *De rerum natura;* and the most recent Loeb translator, Martin Ferguson Smith, uses not the cognate English equivalent *religion,* but *superstition.*

Lucretius is emphatic about the foolishness of believing that the nature of the universe was arranged for the convenience of human beings by divine power (2.167–81). He marshals much evidence to the contrary for his summary history of the earth in book 5. Basically, the environment is too hostile for anyone to imagine it was designed with human habitation in mind. The land mass is mostly mountainous, scorching desert, and permanent frost and surrounded by the waters of the ocean. In the habitable bits humans have to fend off wild beasts and avoid rocks and marshlands. So be it, they are "well accustomed to groan over the stout mattock for very life, and to cleave the soil with the pressure of the plough." Yet the seasons bring disease and untimely death as well as the uncertain harvest of such toil. In an astonishing passage Lucretius contrasts the fragility of human maturation with that of other beasts:

> Then further the child, like a sailor cast forth by the cruel waves,
> lies naked upon the ground, speechless, in need of every kind of
> vital support, as soon as nature has spilt him forth with throes
> from his mother's womb into the regions of light, and he fills all
> around with doleful wailings—as is but just, seeing that so
> much trouble awaits him in life to pass through. But the diverse
> flocks and herds grow, and wild creatures; they need no rattles,
> none of them wants to hear the coaxing and broken baby-talk of
> the foster-nurse, they seek no change of raiment according to
> the temperature of the season, lastly they need no weapons, no
> lofty walls to protect their own, since for them all the earth
> herself brings forth all they want in abundance, and nature the
> cunning fashioner of things. (5.195–234)

Lucretius always seems to be saying, Let's look at the whole picture. Let's look at the environment and at other species. Above all, look at the nature of things over time.

When Ernst Haeckel argued that ontogeny recapitulates phylogeny he was contributing to post-Darwinian *life* sciences.[12] Lucretius went further, typically speculating that the mortality of living organisms recapitulates the history of the universe. "For certainly whenever we see the parts and the members of creatures to be made of body that has birth and forms that are subject to death, we perceive these same creatures to be invariably subject to death and birth along with the parts. Therefore, when I see the grand parts and members of the world being consumed and born again, I may be sure that heaven and earth also once had their time of beginning and will have their destruction" (5.240–47). He has no proof of this beyond the distant analogy, but gods have no part to play in it. Lucretius is at his most Darwinian on the matter of causation itself. Not even the parts of the body were originally designed for the purposes they serve. Bodies evidently varied, evolved over time, and suitable bits were made use of:

> Do not suppose that the clear light of the eyes was made in order that we might be able to see before us; or that the ends of the calves and thighs were jointed and placed upon the foundation of the feet, only to enable us to march forward with long forward strides; that the forearms again were fitted upon sturdy upper arms, and ministering hands given on either side, only that we might be able to do what should be necessary for life. Such explanations, and all other such that men give, put effect for cause and are based on perverted reasoning; since nothing is born in us simply that we may use it, but that which is born creates the use. (4.825–35)

Lucretius is fond of remarking that there is nothing immortal—body or soul, human or inhuman—in the universe. Conceivably, therefore, it was merely literary convention or a concession to his readership that led him to invoke the gods in his several proems. But in a portion of book 5, as if he were an outsider or anthropologist, Lucretius pretty much accepts that people invented those gods (5.1161–1240). Significantly he first registers that religious beliefs and rituals themselves have a history. The altars and shrines that abound in cities and countryside were not built yesterday. The rites and sacrifices are customary, passed along from generation to generation. Lifelike representations of gods first appeared in visions and especially in dreams, and they were of human appearance but handsomer and stronger. Their obvious superhuman advantage is to be quite free from harm and death.

Besides such visions and dreams, humankind has long been impressed by the evidence of order in the universe. The recurring seasons, night and day, phases of the moon, stars in the night sky call out for explanation. Since the cause of these motions was unknown, it was easier to attribute it to the agency of the gods. By extension, gods were very likely responsible for the creation of the universe in the first place. On the other side, the sudden forces of destruction—windstorms, thunderbolts, earthquakes, and tsunamis—terrify and therefore cry out still louder for explanation. Again, the gods provided an answer to unknown natural causes. That the same gods who rule the heavens reap havoc invites the inference, by analogy to the human family and polity, that the divine purpose must be punishment; and humans struck down by these forces accordingly imagine they are somehow guilty. Thus people have taken on faith that there are such beings as superior, possibly cruel gods, under and against which human life is small and not a little contemptible.

Ultimately what is wrong with all this is the resulting self-depreciation of humanity. The installation of this religion casts doubt on advancing our knowledge of the natural world and rationally coming to terms with it; the traditional worship of the gods undervalues human achievement and denies our capacity for self-control: "It is no piety to show oneself often with covered head, turning towards a stone and approaching every altar, none to fall prostrate upon the ground and to spread open the palms before shrines of the gods, none to sprinkle altars with the blood of beasts in showers and to link vow to vow; but rather to be able to survey all things with tranquil mind" (5.1198–1203). It is fear of the gods that really gets to Lucretius, selling humanity short and displacing hope for peaceful social and individual lives. To appreciate the comprehensiveness of this claim, however, it's important to grasp what he means by fear.

The fear is not just a concern, in a given situation, about being targeted by a thunderbolt. It denotes a range of psychological states, from caution in acting without more knowledge to a sense of utter helplessness, from a lack of personal confidence to an automatic surrender to herd behavior. This fear is a very general and, in Epicurean terms, an unnecessary, limiting outlook on life: "For assuredly a dread holds all mortals thus in bond, because they behold many things happening in heaven and earth whose causes they can by no means see, and they think them to be done by divine power" (1.151–54). Mortals are thereby subject to their own imaginary construct, call it either religion or superstition, sanctified by custom over time. To questions that should have been submitted to reason, the gods furnished a ready answer and a quiverful of sharp behavioral inferences: that is, both a narrative explanation and a set of expectations to reinforce this. Such are the ways of the gods, and such is a way to accommodate them. The latter, human result is what Lucretius means by fear: giving in to one's own or the tribe's irrational beliefs.

Famously he illustrates his point in the proem to book 1 by citing the sacrifice of Iphigenia by her father, Agamemnon, leader of the Greek forces at the start of the war against Troy. If we believe philosophy is impious and makes way for crime, he tells us, we should ask what *religio* does in a case like this. Because he wants to make a general case about irrational beliefs, Lucretius chooses an example old enough to be shrouded in myth; but his take on this myth is unmistakable. He enters into none of the soothsaying behind the deed (that the Greek fleet will be forestalled by a calm until the sacrifice is made and so on). He takes for granted we know all that and moves directly to the scene:

> So soon as she saw her father standing sorrowful before the altar, and by his side attendants hiding the knife, and the people shedding tears at the sight of her, dumb with dread, she sank to the ground upon her knees. . . . Uplifted by the hands of men, all trembling she was brought to the altar, not that amidst solemn and sacred ritual she might be escorted by loud hymeneal song, but a clean maiden to fall by unclean hands at the very age of wedlock, a victim sorrowful slain by a father's hand: all in order that a fair and fortunate release might be given to the fleet. So potent was superstition [*religio*] in persuading to evil deeds.

The father is sorrowful, his daughter is sorrowful; what ought to be a marriage ceremony is bloody murder before the assembled company's eyes. Presumably the daughter must be a virgin to appease Diana and release the winds, but what a presumption! Gods and goddesses have nothing to do with the nature of things. In sum, "This terror of mind therefore and this gloom must be dispelled, not by the sun's rays or the bright shafts of day, but by the aspect and law of nature" (1.89–101, 146–48). Lucretius repeats these last lines in the proems to books 2, 3, and 6, lest we forget what he means by irrational fear.

Whether or not Iphigenia was herself a historical person, she was by no means the last human to be sacrificed, buried alive, or burned at the stake in the name of *religio*. Moreover, the degree of foolishness and impudence in presuming to know what a god requires along these lines is bound to vary inversely with the number of gods in question: monotheism would render it all the more shocking. Lucretius adopted the humanitarian stance because humanity is a part of nature. He kept trying to derive the ethics of his position from nature, most cogently from evolving animal species with which humans have direct contact. Both Aristophanes and Lucretius saw how much, except for the regrettable lack of wings, humans have in common with birds. According to Lucretius, birdsong and bird cries possibly inspired the invention of language (5.1078–90). Birds do have a lot going for them, not only song and messaging but formidable airborne powers. The art of Christian times would become strewn with angels, and why should angels have wings? *De rerum natura* was largely lost to view for centuries but became far better known in the early modern and modern era, appealing anew as it did to humanists, scientists, and poets.[13]

3. LAUGHTER OVERHEARD BY CICERO

Lucretius conducted the argument of his poem in his own voice and thereby accepted responsibility for the positions he took, even as he attributed most of what he knew to Epicurus. By resorting to dialogue, Cicero— and Lucian too, in frankly comic or satiric modes—protected himself by speaking through various personae. Philosophical dialogues took this form even though the several participants might hold forth uninterrupted for long periods of time. The dialogues also had a deliberate pedagogical purpose. By exposing students or neophytes to more than one opinion, the method invited them to become more involved and to weigh arguments accordingly. In his last years Cicero increasingly associated himself with the so-called New Academy, which advocated adversarial examination of opposing positions but withholding of judgment. After his forced retirement from political life, he expressly devoted himself to summarizing and translating Greek philosophy in the Latin vernacular. Still, part of the game in reading a Ciceronian dialogue is to figure out who speaks for the author and when. And there is plenty of mischief going on, especially with respect to the gods and divination. Lucian's case will prove to be different, but Cicero never laughs at the gods outright, only at what his opponents believe about them. Because of the adopted dialogue form, readers are privileged to hear the laughter, not necessarily required to join in.

Cicero died in 43 BC, one of the most distinguished losers in the Roman revolution. He composed *De divinatione* the year before and *De natura deorum* the year before that. It is not clear that either dialogue was completely finished before his death. The voices in the typical Ciceronian dialogue are those of historical, real-life friends and acquaintances, practitioners in the courts and politics of Rome, philosophers, and family; but of course it is Cicero who had the last word on what they say. When he assigns a specific setting of a dialogue in time past, the reader may feel the writer is doing his best to recall what was actually said, but not always. Cicero makes the point himself in his dedicatory letter to his friend Varro, one of the participants in *Academica:* "When you read it I fancy you will be surprised at our holding a conversation that never actually took place; but you know the convention as to dialogues."[14] One thing we do not know for sure is Cicero's reaction to Lucretius's great poem. We know he read it, or at least some of it, because in a letter to his brother Quintus in 54 BC he complimented the poet's style and genius. But a single sentence in a family letter is not much to go on. The influence of Lucretius, or of Epicurean principles, at least, on *De natura deorum* and *De divinatione* is nevertheless unmistakable, though none of the speakers in the dialogues ever explicitly alludes to the poem or credits its author.

In an earlier work, *De oratore,* Cicero did provide some analysis of humor and the usefulness of raising a laugh in a course of argument. Even this comes in the form of a dialogue, though there would seem to be nothing controversial in laying out a manual of rhetoric. To discourse on what is laughable and what not is notoriously difficult, however, without spoiling the jokes altogether. The discussion of laughter Cicero ascribed mainly to one Julius Caesar Vopiscus, and his theorizing in book 2 of *De oratore* is quite good of its kind. But Julius acknowledges up front that teachers of rhetoric in this area are likely to prove "so conspicuously silly that their very silliness is the only laughable thing about them." The others agree that laughter is mostly spontaneous, therefore risky for an orator to contrive in any case. Antonius, another participant in the dialogue, remarks that the best laugh lines may come when the orator is on the defensive, stung by the very consciousness of the weakness of his argument. "To retort is human," he declares, and the very quickness of a glancing retort may save the day in court by arousing laughter.[15] Nonetheless Julius does outline a brief systematic approach. The evidence he cites, mostly sample wisecracks uttered by named speakers in various public forums over the years, testifies to Cicero's quite amazing memory. The jokes do not exactly bowl the reader over, but undoubtedly the contrasting seriousness, competitiveness, the stakes involved, or plain boredom of the occasions heightened their effect and made it memorable. Above all, laughter brings people together; it tends to be a collective response. Commonly persons who do not understand the joke or who perhaps did not even hear the joke join right in. It is certainly an advantage to the joking advocate to have people fall in with him, even if the joke has little to do with the point at issue. And to be the butt of a successful joke when serious consequences hang on the debate? That's like receiving a poke from everyone within hearing.

Given Cicero's impressive command of the rhetorical uses of laughter, one can hope and expect that the play dialogues he composes, even on serious matters, may be entertaining. That is certainly the case with *De divinatione*. His scorn for any kind of divination is far more uncompromising and thus easier for readers to take hold of than his beliefs about religion and the nature of the gods. Oracles, augury, astrology or horoscopy, pig entrails or necromancy, bird watching or soothsaying are all so irrational as to be outright laughable. Such so-called arts or sciences of foretelling the future stem from pretensions and superstitions that deserve to be put down. *De divinatione* is technically a dialogue also, and Cicero's express purpose is carefully to rehearse arguments on both sides of the question (1.7).[16] This last dialogue, however, falls into two parts, book 1 turned over to the author's younger brother Quintus, whose job is to present the Stoic position on divination, and book 2 reserved to Cicero himself, who proceeds to demolish the same. One wonders how Quintus felt about all this. He has dutifully read his brother's *De natura deorum*, and before the end of book 2 he breaks in to confess that he basically agrees with everything Cicero is saying about the Stoics' foolish commitment to divination. The fun part of the dialogue is all Cicero's in book 2, where he plays reductio ad absurdum with the arguments set forth by Quintus. At one point he sums up his side by asking, rhetorically, "Need I assert that divination is compounded of a little error, a little superstition, and a good deal of fraud?" (2.83). Yet despite all the author's forensic experience, this is about the only accusation of fraud in *De divinatione*. The game is to ridicule believers, since from the word go "there is no such thing as divination" (2.12).

For the most part Cicero the speaker confines himself to the light comedy endorsed by *De oratore*. He credits the philosopher Democritus himself with joking, for example, before going on to point out that Democritus, who believed in divination, failed to grasp that one would have to examine the entrails of *all* cattle to be positive what entrails portended. This problem long ago occurred to other sages, who concluded that the choice of the specific beast to be sacrificed must first be divinely predetermined, or that the sought-for entrails were somehow magically altered to display the desired signs after the beast was slaughtered (2.30, 35). As recommended in *De oratore*, mimicry invites one's listeners or readers to broaden the application of a witticism. Cicero claims to be "sorry that our Stoic friends have given the Epicureans so great an opportunity for laughter," for he ostensibly disapproves of Epicurus's take on the gods. Or he includes himself, for being so foolish as to bother refuting such arguments (2.39, 51).

Still, what kind of art is it that "makes prophets out of birds that wander aimlessly about—now here, now there—and makes the action or inaction of men depend upon the song or flight of birds? and why was the power granted to some birds to give a favourable omen when on the left side and to others when on the right?" (2.80). And what kind of science? Cicero several times complains of the mixture of fact and fantasy, nature and nonsense, that divination regularly assumes:

> Upon my word you Stoics surrender the very city of philosophy
> while defending its outworks! For, by your insistence on the truth
> of soothsaying, you utterly overthrow physiology. There is a head
> to the liver and a heart in the entrails, presto! they will vanish the
> very second you have sprinkled them with meal and wine! Aye,
> some god will snatch them away! Some invisible power will
> destroy them or eat them up! Then the creation and destruction of
> all things are not due to nature, and there are some things which
> spring from nothing or suddenly become nothing. Was any such
> statement ever made by any natural philosopher? "It is made,"
> you say, "by soothsayers." Then do you think that soothsayers are
> worthier of belief than natural philosophers? (2.37)

In general, soothsayers and the like often grab attention by claiming some miracle and applying the miracle to events and actions to be taken in the real world. Cicero notes that "it may be urged with effect against all portents that the impossible never has happened and that the possible need not excite any wonder" (2.49).

Divination and divinity were as etymologically linked in Latin as these concepts are in English, so in this dialogue the question of the existence of the gods would seem to be critical. Stoicism regarded the two beliefs as inextricable, each dependent on the other. Quintus quite agrees and makes the point up front, only to have his brother promptly object, for reasons that become increasingly obvious: he despises divination yet wishes to preserve respect for the gods (1.9–10). Cicero raises the question himself in book 2 but fails to cope with it very persuasively. He charges the Stoics with sophistry and advises them to be more careful. They may conclude that "there are gods, therefore there is divination." But they might more persuasively proclaim, "There is no divination, therefore there are no gods": more persuasively because that premise is unmistakably factual—there is no such thing as divination, of that we can be sure. In scolding the Stoics for their rashness in coming near to this very negative syllogism, however, Cicero exposes the thinness of his own belief in the gods. He offers no proof of their existence whatever but simply reiterates his conviction that divination is finished yet the gods must be held onto (2.41). The reasons for this opinion are clearer in *De natura deorum* and again at the close of *De divinatione*, but it is already evident that the existence of the gods is a matter of faith.

Cicero's position on the gods is closer to Epicurus as expounded by Lucretius than he chooses to admit. He too spars with Jupiter's thunderbolts, insofar as these are imagined to convey messages from on high. Refutation of this notion evokes the same rhetorical questions that made nonsense of the god's aiming those thunderbolts at human targets: why are so many of them hurled into the ocean, at mountaintops and deserts (2.42–45)? Such phenomena are part of nature and best studied by professionals. So also are experienced generals like Hannibal and Caesar better able to know when to advance or retreat than soothsayers, who pretend to be able to detect the will of the gods. History unfolds "nearly always contrary to the prophecy" (2.51–53). Cicero several times contrasts physicians' caring for human needs with the supposed caring of gods. Dreams are not sent by gods, and he ridicules at length the notion that dreams are reliable messages of any sort. "No; and not even if I wanted to sail a ship, would I pilot it as I might have dreamed I should; for the punishment would be immediate. What would be the sense in the sick seeking relief from an interpreter of dreams rather than from a physician?" (2.123). The gods exist (and in this last part of his argument Cicero mainly uses the singular noun, *deus*). But they do not intervene or advise, and therefore mortals had best meet adversity with courage and, when appropriate, the professional help of fellow human beings.

De natura deorum is the more philosophical and thoughtful dialogue and sometimes nearly as entertaining as Cicero on divination. The author speaks in his own voice only in the frame of the whole, yet even his brief introduction suggests a reading of Lucretius. The very first sentence refers vaguely to a connection between studying the nature of the gods and reaching an understanding about the soul; but indeed the mortality of the soul became a prominent and aggressively argued theme of *De rerum natura*. When Cicero cites next the differences among philosophers about the nature of the gods as his principal ground for writing the present work—"the question upon which the whole issue of the dispute principally turns"—he describes quite accurately the position Lucretius adopts from Epicurus: "For there are and have been philosophers," he writes, "who hold that the gods exercise no control over human affairs whatever." If they are right, he continues, "how can piety, reverence or religion exist?" In his own voice and still without naming names, Cicero then articulates perhaps the clearest summary we have of his own position:

> But if . . . the gods have neither the power nor the will to aid us,
> if they pay no heed to us at all and take no notice of our actions,
> if they can exert no possible influence upon the life of men,
> what ground have we for rendering any sort of worship, honour
> or prayer to the immortal gods? Piety however, like the rest of
> the virtues, cannot exist in mere outward show and pretence;
> and, with piety, reverence and religion must likewise disappear.
> And when these are gone, life soon becomes a welter of disorder
> and confusion; and in all probability the disappearance of piety
> towards the gods will entail the disappearance of loyalty and
> social union among men as well, and of justice itself, the queen
> of all the virtues. (1.1–3)[17]

Cicero never attempts to deliver a proof of the existence of the gods. He marshals here a coherent argument for human need of the gods, in the form of a series of increasing priorities. In order to have grounds for sincere worship and validate the ceremonies surrounding prayer, to preserve custom and order in the culture, and to help stabilize loyalty and justice within the community, there must first be gods to believe in. He gestures toward the same need for traditional religion elsewhere, writes this in a time of revolution after all, and—like Edmund Burke at the time of the French Revolution—is aware of the fragility of the Roman or any other polity.

Once he has positioned himself this way, Cicero can rhetorically waive the importance of his own opinions. Readers "who seek to learn my personal opinion on the various questions show an unreasonable degree of curiosity," he cautions. He also stands firmly by the principles of the Academic school of philosophy: those who wish to advance their under-standing must weigh arguments for and against the issue. "Indeed the authority of those who profess to teach," he says, "is often a positive hindrance to those who desire to learn; they cease to employ their own judgement, and take what they perceive to be the verdict of their chosen master as settling the question." Hence the adoption of a dialogue about the gods rather than a treatise; and a dialogue should also free the author "entirely from ill-disposed criticism." He then proceeds to specify the occasion and introduce the speakers of his dialogue. Some years ago, it seems, his friend Gaius Cotta had invited him to his house, and when he arrived Cotta was already discussing the nature of the gods with two well-qualified spokesmen, Gaius Velleius the Epicurean and Q. Lucilius Balbus the Stoic. With a knowing smile Velleius does point out that Cotta is another adherent of the Academy like Cicero, who responds that he himself will just be "a listener, and an impartial and unprejudiced listener too" (1.10, 13, 17). Here is how the resulting dialogue plays out: with only minor interruptions, Velleius the Epicurean is allotted less than half of book 1 before Cotta commences his refutation; Balbus the Stoic has all the somewhat longer book 2 to himself; Cotta, all of book 3 to refute him—but book 3 of *De natura deorum* is the shortest, some of it either missing or never finished.

Each of the debaters has his say, but obviously Cotta, who has only to rebut first the Epicurean and then the Stoic, is going to have the most fun.

He makes a riotous time of belittling the anthropomorphism that fuels traditional ideas of the gods, though Velleius is scarcely guilty of such. Do we really suppose humans are so beautiful that gods must look like us? or so clever that they would behave the way we do? Do not other species of animal admire and mate with their own kind the way we do, and why wouldn't gods be shaped the way they are? "Although I am not lacking in self-esteem," Cotta modestly confesses, "yet I don't presume to call myself more beautiful than the famous bull on which Europa rode" (1.78). We Romans get our idea of how the gods dress and equip themselves from numerous painters and sculptors who depict them that way. In other lands it seems the gods dress differently and in other languages have different names. Cotta is unquestionably familiar with the advice in *De oratore* about dropping a joke now and then. When he lets loose on Velleius's beliefs, it's easy to imagine him as entertaining a jury. Do Epicureans really believe in a chance coming together of atoms to form the world as we know it, and not in intelligent design? "Are we to think that divine seed fell from heaven to earth, and that thus men came into being resembling their sires? I wish that this were your story, for I should be glad to acknowledge my divine relations! But you do not say anything of the sort—you say that our likeness to the gods was caused by chance" (1.91). This is classic courtroom or debating society sharpness, putting words in the opponent's mouth in order to get a laugh and getting away with it. Cicero shows his mastery of the dialogue style by later having Velleius point this out (2.1), but of course the joke itself—"glad to acknowledge my divine relations"—is subversive of sincere worship.

Striking out in this new direction, Cotta is not notably consistent. At one point he comes close to articulating Cicero's own objections to the Epicurean notion that the gods exist out there placidly enjoying themselves but do not concern themselves with human affairs. Cotta draws the analogy to personal relations: people cannot very well credit and feel gratitude to someone who has done nothing for them. "Piety," he says, "is justice towards the gods; but how can any claims of justice exist between us and them, if god and man have nothing in common?" (1.116). This argument is scarcely congruent with Cotta's relentless mockery of anthropomorphism, the whole idea that gods are quite like us and vice versa. Again, Cicero has the good sense to have Balbus remark, in the interlude before his own delivery of the Stoic position, "I had rather listen to Cotta again, using the same eloquence that he employed in abolishing false gods to present a picture of the true ones" (2.2). Cotta declines to do that, on the grounds that this is a dialogue.

Balbus commences on his role by stating that Stoicism divides the topic of the day in four parts: proof of the existence of the gods, their nature, their governance of the world, and their care for humankind. The first question "seems not even to require arguing," though he ends up devoting as much space to it as Velleius was allowed to expound the Epicurean position as a whole, and one of the first proofs of the existence of the gods is indeed the practice of divination (2.3–4, 7–12). The heat that is suffused throughout the world and the ubiquity of "male and female generative principles" (2.23–32) recall something of Lucretius's emphasis. More mysteriously, "the world is an intelligent being, and indeed also a wise being," especially as evidenced by the "order and regularity" of the stars (2.36, 43). Book 2 of *De natura deorum* anticipates some typical arguments of modern deism. Balbus may not be the most precise reasoner, but he makes up for that with the sweep and enthusiasm of his discourse. When it comes to the nature of the gods, he disputes other physical theories about the ether and the motion of atoms. The form of the divine is spherical, and "in the heavens therefore there is nothing of chance or hazard, no error, no frustration, but absolute order, accuracy, calculation and regularity" (2.55–56). Intelligent design is still more in evidence when it comes to the providential governance of the world, and, perhaps to help make better sense of governance, *deus* is occasionally singular again. Balbus cites both the marvelous beauty of the sky and indeed the anatomy of humans, besides their powers of mind, communication, arts and other skills. Finally, all this was designed to profit humanity—or rather, "for the sake of gods and men" (2.154). With a backward glance, he lists historical and mythical individuals (men, that is, not women) obviously cared for by the gods: "It was this reason which drove the poets, and especially Homer, to attach to their chief heroes, Ulysses, Diomede, Agamemnon or Achilles, certain gods as the companions of their perils and adventures." And there was divination too, for guidance. "No great man ever existed who did not enjoy some portion of divine inspiration" (2.166–67).

Cotta will challenge Balbus's position point by point, he promises, but first he must reaffirm his commitment to "the worship of the immortal gods which I have inherited from our forefathers," and he does so several times. He reminds the others that he is officially a pontiff and as such looks to the hierarchy of Roman high pontiffs for guidance in religious matters. None of Balbus's *reasons* for the existence of the gods have convinced Cotta. Incisively, he now recalls that Balbus began by assuring them that it was hardly necessary to prove the existence of the gods but then went on at great length to do so. The implication of adducing so many reasons for the gods' existence is that none by itself is persuasive: "You did not really feel confident that the doctrine of the divine existence was as self-evident as you could wish" (3.5–9). Also Cotta does *not* believe in divination, "especially as your diviners tell such a pack of lies"; and such divination is no proof of the gods' existence in any case (3.14–15). Although his specific reasons for ruling out divination are missing from the text (see 3.65), one can assume they are much the same as Cicero's in *De divinatione*.

Perhaps because of the lacunae in book 3, or because Cicero sympathizes more with Stoicism, or because his Cotta went overboard in ridiculing Velleius's Epicureanism in book 1, there is less laughter now. Cotta's refutation of Balbus's rather free and upbeat arguments can sometimes be downright sobering. Attempts to surround divinity with too many positive attributions soon result in contradiction. Immortality itself defies both human experience and human intelligence about the surrounding world. Perfection cannot take too many forms at the same time. So with the Stoic understanding of the nature of the gods: to ascribe virtues and reasoning powers to the gods without limit makes no sense. "To a being who experiences and can experience nothing evil, what need is there of the power to choose between things good and evil? Or of reason, or of intelligence? these faculties we employ for the purpose of proceeding from the known to the obscure; but nothing can be obscure to god." Justice and temperance, also, are virtues arising from the needs and shortcomings of human society. To suggest that such virtues enhance the nature of the gods implies that they are in need of them too. "As for courage, how can god be conceived as brave? in enduring pain? or toil? or danger? to none of these is god liable. God then is neither rational nor possessed of any of the virtues: but such a god is inconceivable!" (3.38–39). The sort of anomalies Cotta cites are obviously more crucial for monotheistic beliefs, and this is another passage in which *deus* is singular in the original. (The absence of definite and indefinite articles in Latin also poses a problem for translation.) How could a just god who is both omnipotent and omniscient tolerate evil? When Cotta turns to Balbus's confidence in the providential role gods play in the lives of humans, he asks how that is consistent with so much manifest evil in human behavior. He calls attention even to the representation of evil in the fables of the poets, in tragedy and in comedy as well. More tellingly, he begins to cite notorious historical events: "Why need I mention Socrates, whose death when I read Plato never fails to move me to tears?" (3.82). Then he spells out in some detail the horrors committed by Dionysius the elder, tyrant of Syracuse.

Nonetheless Cotta does make fun of Balbus's belief in the gods. Just how many gods are there? Balbus claims every star in the heavens is a god: that's a great many gods, and some constellations have names like Scorpion or She-goat. Or, "when we speak of corn as Ceres and wine as Liber . . . do you suppose that anybody can be so insane as to believe that the food he eats is a god? As for the cases you allege of men who have risen to the status of divinity, you shall explain, and I shall be glad to learn, how this apotheosis was possible, or why it has ceased to take place now" (3.40–41). Then Cotta goes off on a romp through Greek and Roman mythology. If nymphs are gods, then so are Pans and Satyrs; but the latter are not gods, therefore nymphs are not gods either. He borrows more taunting of Stoic theologians from Carneades of Cyrene, who alleges that "the ancient genealogists name Love, Guile, Fear, Toil, Envy, Fate, Old Age, Death, Darkness, Misery, Lamentation, Favour, Fraud, Obstinacy, the Parcae, the Daughters of Hesperus, the Dreams: all of these are fabled to be the children of Erebus and Night" (3.43–44). Are all these gods too? If rainbows are beautiful enough to be represented by Iris among the gods, what does one say about clouds? (No allusion to Aristophanes is apparently intended.) "Again, why are you so fond of those allegorizing and etymological methods of explaining the mythology?" In the very act of reasoning thus, you and other apologists "clearly admit that the facts are widely different from men's belief, since the so-called gods are really properties of things, not divine persons at all" (3.62–63).

One problem with the rhetoric of overkill, throwing everything one can think of at the opponent, is the likelihood of inconsistency or the contradiction of one's own professed beliefs. Needless to say, the method of the new Academy, purposefully critical rather than constructive, opens itself to this danger. Cotta does not stop to think where the argument may intersect with his own views. It is an acute point to make about most sacred texts and legends that things do not happen that way anymore. Cotta thrusts with this kind of point to underline his disbelief in apotheosis. But like Cicero himself he wants to preserve the old-time Roman religion, which inherits beliefs similarly outdated. He reproves allegorizing and etymologies, fanciful or not, as the work of "idiots" rather than philosophers. Yet he is himself a priest, a member of the Pontifical College, bound not to question doctrines endorsed by the high pontiffs. Three times in the dialogue Cotta speculates that Epicurus merely paid lip-service to the gods in order to placate the Athenians and to stay out of trouble (1.85, 123; 3.3). He does not stop to wonder if Epicurus may have in effect retired the gods but knew better than to abolish them, for much the same motives articulated by himself and Cicero: namely, to preserve shared beliefs that hold a community together.

All in all, *De natura deorum* bears signs of having been influenced by Lucretius on the nature of many things, and evidence for this comes from the lips of Cotta. Early on in his reply to Balbus he says he will show how the world was formed by nature, precisely the thesis of Lucretius and Epicurus, and one Cicero will also emphasize in *De divinatione*. An unfortunate break in the text suggests that a passage has been lost, but in what follows are other important similarities. All nature is in motion, he claims, and "the system's coherence and persistence is due to nature's forces and not to divine power." He never names Lucretius or argues that the universe itself is mortal, but invokes Carneades' argument that every living thing is born, undergoes change, and dies. There is suffering and pain everywhere, and not much dwelling on pleasure (3.26–34). After joking about the godlike power of clouds to bring "rain and tempest, storm and whirlwind," Cotta remarks, in a single sentence, "At any rate it has been the custom of our generals when embarking on a sea-voyage to sacrifice a victim to the waves" (3.51). No names, but nothing in the immediate context to prompt the remark either: just possibly it was triggered by the moving protest against the sacrifice of Iphigenia in the first proem to *De rerum natura*.

Cotta is capable of affecting the reader's feelings also, as when he briefly narrates the evil doings of Dionysius of Syracuse, whose career ended peacefully in bed. "Well," he concludes, "Dionysius was not struck dead with a thunderbolt by Olympian Jupiter." That story, one among any number of such true-life stories, he implies, demonstrates that the gods do not look out for good or evil in this world. Fortunately, human conscience is "so powerful a force in itself, without the assumption of any divine design. Destroy this, and everything collapses"; but "there is no such thing at all as the divine governance of the world if that governance makes no distinction between the good and the wicked." People indeed pray to the gods for good fortune, but not for things within their own control. Virtue and reasoning powers operate within human beings, not from outside. That makes virtue "a just ground for others' praise and a right reason for our own pride, and this would not be so if the gift of virtue came to us from a god and not from ourselves" (3.85–88). These conclusions are all consistent with Lucretius's didactic purposes.

Scholars profess to be baffled by evidence that St. Jerome once seemed to think that Cicero edited *De rerum natura* after Lucretius's death. How could Jerome possibly have imagined anything of the kind, unless it was his little joke about these striking similarities of Cicero's and Cotta's intellectual stance to that of Lucretius? Here is a translation of the passage in question, insofar as it has survived: "Titus Lucretius was a born poet. After drinking a love potion that drove him crazy, he wrote some books during the intermissions of his madness—books that Cicero later revised. He committed suicide at age 44." Surely if Jerome wrote this he was mischievously calling attention to the Epicurean proclivities of Cicero's dialogue?[18]

In any event, Cicero scripted *De natura deorum* to expound and criticize the leading philosophical theories about the gods in his day, represented by the Stoic, Epicurean, and Academic schools. The resulting dialogue could serve as a humanist manifesto. What do public intellectuals among us believe about the gods? and on what grounds? The gods need not necessarily be taken on faith, except "most solemnly to maintain the rights and doctrines of the established religion" (1.61), valued for the support it lends to the state of Rome. This public function notwithstanding, any *truths* about the world that religion may assert are subject to human reason and experience. The whole point of the dialogue is to help determine the best, most defensible intellectual position on religion. Cotta and Cicero both wear two hats, however: that of intellectuals with leanings to the Academic school and that of citizens, more especially of officeholders, in the Roman establishment. Cicero himself was a member of the College of Augurs, though this was a ritual and honorary post rather than a calling to divine future events.

In his peroration to *De divinatione*, Cicero stated that both dialogues were designed to combat *superstitio*, which "has taken advantage of human weakness to cast its spell over the mind of almost every man. . . . But I want it distinctly understood that the destruction of superstition does not mean the destruction of religion." Here again he states, in a single sentence, his principal reason for upholding *religio*. That is, to preserve the gods in order to preserve the state: "For I consider it the part of wisdom to preserve the institutions of our forefathers by retaining their sacred rites and ceremonies." That's all he says; he does not go into details; but this order of wisdom is basically political rather than religious. A second reason, more personal, aesthetic, and less often expressed by Cicero, is also delivered in a single sentence: "Furthermore, the celestial order and the beauty of the universe compel me to confess that there is some excellent and eternal Being, who deserves the respect and homage of men" (2.148). That would seem to be Cicero's last word on this subject. He never tries awkwardly to don both hats at once.

In *De natura deorum*, nonetheless, Cotta threw another light on wearing two hats. At the very beginning of book 3 he tells Balbus, "You are a philosopher, and I ought to receive from you a proof of your religion, whereas I must believe the word of our ancestors even without proof" (3.6). This is somewhat unfair, since Cotta is also a philosopher, though one who believes, like Cicero, in withholding assent from propositions that are uncertain. Here he dons his liturgical hat for rhetorical purposes, to press the burden of proof solely on Balbus. The Academy school is fully committed to the use of reason, however, and appeals to human experience. With their principled noncommittal to theological propositions, Cicero and Cotta thereby admit a proviso: they are *not* persuaded of the truth of the gods' existence. In order to defend traditional Roman *religio* and its replication in art and ritual, which they deem important on other grounds, they have to accept a god or gods on faith. This will become the most common position taken by Christian humanists as well, when the Renaissance and Reformation both play a part in what came to be called the Enlightenment.

Cicero frames the dialogue with narrative in his own voice. His purposes he sets forth at the beginning, and after the briefest exchange of pleasantries following Cotta's refutation of Balbus, he writes, "Here the conversation ended, and we parted, Velleius thinking Cotta's discourse to be the truer, while I felt that that of Balbus approximated more nearly to a semblance of the truth" (3.95). Did he indeed? After Cotta has scored again and again throughout? For an astute reader's recognition of Cicero's irony here, one can look ahead to Hume's mischievous attribution of a winner in his distinctly Ciceronian *Dialogues concerning Natural Religion*. Cicero's writings were never lost to readers in the West, as Lucretius's were, and no ancient thinker made a deeper impression on Renaissance and Enlightenment humanism.

4. LUCIAN LAUGHING OUTRIGHT

Little is known of Lucian except from his writings, in which he can be as mischievous about himself as he was about other beings, human and divine. He came from Syria and lived in several cities of the Middle East before moving in midlife, about AD 165, to Athens. He seems to have practiced law and gone on lecture tours here and there but certainly had mastered Greek and Greek literature before occupying himself chiefly with writing comic dialogues.

Lucian may or may not have performed the dialogues by reciting them aloud. Whether long or very short exchanges, they are quite remarkable compositions, each complete in itself and in that respect very much like English dramatic monologues centuries later. Insofar as setting, circumstances, and actions may be necessary for understanding the conversation, these must be conveyed by what the speakers say. Lucian's chief inspiration was the sort of exchanges that occupy characters in Aristophanes' plays. He knew well both the comedies familiar to us and other Old Comedy scripts that have not survived. Another source was philosophical dialogue, sometimes in the style of Plato but more often in that of the stage—and like Aristophanes he had it in for philosophers. Instead of caring to distinguish between what can be real and what has merely been dreamed up, moreover, Lucian blithely accepts and sports with the supernatural doings of deities. The jokes are almost all delivered deadpan. His gods are so thoroughly anthropomorphed that they think and emote like ordinary human folk. Also Hermes frequently comes on scene, if only to assist other participants and keep the dialogue moving. To balance an act and put things in perspective, Lucian's dialogues sometimes feature ironic self-portrayals too.

A fine introduction to Lucian's laughter at the gods and at himself is the dialogue generally known as "Double Indictment." Essentially the title applies to the last third of the script, where it seems Lucian himself has been indicted in Athens by two plaintiffs at the same time: his change of career from lecturing to composing dialogues has come into question. Unless, of course, the title refers first to local dissatisfaction with the gods and second to the complaints about the scriptwriter. In any event, Zeus speaks first and at such length that one wouldn't immediately recognize this as a dialogue. It's more like a soliloquy, and *his* complaint is that the gods are overworked. He might very well be speaking as the disgusted shop steward of a divine labor union.

Here is how Zeus comes on, in the translation by Keith Sidwell: "Oh to hell with the philosophers who say that happiness exists only among the gods! If they knew what we go through for the sake of human beings, they wouldn't be so eager to envy us the blessings of nectar and ambrosia." He commiserates with the Sun and the Moon, who must travel overhead day after day and night after night. And with Apollo, who has to keep traveling from one shrine to another in no time, whenever one of his priestesses needs him to pronounce an oracle. But as it quickly becomes evident, Zeus feels sorriest for himself, "the father and king of all." He has to supervise the other gods, manage the weather, keep track of everything going on: "People stealing, people perjuring themselves, people sacrificing. Has someone made a libation? Where's the sacrificial smell and smoke coming from? Who has called for me in sickness or at sea?" Like Apollo, he is expected to be everywhere at the same time. "And just say we do nod off for a few minutes? Then Epicurus is immediately justified with his claims that we take no thought for earthly affairs. And it's not a negligible danger we face if people believe what he says. As a consequence we'll have no garlands on our temples, no smell of roasting in our streets, no libations poured to us from the mixing-bowls, the fires will go out on our altars and there'll be a total lack of sacrifice and offering. We'll certainly starve" (1–2).[19] Obviously Lucian is aware of—and no doubt Zeus himself recalls—what happened in Aristophanes' *Birds*. This Zeus, father and king notwithstanding, is more working class, and the pathos is heavy. In one of the briefest of Lucian's dialogues of the gods, "Eros and Zeus," the father—forget about king—bitterly complains that Eros has never made any woman fall in love with him: "No. . . . It's the bull or the swan *they* make love to; if they catch sight of me they're scared to death."[20]

As the long-winded Zeus concludes his seeming soliloquy and lament, he mentions the backlog of lawsuits he can never get around to resolving as still another cause of people's complaining. At this point in "Double Indictment" Hermes speaks up: obviously he has been standing by Zeus's side all the while, ready to assist. The multiple appearances Hermes makes in the dialogues are another compliment to the negotiations between gods and men that he helps carry out in Old Comedy. In one of Lucian's shorter dialogues of the gods, Hephaestus and Apollo manage to compress the same yarn about Hermes' first two days of life to less than a tenth the length of the *Hymn to Hermes* itself. The literary feat in both these entertainments, composed nearly a thousand years apart, was to *narrate* the story in distinctive genres, hymn and dialogue, respectively. In "Hermes and Maia" Lucian gives an adolescent Hermes a chance to bemoan, like Zeus, how much work he has to do. His mother tells him just to do what he's told. In "Voyage to the Underworld," a longer dialogue, Hermes labors along with Clotho and Charon to collect and ferry across to Hades the shades of the dead. Needless to say, this is a daily task and a struggle with predictably difficult personalities among the shades. By extrapolating from the mythical powers of the gods the routines they would be caught up in, Lucian slyly exposes those powers as—myth.

In "Double Indictment" Hermes in effect takes over the proposed action from Zeus. He both advises his father and carries out his wishes—or attempts to. He flies off to Attica with his half sister Justice to see what can be done about the court cases that are piling up. She is very reluctant to go along: "What? You want me to go back to earth again? All that will happen is that I'll have to run away from human life once more when I can't stand the mocking laughter of Injustice" (5). Justice is recognizably Astraea, but Lucian prefers the personifications for purposes of his satire: compare Better Argument and Worse Argument in Aristophanes' *Clouds*. Even before Hermes and Justice come in for a landing the conversation has turned to philosophers, and then they run into Pan, who has not been doing very well in Attica either. "Who are these philosophers you're talking about?" Pan asks. "Do you mean those depressives who huddle together in groups, the ones with beards like mine, the natterers?" (11).

Yet the law cases the gods take out of storage and get moving again are argued by philosophers, and it seems personification is rife among human plaintiffs and defendants also. One female Intoxication is suing Academy, who presumably kidnapped and sobered up Intoxication's only dependable slave. The plaintiff is in no shape to argue her own case but drunkenly asks Academy to speak for her as well as for the defense, and Justice concurs. As an Academic, naturally, Academy would not on principle take a strong position one way or the other. Call the next case. In Stoa vs. Pleasure, it is one woman against another, for seducing the plaintiff's lover. Stoa pleads her own case, and of course, Epicurus represents Pleasure. Both these jokes are elaborately told. In each case Hermes polls the jury: Academy wins the first for the defense, and Epicurus the second.

The most touching case, alluded to in the title of the dialogue, involves Lucian himself thinly disguised as "a Syrian," and that trial is said to draw a large crowd. The Syrian has to defend himself from two rival plaintiffs, his sometime wife, Rhetoric, and his new love, Dialogue. After my husband learned everything he knew from me, Rhetoric protests, "he fell passionately in love with that bearded fellow, Dialogue . . . who claims to be the son of Philosophy. He's with him now—love for the 'older man,' I suppose" (28). The Syrian replies that he was tired of the life he led in practicing the law and in speechifying against tyrants or praising princes. Besides, "I was almost forty years old. . . . Time to wander round with my very good friend Dialogue, engaging in gentle conversations which have no need of ovations and applause." Dialogue sees their relationship differently, of course, or he wouldn't have brought his case. He proceeds to tell the jury how the Syrian has "wronged and mistreated" him: "I used to be majestic. I inquired into subjects such as, 'the gods,' 'nature,' 'the universal periodic cycle'" and so forth. Now Dialogue has become some sort of clown, he complains: "I'm not prose and I'm not poetry." Our Syrian defendant pretends to be surprised by such accusations and defends himself by declaring, "The most important thing I did was to yoke him [Dialogue] up with Comedy." What's really bothering old Dialogue must be that "I don't sit down and engage in all that nit-picking logic-chopping with him. 'Is the soul immortal?' 'How many ladles of the unmixed essence of real being did the god pour into the mixing-bowl in which everything was combined when he constructed the universe?'" (32–34). Happily, in "Double Indictment" the jury votes for the defendant in both prosecutions for alienation of affection; and although the gods have barely made a dent in the backlog of Athenian lawsuits, Hermes calls it a day.

In "Philosophies for Sale" Zeus and Hermes both come down to earth in order to make fun of philosophy at length. In a sequel, a dialogue known as "The Fisherman," the philosophers fight back, affording an opportunity for Lucian to defend himself in his own name. Better still, a magnificent cast of Olympians emit both prose and verse in Lucian's "Zeus Tragoedus." With good reason Lionel Casson translates this one as "Zeus the Opera Star," and the dramatic irony throughout affords another splendid picture of Lucian's view of the gods.

The opening scene finds the father of the gods in an even more grim and despairing mood, but Hermes speaks first: "O Zeus, what means this furrowed brow, these words / Addressed unto yourself, this pacing back / And forth?" Then Athena: "Hear me, O Father, O dread son of Cronus, O ruler almighty! / Owl-eyed Athena, your daughter, the Tritogeneia, implores you: / Speak to us, tell us your secret. . . ." And his wife, Hera: "Enough hysterics, my dear Zeus. I don't have the flair for comedy or grand opera that these two have, and I have not swallowed Euripides whole. . . ." Hera, naturally, believes that it's just another love affair he is moaning about. Zeus decides to put her straight and responds, also in prose, that what worries him is something that all the gods should be concerned about: "The gods' situation is desperate. . . . It's anybody's guess whether we'll continue to be worshipped and respected on earth or be considered nobodies and be completely ignored" (1–3). Yesterday, he explains to this inner family circle, a debate occurred down below between Timocles the Stoic and Damis the Epicurean about providence. A crowd was gathering. Timocles was doing his best, but Damis contended that gods do not even exist, and he appeared to be winning when both agreed to continue the discussion another day.

As in a human family, father Zeus hears conflicting suggestions as to what they should do. A consensus builds that they should convene a meeting of all the gods, and that is no small number. Zeus and Hermes launch into the question of proper seating arrangements and come up with something like that prevailing in the theaters of ancient Attica—with

an underlying joke that seating divine attendees will be like seating stone
statues of the same. At least gods of any weight can assemble rapidly, but
when they have all arrived Zeus panics, tongue-tied, until Hermes
steadies him again. Once he begins to narrate what has happened, in
greater detail this time, it becomes clear that Zeus stumbled on the debate
between Damis the Epicurean and Timocles the Stoic quite by accident.
Unlike Homer's king of the gods, who could see pretty much whatever he
needed to see from on high, Lucian's was passing the time on foot in the
arcade of the public square in Athens when he noticed the crowd gathering around Damis and Timocles: "The whole discussion, it seems, was
about us." By now Zeus has overcome his panic, and he concludes,

> Fellow gods, this is why I have called you together—no small
> reason when you consider that our honor, our prestige, and our
> revenues all depend upon men. If they're convinced that gods
> don't exist or that, if we do, we take no thought for them, it
> means the end of sacrifices, gifts, and honors for us from down
> below. We'll sit around uselessly in heaven and starve. . . . I say
> it's the duty of everyone here to rack his brains for some way to
> save us in this crisis, some way to give Timocles the stronger
> case and a victory and to get the audience to hoot Damis down.
> Unless we do something for Timocles, I don't have much
> confidence in his winning on his own. (17–18)

Hermes calls on the other gods to speak, and at first Momus is the only
one who takes the cue. Distinctly an outsider, not one of your Olympians,
Momus cynically comes forward on the Epicurean side. Considering the
inequities of the human lot, criminals who get off free, and innocents
who suffer punishment, why should people believe in the gods in any
case? Momus cannot help himself from mocking or importuning his
superiors, and his advice is received accordingly. Poseidon on the other
hand is for doing the thunderbolt thing, and Heracles offers to shake the
arcade down on Damis's head; but Zeus counters that only the Fates can
determine on such actions.

    One Hermagoras enters at this point with news that a crowd is gath-
ering again below, as Damis and Timocles renew their debate. Zeus
orders the clouds to be rolled back so that the gods may see for themselves. Timocles will be "no match for Damis," he predicts, but "we'll do

all we can for him—we'll pray" (34). Lucian now unfolds a tour de force of comedy, a play within a play, dialogue within a dialogue. He scripts both the debate between the Stoic and Epicurean philosophers below and the ongoing dialogue among the gods above. It's like having a bird's-eye view of another Ciceronian *De natura deorum* being overheard by the very gods in question, and the dramatic irony abounds. Damis and Timocles go right at it. "Why this inflaming the public against me, Timocles? Who are you to carry on like this for the gods when they don't choose to do so for themselves? They've yet to do anything terrible to me and they've been hearing me talk for years—assuming, of course, that they can hear." Timocles: "They can hear, all right, and they'll go after you when the time comes." Damis: "How can they have time for me? You've told me yourself how many jobs they have, how they have to run the universe with its infinite mass of things" (37). Unknown to the debaters, they *are* being overheard by the gods; and, unknown to the gods, they are being overheard by Lucian's listeners or readers. It's delicious.

Almost all the arguments are familiar, and they all go Damis's way, as the gods above understand all too well. Timocles ventures to put the plays of Euripides in evidence. "Ah," Damis replies, "if it was our writers of tragedy who convinced you with such stuff, there are only two possible conclusions: either you must hold that the gods temporarily took the form of [famous actors] or, what's worse, that they took the form of the masks with gods' faces, the buskins, trailing robes, cloaks, long sleeves, belly pads, body pads, and all the other paraphernalia. . . . This is ridiculous." Timocles demands to know how all the people in the world who believe in the gods could be mistaken; and Damis runs through a counter-litany of all the variety of gods and rituals of worship: villagers there are who "worship half a skull or a clay cup or bowl" (41–43). Timocles finally tries this one: "See whether this syllogism isn't valid and whether there's any way you can capsize it. If there are altars, then there must be gods. But there *are* altars. Ergo, there must be gods. What do you say to *that*?" (51). Damis bursts out laughing, and says if that's all Timocles has to offer they can stop right now. Timocles first contends that if Damis wants to quit, then he is the loser. He then becomes furious at being made fun of.

This denouement of the philosophers' dialogue provides Lucian a perfect moment to close down the dialogue among the gods without further ado. Zeus and Hermes exchange just three more comments.

Readers are indebted to Zeus for observing that Damis goes running from the public square, "laughing his head off, with Timocles on his heels." So what should the gods do now? As usual, Hermes has an answer. He quotes from a comedy by Menander, "You feel no hurt—if you pretend there's none." As far as Hermes is concerned, it won't matter if some in the crowd below have been convinced by Damis, since plenty more will still be believers—"Greek *hoi polloi* and all the barbarians," for sure. Zeus pauses to reflect; and he gets the last word: "Still, Hermes, there's a lot to that remark Darius made about Zopyrus; I'd rather have one Damis on my side than own ten thousand Babylons" (53).

That Lucian was inspired by the comedies of Aristophanes goes without saying, and his dialogues bear witness to a considerable familiarity with the plays five or six hundred years after they were first performed. Lucian's treatment of Euripides both here and elsewhere is modeled on Aristophanes'. The very plot behind "Zeus Tragoedus"—if that's the word for an action that merely threatens the gods—derives from the penultimate action in *Birds*. The immortals in that comedy instructed their ambassadors to cut a deal with Peisetaerus because mortals are no longer favoring them with smoke from sacrificial fires. But in effect Lucian goes Aristophanes one better. One point of view he creates is that of the gods themselves, how they are first noticing something, then feeling and reacting. To be sure, divine and human beings express themselves strictly by the same means: dialogue. The two camps, with their variety of personalities and opinions, are set off from one another, as if for comparison. There are no ingenious clownlike protagonists such as Aristophanes' Peisetaerus or Strepsiades to spur the action. Yet by means of his play within a play in "Zeus Tragoedus" Lucian gives both sides equal time.

Incidentally, Lucian devoted a short, smooth-talking dialogue to the gods' punishment of Prometheus for creating human beings and giving them fire. In that dialogue Hermes and Hephaestus have the assignment of crucifying him in the mountains where an eagle can gnaw eternally at his liver, and they matter-of-factly go about this while Prometheus pleads his innocence. And Lucian's Prometheus certainly defends himself very ably. He has always looked out for the common good, he notes, and one of his reasons for creating humans was to help out the gods. After all, "there were no altars or temples" before he made humans. "You see"—this is another of Casson's translations—"I felt that being a god lacked something in not having a counterpart to set it off, something which, when used as a standard of comparison, would show what a very good thing divinity is. I further felt that this counterpart, although mortal, should be highly ingenious and intelligent and aware of the better things in life" (12). This comparison, implicit in many of Lucian's dialogues, holds out a hand to humanist comedy—for which side needs the other more? What could immortality signify if it were not for mortality? Despite Damis's laughter, those altars that Timocles wraps in his so-called syllogism make a telling point. If there were no humans there would be no altars.

Lucian's talents were not lost to posterity. Humanists with a sense of humor did not fail to take up the dialogues and work with them.[21] In quattrocento Italy the multi-tasking Leon Battista Alberti could scarcely keep Lucian away from his own literary endeavors. His bold *Momus*, silly but also satiric dialogues bound together in a deliberately improbable narrative about another crisis in the relations between gods and men, is obviously inspired by the lesser part played by Momus in Lucian's "Zeus Tragoedus."[22] Both Erasmus and Sir Thomas More, the friend to whom the *Praise of Folly* was dedicated, enjoyed translating the dialogues (into Latin) and borrowing from Lucian's wit and moral scores. There were even one or two mock encomiums that may have directly influenced Erasmus, such as Lucian's "Praising of a Fly"—*Musicae Encomium* becomes *Moriae Encomium*, so to speak.

Lucian's "Death of Peregrinus," on the other hand, was the very opposite kind of piece. Peregrinus was both a desperate show-off and some kind of psychopath who for a time managed to invent a role for himself in a Christian sect. Lucian despised the man and reacted accordingly, but that episode gave him room for a little bemused mockery of the teachings of Christianity as well—belief in life after death, contempt for worldly goods, and worship of the crucified Jesus. Lucian's method of scripting dialogues certainly captured the imagination in modern times.[23] Think of twentieth-century radio plays and skits.

ACT TWO

Humanist Games in Christian Times

What is Truth? said jesting Pilate; and would not stay for an
answer.
—Francis Bacon, *Essays*

The mental capacities of people are completely different, and
they readily put up with different beliefs. What inspires one
person's religion moves another to laughter.
—[Baruch Spinoza,] *Tractatus theologico-politicus*

Humanism can mean many things, but most commonly the word refers to a pronounced movement of ideas among the cognoscenti in the West that was well under way by the fifteenth century. This movement featured, above all, the use of reason and took a skeptical view of received wisdom, more especially anything that could be viewed as superstition. Humanity with its distinct societies had a history and, given those reasoning powers, theoretically could take charge of its own future. The movement was the offspring of both the Renaissance and the Reformation: the Renaissance inspired it to dig out and ponder classical literature and philosophy; the Reformation served as a model of changing doctrine. Freedom of thought was a desideratum, and sooner or later religious tolerance became a common cause among thinking people. John Donne might worry that "new philosophy calls all in doubt," but John Milton would try such matters "by dint of argument" rather than display "weakness and cowardice in the wars of Truth." Increasingly the natural world would be the focus of study, with humanity understood to be continuous with nature. All the major writers to be discussed here were humanists in this broad historical sense, though by the end of the nineteenth century much science and scientific knowledge had become too specialized to be comprehended by generalists.[1]

Scholars have sometimes conjectured that one or more of these writers—Hobbes, perhaps—simply kept their disbelief in God to themselves. With the exception of David Hume, however, none of these humanists was an atheist, and we have separate grounds for Hume's atheism not associated with his posthumously published *Dialogues concerning Natural Religion*. (The same can be said of the part José Saramago plays in act three. Saramago was an atheist, but in *The Gospel According to Jesus Christ* he carefully avoided denying the existence of God or indeed the miracles recorded in the gospels of old.) The humanists of act two were not professional comedians either, of course, and not amusing according to most scholarly opinion about their work. Nevertheless they could and did engage in play. A sheer delight in argument, a kind of triumphalism, could carry them away even as it carried the ancients away. Laughter at missing evidence or at another's poor logic took for granted the value of true reasoning; reductio ad absurdum abounded. Sparring with opponents may have left the outcome in doubt but combined safety with surprise. Milton was Milton, but these humanists excelled in the games of truth rather than the wars. Like their classical precursors, some fenced with divinity in general. For where did the future lie, with divine providence or with nature and humanity? The fencing need not produce a winner in order to meet the humanist goal of the advancement of learning.

Francis Bacon's position was not atypical. Bacon was a Christian humanist but never tired of playing one tradition off the other. He was tolerant of atheism because atheism was preferable to superstition. Atheists could at least be open-minded, whereas the superstitious panicked and were swayed by the mob. For comparisons and sorting of philosophical positions, Bacon turned repeatedly to the classical past. He understood full well the relatively relaxed commitments of polytheistic religion as compared to the monotheism of the Abrahamic faiths. In the third of his fifty-eight *Essays* he called for unity of religion because that was what Christian communities required and were failing to achieve. "The quarrels and divisions about religion were evils unknown to the heathen. The reason was, because the religion of the heathen consisted rather in rites and ceremonies than in any constant belief. For you may imagine what kind of faith theirs was, when the chief doctors and fathers of their church were the poets. But the true God hath this attribute, that he is a *jealous God*; and therefore his worship will endure no mixture nor partner."[2]

Like Thomas Hobbes after him, Bacon was principally targeting Roman Catholicism. He contended that quarrels within the church invited scorn from outsiders and mortified insiders; that trivial differences should be forgotten and serious ones worked out according to reason; and above all, that Christians should not "propagate religion by wars or by sanguinary persecutions to force consciences." He followed this up, not inappropriately, with a direct appeal to Lucretius's *De rerum natura*: "Lucretius the poet, when he beheld the act of Agamemnon, that could endure the sacrificing of his own daughter, exclaimed: *Tantum Religio potuit suadere malorum*. What would he have said, if he had known of the massacre in France or the powder treason of England? He would have been seven times more Epicure and atheist than he was."[3] Bacon did not need to elaborate on either of these allusions to contemporary history, the notorious massacre of Huguenots on St. Bartholomew's Day 1572 in France and the foiled gunpowder plot of Guy Fawkes against Parliament on 5 November 1605 in London, which resulted in the brutal execution of the conspirators. The Latin, which translates, "So great an amount of evil religion was able to inspire," is the frequently quoted final line of Lucretius's moving précis of the fate of Iphigenia (1.101). Among ancient philosophers Bacon tended to identify with Epicurus and Democritus rather than Plato or Aristotle.

Bacon's famous saying about jesting Pilate is the opening line of the first of the *Essays*, "Of Truth." (This too he followed with an allusion to Lucretius's poem—a paraphrase of the proem to book 2.) Pilate's question comes from the Gospel according to John (18:38), which has a fuller account of the Roman praetor's role in the passion of Jesus than any of the synoptic gospels. It is certainly possible to read into this and other of Pilate's remarks a sarcastic tone, but even so this is Lord Francis Bacon the prosecutor setting the tone, calling Pilate a jester. The truth in question is that of Jesus's teachings, which here and elsewhere Bacon is careful to hold separate from the knowledge of humankind and of nature that he promotes as a humanist—a position congruent with the Epicurean separation of the gods from evolving nature and human affairs both. Bacon infers Pilate was involved in the mocking of Jesus and crown of thorns as well as in the crucifixion itself. That mockery of bystanders fixes in the mind the disturbing account of the passion in all four gospels, which Erich Auerbach rightly saw as a turning point in the course of Western literary realism.[4]

Comedy is most at home on the stage. There can be no disagreement that Aristophanes scripted and went on to produce marvelous comedies. These were followed in Attica by the New Comedy, chiefly known to us via adaptations by Plautus and Terence for the Roman stage—or via pantomime and commedia dell'arte, modern theater and motion pictures. Yet for all that time comedy has never been confined to the theater; it can be spontaneous, contained and passed on by narrative, or deliberately utilized in a trial or public forum. What is questionable is whether comedy can ever be separated from some sort of performance; and performance is never single-minded. *To perform*, whether the transitive or the intransitive verb, means to manage at least two things at once, since performers are conscious of their appearance, words, gestures and of the possible reactions of an audience, whether listener, reader, or lookers-on. A comic performance has a tentativeness about it, a mischievous hope to share a laugh or, if not, to hit the escape button. If a performance should be unintended, then the performer may become the object of laughter: but note that clown acts are still acts, consciously inviting laughter. In sum, comedy, witty rejoinders, jokes—and needless to say, so-called practical jokes—are all performances.

Bacon famously called for the advancement of learning, for which religious tolerance would at least help clear the way. Can it be possible that comic performances should actually contribute in their way to the advancement of learning? A great number of prose tracts on serious subjects do raise a laugh when they engage in conscious performance. It is as if the type and duration of argument took precedence over the conclusion. Lucian's comic dialogues borrow directly from the theater, but even Ciceronian dialogue can verge on comedy. Bacon's essays have an edge and wordplay that entertain as well as instruct. Montaigne's *Essais*, from which Bacon frequently quotes, clearly inspired his own. Montaigne, who more than any other early modern writer also quotes Lucretius, kept reworking his essays, so that it has become customary for editors to indicate these expansions of the argument and for readers to try to grasp the author's performance over time. For practical reasons Pierre Bayle's *Pensées diverses sur la comète* is the one text of his examined here, but notoriously Bayle's principal work, the nonstop *Dictionnaire historique et critique*, was compounded in successive editions of boundless discursive remarks. Hobbes and Spinoza exulted in proving ridiculous the kind of nonsense that others create when interpreting the Bible. In their clearing of the decks, the laugh shall be on the side of the sweeper. Hume, it can be said, took up performing where Cicero left off. And Arnold jousted so faithfully that it is as if he began to engage in self-parody.

1. ERASMUS'S PRAISE OF FOLLY

Without question Desiderius Erasmus scripted a memorable performance and handed the leading role to Stultitia, the goddess Folly. Under her author's ironic direction, she both satirized human pretensions to theology and acted the serious part of Christian commitment to foolishness. *Praise of Folly*, begun possibly as early as 1509 and first published in 1511, was modeled on a standard type of classical speech making, the praise or encomium. Such speeches would regularly be anticipated as a special performance, the celebration of a god or praise of a victorious military commander. But the very title of this one promises a comic performance. The irony of praising the laughable—that is, the opposite of what is normally admired—is unmistakable. Wisdom, good sense, achievement, all out the door? Yet before he is done, Erasmus's rhetorical gambit moves down and up again through layers of fresh ironies, scoring point after point. Besides, right from the start and in violation of all the rules, the performer announces that she, Folly herself, will praise herself.[5]

Like so many writers ancient and modern, Erasmus takes advantage of the plurality of old-time gods to make free with their powers and differences. Folly informs us that she is the daughter of Plutus, the god of wealth, but Plutus when he was young and reckless, not the blind and aged god of Aristophanes' play. Her name, like his, results from a deification of the quality itself, *stultitia*, or foolishness. She thereby warrants an extended family of deifications: in Betty Radice's translation from the Latin, "I certainly don't envy the 'mighty son of Kronos' his she-goat nurse, for two charming nymphs fed me at their breasts, Drunkenness, daughter of Bacchus, and Ignorance, daughter of Pan." Among her other attendants are Self-love, Flattery, Forgetfulness, Idleness, Pleasure, and Sensuality. By this point feminists must rightfully be protesting, but Folly slyly adds, "You can see there are also two gods amongst the girls; one is called '*Comus*,' Revelry, and the other '*Negretos Hypnos*,' Sound Sleep" (17–18).[6] The notion of Folly among all this good company sets Erasmus's spokes-goddess off on a witty romp unmatched in literature. Basically there is an awful lot of foolishness at large in this world, and every individual member of the human tribe ought to confess that he or she has more than once played the fool. Thus Folly can justly boast that she has more followers among humanity than any other god.

Erasmus prompts her to articulate another sweeping generalization, this one about professional fools. When wise men speak the truth, people in charge don't wish to hear it; but fools have a special license: "They're the only ones who speak frankly and tell the truth, and what is more praiseworthy than truth?" Possibly, fools speak the truth because they have no idea of what will offend, whereas professional advisers do understand and tell only what their bosses wish to hear. But it's more than that; fools have a way of telling truths: "They can speak truth and even open insults and be heard with positive pleasure; indeed, the words which would cost a wise man his life are surprisingly enjoyable when uttered by a clown. For truth has a genuine power to please if it manages not to give offence, but this is something the gods have granted only to fools" (56–57). This principle goes a good way toward explaining how jokes communicate even as they entertain. Even jokes at the expense of a god? The gods (plural) don't mind. Erasmus's goddess then darkly reflects on people like her author:

> Let's now compare the lot of a wise man with that of this clown. Imagine some paragon of wisdom to set up against him, a man who has frittered away all his boyhood and youth in acquiring learning, has lost the happiest part of his life in endless wakeful nights, toil, and care, and never tastes a drop of pleasure even in what's left to him. He's always thrifty, impoverished, miserable, grumpy, harsh and unjust to himself, disagreeable and unpopular with his fellows, pale and thin, sickly and blear-eyed, prematurely white-haired and senile, worn-out and dying before his time. Though what difference does it make when a man like that does die? He's never been alive. There you have a splendid picture of a wise man. (57)

It is simply not the case that Folly is incapable of reasoning. She is like a debater employing whatever argument comes to hand, and when she scores the reader cannot help but smile.

Folly has an ear for rant and an eye for the grotesque. Early on she worries politics, disgusted with the way men stand up and ask for votes so that they can become famous as leaders and end up in the history books. But that's the way they are, and "this same folly creates societies and maintains empires, officialdom, religion, law courts, and councils—in fact the whole of human life is nothing but a sport of folly." So which side is she on? Are politics offensive, stupid, *and* necessary? Similarly warfare is a path to fame and empire—and perhaps domination over an alien religion. But warfare is bloody awful, a field of mangled corpses. Who wants that? Only a bloody fool—a fool with courage, no doubt, but taking terrible chances. Nevertheless, such foolishness teaches genuine prudence: "The wise man seeks refuge in his books of antiquity and learns from them the pure subtleties of what the ancients say. The fool tries everything, meets his dangers at first hand, and thereby acquires what I'm sure is genuine prudence." From this kind of reasoning Folly is able to generalize about entrepreneurial success and, by extension, the advancement of society. Experience is what is required, and "the two main obstacles to learning by experience are a sense of propriety which clouds the judgement and fear which advises against an undertaking once danger is apparent. Folly offers a splendid liberation from both of them. Few mortals realize how many other advantages follow from being free from scruples and willing to venture anything" (42–43). This is Folly herself speaking, and that might be grounds for throwing out the whole argument. But Erasmus is not satirizing one position or the other here. He prefers to leave these paradoxical, purely secular theses about history up in the air. He admits that men of action may change society more radically than armchair intellectuals like himself. The case that Folly makes for the ubiquity of her followers stands.

Elsewhere *Praise of Folly* does unmistakably engage in satire. Although the notion of Folly railing at folly does give pause, satire itself is less enigmatic than prolonged contemplation of foolishness. Generally speaking satire is a very satisfying exercise, a combination of ridicule and attack on a specific target or targets. It is a mistake to think of it primarily as the means to reform. That may now and then be the result, but in that rare event satirists will simply feel deprived of their enjoyment and the chance to work out their aggression. To satirize is undoubtedly satisfying, and Folly herself can rest easy. For as she is fond of reminding us, there are plenty of human activities and agents out there worthy of ridicule. About halfway through the *Praise* Erasmus turns, first tentatively and then more spiritedly, to satire. The targets that come immediately to Folly's mind are mainly conventional: gentlemen hunting wild game as a weekend sport; the practice of alchemy or astrology; gambling and quarreling over a throw of the dice; infatuation with ghost stories, tales of miracles, and the like; people who prearrange their funeral services down to the last obsessive detail; people who trace their ancestors back to Aeneas, say, or Brutus; people whose self-admiration equates them with Euclid because they can draw circles with a compass; others who credit themselves with what their servants have done; performers on the stage who cannot get over how well they do their thing. The list, hardly anything more than that, is capped with a nice paragraph on national characteristics vaunted by the peoples of Europe, as illustrative of their self-love (60–69). The classical inspiration for some of this point scoring can be traced to Horace's *Epistles*. Others, like the unnecessary torture and mangling of wild game, were shared by Erasmus's friend Sir Thomas More in his *Utopia* (1516).[7]

With sights trained next on flatterers, the satire becomes more rewarding. Folly first mischievously concedes that "no animal fawns so much as a dog, and none is so faithful." But there are problems with human fawning: cowardice, insincerity, and often calculated deception. She condemns all that as a matter of course, however, then devotes more words to one of her typical argumentative dichotomies. There is a second kind of flattery that Folly takes to heart, without which family and social life could hardly survive. We need to be deceived, are accustomed to being fooled, and do not wish to know what people we deal with everyday really think about us. Without such polite consideration and, yes, hypocrisy life would be much more unpleasant. On a professional level, flattery is partly what is meant by eloquence or by poetry, to say nothing of a successful medical practice. Ingeniously, Erasmus has scripted another comic surprise and enlarged the target of satire to include everyman. What starts as a predictable assault on a noxious type, flatterers, turns on all of us, just as we were settling down to enjoying the spectacle. As Folly concludes, "Man's mind is so formed that it is far more susceptible to falsehood than to truth. If anyone wants an immediate, clear example of this he has only to go to church at sermon time, where everyone is asleep or yawning or feeling queasy whenever some serious argument is expounded, but if the preacher starts to rant (I beg your pardon, I mean orate) on some old wives' tale, as they often do, his audience sits up and takes notice open-mouthed." Even when, as is frequently the case, she engages in a little self-flattery, she drives home the main point: "I don't leave a single mortal without a share in my bounty, though the gifts of the other deities are unevenly bestowed." To prove her case, she runs through the traditional Olympian gods and the favors they bestow by name (69–73).

She next attacks the learned professions, scarcely unique to Erasmus as the object of satire. Leading off come schoolmasters, poets, and rhetoricians, the last including those who have written "so many painstaking passages on the theory of joking." The authors of any book court fame, and the more specialized and learned the book, the harder fame is to come by. Folly pities their struggles to complete their task: "They add, change, remove, lay aside, take up, rephrase, show to their friends, keep for nine years"—and wear themselves out. "Yet the wise man believes he is compensated for everything if he wins the approval of one or another purblind scholar." Lawyers hardly need mentioning, having been satirized for so many centuries past; they are completely self-satisfied, endlessly find work for themselves, and talk nonstop. And what can be said for philosophers? They believe there *are* no wise men save themselves. Philosophers purport to know everything. "They never pause for a moment, as if they were private secretaries to Nature, architect of the universe, or had come to us straight from the council of the gods. Meanwhile Nature has a fine laugh at them and their conjectures, for their total lack of certainty is obvious enough from the endless contention amongst themselves on every single point" (78–85).

Then it becomes the turn of theologians and monks, the so-called religious. As in the case of lawyers and philosophers, there was nothing new about satirizing the religious. Priests and friars who did not rise to their calling were fair game in the Middle Ages. But the callings were specifically Christian, and criticism from Erasmus had its humanist bent. In her initial list of satiric targets Folly had already included a bundle of related targets, such as people who confuse the saints with heathen gods, those who imagine that purgatory will prove an easy trip for them but still wish to put off death, those who trust that reciting the same magic verses from the Psalms everyday will assure their happiness, or who believe that a nod from the Virgin Mary matters more than following the teachings of Jesus (63–65). More significantly, after the edition of 1511 Erasmus greatly expanded the number of pages in the *Praise of Folly* devoted to ridiculing theologians and religious both. The added paragraphs spin out his transition from satire to a serious embrace of what Paul, especially, wrote about foolishness. In some places Erasmus pretty well abandons the persona of Folly, and not all the additions represent his best writing.

She gets off to a good start on theologians, however, by remarking how they look down on the rest of humankind from "a sort of third heaven" of their own. Such a heaven they have undoubtedly earned by all their logic chopping, for they boast that they could untie the knots in the steel net that Vulcan wove by sheer argument. It is not clear whether the heights of Olympus, in the story sung by Demodocus in book 8 of the *Odyssey*, count as the first heaven or the second—or whether Folly alludes to Paul's misgivings in 2 Corinthians 12:1–7. But theologians apparently don't stop to reason why they, rather than Mars and Venus, might be thus enclosed, nor do they even notice the laughter of the other gods. Folly charges them with self-love, but mainly she belittles the kinds of distinctions they make in endless debates about the liturgy—or scripture, such as how long Jesus resided in Mary's womb. Their disputes have spread and become sectarian, so that it has become impossible to escape "from the tortuous obscurities of realists, nominalists, Thomists, Albertists, Ockhamists and Scotists." Worse, theologians so thoroughly lose their sense of proportion that they reach absurd moral conclusions: such as, that it is better to kill a thousand fellow human beings than to break the Sabbath by cobbling a shoe, or to let the whole world perish rather than tell a lie (86–88).

There is more of this, and Folly recommends that Scotists, Ockhamists, and Albertists be sent off with a troupe of sophists to make war against the Turks. But there are also marked alterations in tone, especially in some of the passages added after 1512. The satire lets up, and Folly differentiates between such petty doctrinal disputes and a more thoughtful teaching of charity and grace—and far better to teach by example than by syllogism in any case. She contrasts the contributions of Paul and the Apostles with all that logic chopping of the sects and aloof theologians. This means going back to the Bible, and she refers her listeners explicitly to 1 Corinthians 13. The reference speaks for itself. Erasmus judges that there is no need to quote it, since this is the chapter from Paul's letter beginning, "If I speak in the tongues of men and of angels, but have not love, I am a noisy gong or a clanging cymbal," and concluding, "When I was a child, I spoke like a child, I thought like a child, I reasoned like a child; when I became a man, I gave up childish ways. For now we see in a mirror dimly, but [in the future] face to face. Now I know in part; then I shall understand fully, even as I have been fully understood. So faith, hope, love abide, these three; but the greatest of these is love."[8] Folly, of all goddesses, chides those of her followers who, amid their complacent fooleries, cannot find "a spare moment in which to read the Gospel or the letters of Paul even once through" (89–93).

In some ways Erasmus seems even more disgusted with religious orders than he is with theologians. This may be a kind of class bias; it seems a great many monks were not even literate. At any rate, he allows Folly to charge them with being proud of their ignorance and illiteracy and living strictly by the rule, day in day out. And then there are the names of all the different orders, "as if it weren't enough to be called Christians." Erasmus and his spokes-goddess go way off base, in one of the added passages, when they imagine and represent in direct discourse what Jesus would say to these monks, calling them a "new race of Jews" no less (97–98). They are on safer ground (and back to the 1512 text) when the satire addresses kings and courtiers as still another target. Leaders of the secular world have a lot to live up to, hence many shortcomings of behavior, competence, and attitude for Folly to take down. And she notice-ably warms to the task once more when comparing churchmen with these aristocrats: "Such practices of princes have long been zealously adopted by supreme pontiffs, cardinals, and bishops, and indeed, have almost been surpassed." The hierarchies in question are similar and make for laziness. Forms of address, such as your Beatitude, Reverence, or Holiness, are insisted upon by the protocol. Thus the forms, extent, and means of secular rule have been adopted by the church: "Lands, cities, taxes, imposts, and sovereignties are all called Peter's patrimony, despite the words of the Gospel, 'We have forsaken all and follow thee.'" Still more absurdly and wickedly, the custom of warfare among secular powers has been taken over by a church engaged in holy wars:

> Since the Christian church was founded on blood, strengthened by blood, and increased in blood, they continue to manage its affairs by the sword as if Christ has perished and can no longer protect his own people in his own way. War is something so monstrous that it befits wild beasts rather than men . . . so impious that it is quite alien to Christ; and yet they leave everything to devote themselves to war alone. . . . And there's no lack of learned sycophants to put the name of zeal, piety, and valour to this manifest insanity, and to think up a means whereby it is possible for a man to draw a murderous sword and plunge it into his brother's vitals without loss of the supreme charity which in accordance with Christ's teaching every Christian owes his neighbour. (107–11)

In such a passage the question of the consistency of Folly's voice seems beside the point. Too many wars *have* been fought in Christ's name. But Erasmus permits her to score still another hit against the secular ways of the church—the worship of money. One further, telling paragraph contends, in sum, that "wherever you turn, to pontiff or prince, judge or official, friend or foe, high or low, you'll find nothing can be achieved without money; and as the wise man despises money, it takes good care to keep out of his way" (114). With still about a sixth of her speech to go, Folly signals that she will soon be done, and this clearly marks a turning point.

How does one close and tie up such a bundle of ironies, especially a bundle as entertaining and profound as this one? Did Erasmus plan his way from the start? The *Praise of Folly* throws dramatic consistency to the winds and settles for surprise, by turning its message about folly outside in. Folly now declares that she will persuade Christians to take her side by reviewing "the evidence of the Holy Scriptures" (115). Needless to say, this last portion of the *Praise* is the hardest to interpret. Confidently to say what Erasmus is up to here would take an exhaustive study of his own reading of the scriptures, especially of the gospels and the letters of Paul.

A number of Folly's specific allusions to the Bible are to the first four chapters of 1 Corinthians and the last four chapters of 2 Corinthians because these include not a few explicit appeals to foolishness. It may well be that Erasmus identified with the apostle Paul, who had a difficult relation with the Christian congregation of Corinth. Actually, 2 Corinthians 10–13 seems to be a fragment of a third or fourth letter to the congregation, with whom, underneath the irony and a certain defensiveness, Paul is angry. "I wish you would bear with me in a little foolishness," he writes. "Do bear with me! I feel a divine jealousy for you, for I betrothed you to Christ to present you as a pure bride to her one husband. But I am afraid that as the serpent deceived Eve by his cunning, your thoughts will be led astray from a sincere and pure devotion to Christ" (11.1–3). Here foolishness refers to his pleasantry, the imaginative allegory of their relationship. In this allegory Paul does not quite elevate himself to divinity. Although he speaks with apostolic authority throughout the epistles, in 2 Corinthians he also plays the fool. "I am talking like a madman" (11.23), he exclaims, in one of the expressions picked out by Erasmus's Folly. In this epistle Paul keeps being ironic and then withdrawing the irony. He knows whereof he speaks, and he is not pleased with the Corinthians' backsliding and desertion. On Folly's side, so to speak, he does plead the license of a fool, but only rhetorically: "I repeat, let no one think me foolish; but even if you do, accept me as a fool, so that I too may boast a little. What I am saying I say not with the Lord's authority but as a fool in this boastful confidence; since many boast of worldly things, I too will boast." And he adds, a little sarcastically, "For you gladly bear with fools, being wise yourselves!" (11.16–19). The sarcasm of his joke—for that is what it is—effectively cancels the fool's license. But it was a mock license in the first place.

The appeals to foolishness in 1 Corinthians are another matter. The addressees may be of the same tribe, but this epistle is concerted and far more coherent, memorable for its eloquence and outreach and warmth. It begins with at least nine invocations of Jesus Christ, almost one every sentence, in which the Corinthian congregation is implicitly invited to join. The appeal to foolishness commences at once and proves quite serious, a play on the extrinsic but also intrinsic foolishness of Jesus's teachings. Paul has been sent by Christ "to preach the gospel" but "not with eloquent wisdom, lest the cross of Christ be emptied of its power." That is, the example of Jesus is even more compelling than the teaching (a proposition Erasmus would accept): "For the word of the cross is folly to those who are perishing, but to us who are being saved it is the power of God" (1.17–18). Then he quotes the last two lines of Isaiah 29.14, a glance at the wisdom literature of the Hebrew Bible. (Erasmus's Folly borrows lines from Proverbs and Ecclesiastes as often as she does from the New Testament.) Paul's opening thrust here speaks directly to the belief in life after death that rapidly became, partly because of his teaching, a principal reward of Christian faith. In the synoptic gospels Jesus says almost nothing of this promise, let alone of the immortality of human souls in general. Paul preaches it continually and very eloquently indeed in 1 Corinthians 15. But only the followers of Jesus Christ and the apostles will be saved, not unbelievers, to whom it is all foolishness.

Thus one meaning of foolishness for Paul is extrinsic to the faith. Christians certainly look foolish to outsiders. In scolding the rather limited, conceited, and potentially disloyal Corinthian congregation, Paul ironically exaggerates that point of view: "For I think that God has exhibited us apostles as last of all, like men sentenced to death; because we have become a spectacle to the world, to angels and to men." Whereas the Corinthians imagine they are just fine, wise and strong, "we are fools for

Christ's sake. . . . we hunger and thirst, we are ill-clad and buffeted and homeless, and we labor, working with our own hands." Besides this humbling—that is, in the world's view of social standing—the practice of turning the other cheek renders appearances even worse: "When reviled, we bless; when persecuted, we endure; when slandered, we try to conciliate; we have become, and are now, as the refuse of the world, the offscouring of all things" (4.9–13). One vector of becoming a fool for Christ's sake results in this unintended performance for the unsaved, who are the many, the worldly of this world. And this is scarcely the only reference to foolishness in this sense in Paul, the gospels, or the wisdom literature of old.

But the teachings of Jesus were also intrinsically foolish, consciously so in the commitments asked of believers and their acceptance. Paul touches on this foolishness, too, in the same absorbing 1 Corinthians. "Has not God made foolish the wisdom of the world? . . . it pleased God through the folly of what we preach to save those who believe. For Jews demand signs and Greeks seek wisdom, but we preach Christ crucified, a stumbling block to Jews and folly to Gentiles, but to those who are called, both Jews and Greeks, Christ the power of God and the wisdom of God." Just a reminder of the crucifixion and the mocking of onlookers as the culmination of Jesus's life on earth is enough to evoke the craziness of his mission. He deliberately sought out the unfortunate, the very people whom others looked down upon and made fun of. Here Paul strikes a more comradely note. He reminds his Corinthians that they were not especially smart or successful or of notable families either: "But God chose what is foolish in the world to shame the wise, God chose what is weak in the world to shame the strong, God chose what is low and despised in the world, even things that are not, to bring to nothing things that are, so that no human being might boast in the presence of God" (1.20–24, 27–29). This might be called a revolution, and there is plenty of evidence in the gospels that Jesus persistently addressed the unfairness of human lives in lower social strata or in circumstances beyond their control. An unmistakable leveling tendency moves through the gospels, the origins of Christianity as a whole, and the Sermon on the Mount in particular. A moral egalitarianism is implicit in the so-called golden rule that Jesus embraces (and Paul will amplify in Romans 13.8–10). The beatitudes, especially as recorded in the gospel according to Luke, are revolutionary. Blessed are the poor, those that hunger, and those who weep; and, "Blessed are you when men hate you, and when they exclude you and revile you, and cast out your name as evil," as a follower of mine. "But woe to you that are rich, for you have received your consolation. Woe to you that are full now, for you shall hunger. Woe to you that laugh now, for you shall mourn and weep. Woe to you, when all men speak well of you, for so their fathers did to the false prophets" (Luke 6.20–26).

Matthew's version of the beatitudes is less materialistic: blessed are the poor in spirit, those who mourn, and the meek. But such considerations of the inward person, some will say, pose an even more profound revolution. Anger, for example, may spur a crime like murder, "but I say to you that every one who is angry with his brother shall be liable to judgment; whoever insults his brother shall be liable to the council, and whoever says, 'You fool!' shall be liable to the hell of fire." Similarly with those who lust after a woman and commit adultery in their hearts (Matthew 5.3–5, 22, 28). Given the hypocrisy of the world, turning the other cheek sometimes so surprises and shames the powers that be that it results in action. Frequently Jesus invokes God the Father as the guarantor—and policeman—of all these teachings; but many may readily be interpreted as sound secular psychology for living. Either way, the attention to interior feelings and judgments can be salutary. Most of human life is far from speaking out; much control can be exercised from within; mental attitudes count, for contentment and survival as well as outward behavior. "For whoever would save his life will lose it . . . what does it profit a man if he gains the whole world and loses or forfeits himself?" (Luke 9.24–25). Hope is in the nature of things benevolent, especially good for the poor or poor in spirit, for whom experience suggests it is foolish. Such is the intrinsic foolishness of Christianity, not to be laughed at.

So, in the last portion of Erasmus's *Praise of Folly* is Folly's view of the foolishness witnessed in holy scripture that of an outsider or an insider? The answer is both, at some expense to the consistency of character in the performer. But two things can be said about that. As low characters, clowns and fools are not expected to be consistent; and as a high matter, humanist authors regularly cited classical texts, even loose applications of Greek and Roman gods in support of arguments with serious Christian intent. Stultitia is another one of those goddesses, you see. The burden of consistency finally lies with Erasmus (and, to be sure, the *Praise* and other writings drew plenty of fire from less imaginative contemporaries). In the end Erasmus's Folly does touch down on some of the intrinsic as well as extrinsic foolishness of the Christian faith, and her creator takes advantage of laughter's two-sidedness to get off free.

Folly knows 1 Corinthians well, but she appeals to other books of the Bible also in positive ways. Mostly she doesn't cite texts, let alone expound them, and counts on her listeners' familiarity with the passage. Thus she glances at a few of Jesus's parables and generalizes as follows: "He . . . made his appeal through the example of children, lilies, mustard-seed, and humble sparrows, all foolish, senseless things, which live their lives by natural instinct alone, free from care or purpose." Never mind that any one of such parables has before now elicited countless abstruse sermons, Folly features their simplicity. Everyone knows that children are foolish, and most love them that way. Jesus held them out as an example. He "seems to have taken special delight in little children, women, and fishermen." Christ "preferred to ride a donkey, though had he chosen he could safely have been mounted on a lion; and the Holy Spirit descended in the form of a dove, not of an eagle or a hawk" (125–26). Folly also knows how important forgiveness is for Christians and (in a paragraph added after 1512) detects a connection with foolishness. She wants to insist that foolishness is forgivable and is happy to point out that when people admit to others or to themselves that they have been fools, they are likely to be forgiven. Here she cites some specific instances in the Hebrew Bible, notably the memorable exchange between the warring Saul and David in 1 Samuel. And she quotes the last words of the crucified Jesus, as given in the gospel of Luke—and only in Luke: "Father, forgive them; for they know not what they do" (23.34).

When Folly has done with scripture and summarizes her estimate of Christians' foolishness, she might as well be speaking as an outsider again: "Finally, the biggest fools of all appear to be those who have once been wholly possessed by zeal for Christian piety. They squander their possessions, ignore insults, submit to being cheated, make no distinction between friends and enemies, shun pleasure, sustain themselves on fasting, vigils, tears, toil, and humiliations, scorn life, and desire only death." And pointedly she concludes, "They seem to be dead to any normal feelings, as if their spirit dwelt elsewhere than in their body. What else can that be but madness?" (128). In truth, Erasmus the humanist is also shifting ground here. There is madness and madness. He wonderfully maintains the irony in scripting Folly's part, but the authority for what follows, a brief discourse on the difference of body and soul, is Platonic. As she puts it, Christians and Platonists agree that the soul is distinct from the body and must study to be free. The soul needs to escape from prison: a metaphor she explicitly borrows from Plato's parable of the cave in the *Republic*. It *is* a sort of crazy parable. The men in the cave, remember, are chained in place so that they can see only shadows. They mistake these shadows for reality; thus the solid bodies that cast shadows allegorically stand for the higher, abstract Platonic reality, which most people never comprehend because they fail to escape from the prison of the body. In the same part of the *Republic* (book 7) Socrates goes on to outline the near lifetime education of the guardians of the state, for which only a few citizens qualify. Knowledge is the prerequisite, and striving for it entails the cultivation of reasoning and will rather than of the senses associated with the body. Similarly, only the most pious Christians succeed in transcending the body.

A promise to be saved from death often seems crude to later humanists, though that is what most obviously counters the evidence of the body—and bringing in Plato may encompass the aim of perfecting the present life. But then Erasmus prompts Folly to explain the sacrament of the Eucharist, and so she does: "It represents the death of Christ, which men must express through the mastery and extinction of their bodily passions, laying them in the tomb, as it were, in order to rise again to a new life wherein they can be united with him and with each other." And once Folly gets going, she segues from Platonic love to imaginings of ecstasy, such as the pious are liable to, "so much does the spiritual surpass the physical, the invisible the visible." She calls on the prophet Isaiah, as quoted by Paul in 1 Corinthians—"Eye hath not seen, nor ear heard, neither have entered into the heart of man, the things that God hath prepared for those that love him"[9]—and comments, "So those who are granted a foretaste of this—and very few have the good fortune—experience something which is very like madness" (131–33). She has been anticipated, one might say, by Paul's conversion on the road to Damascus; or better, his querulous report of another such experience in 2 Corinthians 12.2–9.

Folly, it seems, has been quite carried away. She catches herself just in time and, rather sweetly, apologizes before saying goodbye to her listeners and the reader: "But I've long been forgetting who I am. . . . If anything I've said seems rather impudent or garrulous, you must remember it's Folly and a woman who's been speaking" (134). The comedy is over.

In order to assess this last, Christian portion of Folly's performance, it helps to hold the *Encomium* up against a more straightforward account of Erasmus's beliefs and compare them. Such a standard is provided by the *Enchiridion militis christiani*, or *Handbook of the Christian Soldier*, of 1503. This was also a short and highly successful publication in Latin, with many editions and translations in Erasmus's lifetime. The soldier of the title is a Pauline metonymy for any—or at least any male—Christian believer. This too is a performance of sorts, not strictly in the writer's own voice until the last few pages, but if so, the *Enchiridion* is a sober, didactic performance. The center of it consists of twenty-two variously elaborated rules for a Christian soldier to follow in order to get a hold on his life and perhaps to be saved. As in the *Praise of Folly*, there is a mix of humanist and religious themes, an emphasis on knowledge, on knowing oneself, behaving well to others, and perhaps doing some reading in the classics, along with a steady adherence to God's word. Once again it seems Plato can assist in both camps. The soldier must be commanded by Christ, who *is* God, "although he became man for your sake."[10]

Both these works by Erasmus rely heavily on the speculative division of each human being into body and soul that is probably as old as humanity itself. In the *Enchiridion* he attributes to Origen as well as Paul a triple partition into body, soul, and spirit, of which the last may well be the most uncertain. Erasmus is also fond of referring to *mind* and body rather than soul. The insistence on soul versus body in Christianity has much to do with its traditionally very harsh view of human sexuality and its lack of interest in material progress, which in turn discouraged science. (The last may be beside the point here, but without question Erasmus is rougher on sex between man and woman, whether lust or love, in this work than in *Praise of Folly*.) In the tripartite case, the soul wavers between body and spirit. He quotes Paul, 1 Corinthians 6.16–17: "Do you not know that he who joins himself to a prostitute becomes one body with her? . . . But he who is united to the Lord becomes one spirit with him." One may agree that will, reasoning, language, and other capacities of the mind may be more valuable—more human—than functions shared with animals or even plants, but if so, the ground of Paul's comparison is a stretch. Can being with God meaningfully even be contrasted to being with a whore? Typically the spirit, whether part of a god or of a human, is never precisely determined or defined. Erasmus goes on to adduce some passages from Proverbs, but these apply to the point in question only as allegory.

The fifth and longest rule of the *Enchiridion* broadly urges "despising visible things in comparison to those that are invisible" precisely because seeing, the surest of human senses, is a common metaphor for knowing. The problem is that all the evidence goes out with the visible; the invisible remains invisible, impossible to make out or to describe. Erasmus's only recourse is to keep reminding the reader how often the scriptures have recourse to the same word, *spirit*, but the added authority does not supply more content. For John, especially, God is spirit, and "it is the spirit that gives life, the flesh is of no avail" (6.63). The first time Erasmus quotes this bit in support of his fifth rule, he prefers to qualify it: after all, the flesh does play a part. But then he immediately defers again to the higher truth of the gospel. The one promise common to John and Paul that is comprehensible to the poor reader is that of souls not perishing along with the body. Some later humanists will put that down to a selfish motive for keeping the faith.

But that is not all there is to the *Enchiridion*. Alongside the allegorizing of the Hebrew prophets and so much deferral to the exact diction of the apostles, the handbook calls independently for learning and thoughtful interaction with others, and above all, self-knowledge and self-command. It assumes the Christian soldier's willing concurrence with the Bible, once he has been reminded of what it says; but for a more rounded and satisfying life he might wish to be acquainted with Plato and classical literature. The rules set forth by Erasmus tend to get shorter, and some do not overtly appeal to scripture. Once they are all in place he concludes by spelling out more remedies for rule breaking and advice for everyday living. The assumptions and conclusions are more humanist, less necessarily religious. For his twentieth rule Erasmus states that virtue is its own reward and needn't wait on Christian salvation. What is more obvious, he asks, than to prefer everlasting life in heaven to everlasting

torment in hell? What operates more subtly, however, is the consciousness of right and wrong in the present life: "tranquility of mind and . . .
joy" as against "the anguish of a mind conscious of its guilt." The twenty-
first rule is simply a reminder that no one knows how long they will live.
The twenty-second and last rule of all is to beware of impenitence. Instead
of scripture, and without feeling it necessary to give the source or to
explain his allegorical reading of it, Erasmus quotes a line and a half
from Virgil: easy is the descent to hell, remember, "but to retrace one's
step and pass to the upper airs, / that is the task and that the toil" (*Aeneid*
6.128–29). This is the voice of the Sybil, pointing the way at the beginning of Aeneas's journey to the underworld. Erasmus is himself again;
and if he had had the literary genius of a Dante and taken the reader along
on another such tour, his picture of the afterlife in store for humanity
would not be so empty.

In his *Essays* Bacon might seem to be mocking the ancients: "You
may imagine what kind of faith theirs was, when the chief doctors and
fathers of their church were the poets." But he was not being dismissive,
because the reason for invoking classical times in the first place is that
they were free from the evils, the quarrels and divisions that plague the
religion of his own time—the very kinds of things that troubled Erasmus
also. Humanists felt something like nostalgia for divinity as pictured by
the Greeks and Romans, with its polytheism and pronounced anthropomorphism; there were mortals and there were the immortals, the latter
with particular cares and understandable emotions, extraordinary yet ultimately limited powers. Bacon put his finger on the difference even as he
ironically understated it as "this attribute" of the true God, "a jealous
God."[11] Those key words come from the second commandment (speaking
of rules) as reported by Moses; and of the ten commandments only the
first two are couched in the first person: "For I the Lord your God am a
jealous God," and he explains what that means. The commandment
which commences by ruling out the worship of graven images ends by
God's promising to love his followers but to punish those who hate him
(Exodus 20.2–6). Bacon understood that the exclusivity of the Judeo-
Christian God motivated believers, hence the divisions and quarrels but
also the rise of a new church in the West, as against Jews and others. If
there is only one God, and you happen to know what he favors, the rest is
history. If you remain a member of the minority, one of the chosen, all the

better. A kind of inverse snobbery has its appeal. In sum, both Jesus and the apostle Paul stressed that many are called but few are chosen, with two effects. One was revolutionary: if the few could win out over the many, the weak could become strong. The second was consolatory: if you failed to make the cut, you had plenty of company. Both effects contributed to a third, the likelihood of schisms still to come.

Erasmus clearly subscribes to the principle of the few versus the many. The *Enchiridion* takes the privilege of the few for granted throughout. In expounding the sixth rule, for example, Erasmus invokes Plato against the ignorance of the majority and the danger of running with the mob. But the finely honed sentences on the theme tend to echo the gospels: "Those who take to heart Christian simplicity, poverty, and truth are but a tiny flock, and they always will be. It is tiny, but blessed, since to it alone is owed the kingdom of heaven. The path of virtue is narrow and trodden by very few, but no other leads to life."[12] This is one of those areas, like the sharp differentiation of body and soul, where the *Encomium* concurs with the *Enchiridion*. At least in the last pages of the *Encomium*, Folly half a dozen times contrasts the commitment of the pious few with being swayed by the crowd. Erasmus never gives the impression that true Christianity is for the masses.

A few pious scholars think *Praise of Folly* is the inferior work, but they are wrong. It works as satire and as a thoughtful probing of Christian belief and is very entertaining. Erasmus's humanism is not entirely comfortable with the promise of salvation literally construed, but unproven, as life after death. The license of comedy allows him to pull up short where the evidence runs out and rest content. In a long section added to the *Praise* after 1512 Erasmus glossed one of the tricky sayings about foolishness by Paul that he had already partially quoted (2 Corinthians 11.23). There was clearly a problem in how to punctuate or even pronounce the words, "I speak as a fool, I am more." Erasmus's Folly kindly puts herself in Paul's place and offers this interpretation: "He wanted this to carry conviction without his words sounding arrogant and offensive, so he made folly his pretext to forestall objections, writing 'I speak as a fool' because it is the privilege of fools to speak the truth without giving offence" (119). Just so, Erasmus seized the privilege and composed what remains his most popular book, whether in skeptical circles or in divinity schools.

2. MONTAIGNE'S *QUE SAIS-JE?*

Montaigne wrote his *Essais* over a period of roughly twenty years, starting around 1571 and continuing until his death in 1592, when he was in his sixtieth year. They functioned mainly as a commonplace book at first, in which he recorded his thoughts along with passages from his reading that inspired them or came to his attention later. But as the essays accumulated he decided to publish them, gave them titles, and eventually divided them into three books. When he republished them he not only added essays but second thoughts and more quotations to those already in print—a kind of performance, laying out his mind and the minds of those who had come before in front of the reader.

The essays that evolved are replete with quotation and paraphrase from classical antiquity: above all, Cicero and Lucretius, Plutarch and Seneca, Virgil, Ovid, and Horace. Montaigne was essentially a reader of Latin, not Greek, but he frequently invokes Plato and occasionally fences with Aristotle. Among Christian texts he often cites Augustine's *De civitate dei*, especially passages in which Augustine himself was coping with Cicero and company. He was evidently acquainted with some of Erasmus's writings, but unlike Erasmus he rarely wrote out or commented on passages from the Bible. Montaigne's last, substantial essay, "Of Experience," gets under way with a remark that is quite to the point: "Those people must be jesting who think they can diminish and stop our disputes by recalling us to the express words of the Bible" (3, 13, 815/1042 B).[13] *Our* disputes are either generic here or refer to the French wars of religion. Montaigne does not engage in disputes if he can help it. The thoughts he sets down in the essays are mostly just that: something to think about. He loathes "that aggressive and quarrelsome arrogance that believes and trusts wholly in itself, a mortal enemy of discipline and truth" (823/1052 B). Intellectual disputants take positions on very little evidence and then argue as if they were handing down proofs. Montaigne, on the contrary, offers a very low estimate of what one can know in the first place. Richard Popkin unhesitatingly identified him as the most influential practitioner of the new Pyrrhonism of early modern times.[14] But Montaigne also stresses how much of what we think and believe depends on our upbringing and where we hail from. In "Of Custom," but not only there, he cautions that habit can be stronger than reason and credits Cicero with the same observation (1, 23, 79/109 A, C). Montaigne can be devastating on human vanity and foolish habits. He does not count on the common people, mostly illiterate, exercising reason. But he is open-minded and a strong believer in his own mortal self, determined to go on learning as he can.

The question "Que sais-je?" that expresses this minimalist stance occurs more than a third of the way through his book-length essay titled "Apology for Raymond Sebond" (2, 12, 393/508 B; modernized spelling). What do I know? Montaigne puts the question in order to avoid the Pyrrhonist trap of asserting, "I do not know," which defeats itself by denying that one knows that one does not know. (Compare the same problem with "I lie.") He imagines the words *Que sais-je?* inscribed over the emblem of a pair of scales. His motto will be to weigh carefully what he knows and does not know. Given that by this point Montaigne has amply ridiculed those who say much more about gods and God than they possibly can know, "Que sais-je?" also functions as a generalized rhetorical question: What do any of us know about divinity? He falls back on his genuine modesty, touched with a bit of noblesse oblige, to admit that he does not have any independent knowledge of God either. The "Apology for Raymond Sebond" provides the best continuous record of Montaigne's thoughts on religion, and in it he constantly returns to questions of what can be known and how. Sebond wrote his *Theologia naturalis* in the fourteenth century. The book came into the hands of Montaigne's father, who asked his son to translate it into French for him; Montaigne dutifully did so in 1569, and the translation was subsequently published. The "Apology," composed a decade later, says little more about Sebond or his book than this, though the book's subject matter became that of the extraordinary essay.

In the Reformation and its aftermath, Christian doctrines as well as churches split off anew. Differing church leaders and attendant theologians decreed that salvation depended on accepting certain propositions literally as dogma. Meanwhile for humanists the notion of comparing religions once again took a scholarly turn as opposed to ritual engagement, and this had consequences for later religious debates.[15] Historians of ideas sometimes aver that Montaigne's "Apology" is mostly just anti-Protestant, but that hardly does justice to his position. Rather, he registers right away that doctrine is not enough and often has little to do with practice. He even speculates that pagans were more likely than present-day

Christians to act on their beliefs: "We ought to be ashamed that in [other] human sects there never was a partisan, whatever difficult and strange thing his doctrine maintained, who did not to some extent conform his conduct and his life to it"; whereas—and here the voice takes on a sardonic edge—"so divine and celestial a teaching as ours marks Christians only by their words" (322/419 A). Thus near the beginning of his essay he writes of *religions* in the plural but protests that "men are the leaders here, and make use of religion; it ought to be quite the contrary." Ironically words are held aloft to justify even worse kinds of conduct, for "we burn the people who say that truth must be made to endure the yoke of our need. And how much worse France does than say it!" (323/420 A, C).

In truth the study of comparative religion was *re*started in early modern times, since two of Montaigne's major sources, Cicero and Lucretius, had written of religions—plural—in classical times, even though they characterized the spokesmen involved as philosophers rather than churchmen. From start to finish Lucretius is more frequently quoted in "Apology for Raymond Sebond" than anywhere else in the *Essais*. Montaigne does not fail to recall the famous line "Tantum religio potuit suadere malorum" with which Lucretius concluded his summary of the sacrifice of Iphigenia; and he includes other lines from that moving passage (388/502 B). Like Erasmus, he devotes a good many pages to the matter of souls and the relation of a soul to the human body; but unlike Erasmus he does not finally believe in an afterlife: rather, he follows closely the teaching of Lucretius on this subject, again touching down on appropriate lines from *De rerum natura*. In book 3 Lucretius cannily argued that animals have many of the mental capacities of humans, and as in humans these capacities wax and then wane over the years. The evidence suggests that consciousness slows altogether to a stop with the death of the body. And where can immortal souls come from, where are they bound to, if the test of ordinary recollection is applied? For purposes of his own argument Montaigne quotes—first one sentence and then the other—six successive lines from Lucretius (3.671–76). Here they are in Donald Frame's verse translations: if the spirit is immortal and "slips into the body at its birth, / Why do we not recall our bygone life on earth, / And keep at least some traces of the things we did?"

and "For if the power of mind has been so changed / That all remembrance of the past has fled, / That is not far, methinks, from being dead." At this point Montaigne disturbingly, or mischievously, raises the question of the justice of an afterlife. For better or worse, how one behaves in *this* life is vulgarly supposed to govern what will happen for eternity. But the duration of the present life varies: "perhaps one or two hours, or at worst a century, which is no more in proportion to infinity than an instant." Insofar as reward or punishment is the issue, this is clearly a problem. "It would be an inequitable disproportion to receive eternal compensation in consequence of so short a life" (410–11/530–31 B, A).

Montaigne's conviction about how little he or anyone else can actually know about divinity both enables and follows from his mocking of the rampant anthropomorphism of believers. Here he is very much indebted to Cicero as well as Lucretius, especially to Cotta's initial refutation of Velleius in *De natura deorum* (1.76–96). It is not just a matter of the all-too-human nature of the ancient Greeks' gods; it is very difficult for humans to conceive of one or many gods except in their own image, especially if they predicate any shared concerns and a common language. It is one thing to enjoy a laugh with Aristophanes or Lucian at the antics on Mount Olympus but another to fathom the God of Abraham. Montaigne's ponderings of what one can or cannot know about God turn to the positive attributes of divinity. In a late passage, also inspired by Cicero's Cotta (3.38–39), he questions how an almighty God can exercise even the highest human virtues—or why he would stoop to using a foreign tongue in doing so.

> How can wisdom, which is the choice between good and evil, fit him, seeing that no evil touches him? What has he to do with reason and intelligence, which we use to arrive at apparent things from things obscure, seeing that there is nothing obscure to God? Justice, which distributes to each man what belongs to him, created for the society and community of men—how can it be in God? And what of temperance, which is moderation in bodily pleasures, which have no place in divinity? Fortitude in bearing pain, toil, and dangers, appertains to him as little, since these three things have no access to him. (369/479 C)

Montaigne devotes far more space than this to remarking and ridiculing the attribution of more common anthropoid appetites, passions, and behavior to divinity but generally associates this tendency with polytheism: "Antiquity thought, I believe, that it was doing something for divine greatness by likening it to man, investing it with his faculties, and presenting it with his fine humors and his most shameful needs . . . cajoling it with the odor of incense and the sounds of music . . . flattering its justice with inhuman vengeance . . . filling its altars, besides, with butchery" (387/501 A and C).

The ancients had nearly as many theories of divinity as they had gods. Montaigne is struck not only by the anthropomorphism but also by the differences of opinion about the gods that Cicero made the subject of his dialogues. With explicit reference to book 1 of *De natura deorum* (1.25–41) he turns out a list of twenty-seven classical philosophers all of whom more or less disagreed about god or gods. Velleius, who delivers the list in the dialogue, is rather more caustic in his remarks and assessments; but by compressing the long passage Montaigne makes it read even more like a satiric catalogue (381–83/495–97 C). It is not only philosophers or religious or theologians who differ. For most people, what they believe depends on where they come from. Montaigne is quite sure on this point. "We receive our religion only in our own way," but so do others—in their way. "We happen to have been born in a country where it was in practice; or we regard its antiquity or the authority of the men who have maintained it; or we fear the threats it fastens upon unbelievers, or pursue its promises. Those considerations should be employed in our belief, but as subsidiaries; they are human ties. Another region, other witnesses, similar promises and threats, might imprint upon us in the same way a contrary belief" (324–25/422 A). These observations, drawn from his studies, hold for contemporary times. Montaigne is famous, in "Of Cannibals," for example, for his awareness of the new world being explored in the sixteenth century and its implications. Before the end of the "Apology" he reflects more than once, as a modern anthropologist might, on the correspondences as well as differences of distinct cultures, including "the coincidences between a great number of fabulous popular opinions and savage customs and beliefs" (431/556–57 C). The Reformation and so-called religious wars in France give him occasion to remark changing and frequently contentious beliefs during his own lifetime. Surely it is contemporary history that causes him bitterly to add, near the beginning of the essay, "There is no hostility that excels Christian hostility. Our zeal does wonders when it is seconding our leaning toward hatred, cruelty, ambition, avarice, detraction, rebellion. Against the grain, toward goodness, benignity, moderation, unless as by a miracle some rare nature bears it, it will neither walk nor fly. Our religion is made to extirpate vices; it covers them, fosters them, incites them" (324/421 C).

How shall Montaigne bring the extensive and intensive pondering of religion to a close? Where does he finally stand? The last stretch of the "Apology" he devotes to epistemology again. The senses provide the grounds for what we know, yet the senses too can mislead, and he can call on Lucretius (4.513–21) to back him on this. But alas the conclusion is handed over to Plutarch, with a bit of Seneca thrown in plus four more lines from Lucretius. In other words, this is still the *Essais* as commonplace book. Not that what Plutarch has to say is commonplace, for here in his *Morales* he decodes "The E at Delphi." Supposedly the Greek letter E was inscribed there—by Apollo? And what did it signify? It takes an acquaintance with the occult, and even numerology, for Plutarch to say.[16] The part that interests Montaigne is a definition of *being* associated with Stoicism that applies to nothing in the universe except god. Everything else has a before and after, is caught up in time, and therefore never *is*. And that includes humans, who are obviously aware of mortality as they contemplate their own lives. Apologizing for going on so long, Montaigne brings to a conclusion Plutarch's reading of E with an exclamation from Seneca (without naming him): " 'O what a vile and abject thing is man' he says, 'if he does not raise himself above humanity!' "[17] But this is not possible, Montaigne retorts; man cannot raise himself: "He will rise, if God by exception lends him a hand; he will rise by abandoning and renouncing his own means, and letting himself be raised and uplifted by purely celestial means." Subsequently he added, "It is for our Christian faith, not for his Stoical virtue, to aspire to that divine and miraculous metamorphosis" (457/588–89 A, C). And thus the "Apology" comes to an end, with a perfunctory statement of Christian faith, but the applicable reasoning (and occult fantasy) attributed to classical sources.

Elsewhere in the long essay Montaigne makes a number of such brief affirmations of the faith. But the article of faith is never spelled out, and the moment is lost as rehearsals of the problem of knowing and the ridicule of anthropomorphic beliefs roll on. And remember, Montaigne scorns selective recall of "express words of the Bible." That tactic merely fuels disputes about what the words mean, and whatever the reason, he seldom himself resorts to words of the prophets, the apostles, or Jesus. The spirit of the "Apology" is critical, searching, and comical in more than one sense. "Absurd" (C) is another epithet applied latterly to the quotation from Seneca above. Sometimes the irony can get turned around, however, or become more sweeping than intended. So what is truth? The statement of faith that concludes the essay is qualified by an "if," and perhaps what God does "by exception" refers to grace. Being "raised and uplifted by purely celestial means" suggests going to heaven, though Montaigne never puts much stock in that. But if this is the message, how is it exempt from generalizations laid down earlier and from manifest irony with respect to religious beliefs? For instance, "Man fabricates a thousand ridiculous associations between God and himself. Is he not his compatriot?" (399/516 C). With so much juggling of assertions like this some are bound to strike home. Montaigne's longest essay can best be read as a humanist comedy.

Anthropomorphism is the most prominent and lively theme in the essay: puny man creates God in his own image. By starting with the limitations and foolishness of the species Montaigne begins modestly enough, for he is one of them, and what does he know? By adopting the humanist's privilege of surveying bygone religions alongside his own, he achieves the multiple, suspended allowances of comedy. Do the gods exist? is not a question he addresses as frankly as those Roman precursors Lucretius and Cicero. But the laughable antics of the gods of antiquity in his account reflect the foolishness of their worshippers. "Immortalia mortali sermone notantes" is a line from Lucretius (5.121)—"denoting things immortal in mortal prose" (369/479 B)—that says in four words what Montaigne is mocking. In what sense *would* immortal gods exist without mortals to invest in them? The laughter cuts both ways, the worshipped and the worshippers. Beware also of the aphorisms that seem to come so readily to his pen: "It is far from honoring him who made us, to honor him whom we have made." Without more knowledge to gainsay this, Montaigne the humanist thereby empties out entirely the independent being of God, Plutarch to the contrary notwithstanding. A few sentences further on he inserts another aphorism to back this one up:

"Man is certainly crazy. He could not make a mite, and he makes gods by the dozen" (395/511 C). And one suspects that for Montaigne, as for Lucretius, mites are so minuscule that they are in any event products of nature rather than of divinity. Shades of Darwinism still to come perhaps.

For this scion of the French nobility cheerfully situates humanity in nature as a whole. More than a few pages of the "Apology," qualified at the start by an aside on his cat—"When I play with my cat, who knows if I am not a pastime to her more than she is to me?" (331/430 C)—he devotes to animals. With repeated backups from Lucretius once again, Montaigne concentrates on the ways many animals outperform humans: "Moreover, what sort of faculty of ours do we not recognize in the actions of the animals?" He respects their mental powers; they may not be able fully to understand us, but neither are we always able to communicate with them. Birds and other animals construct suitably designed nests and shelters; spiders tie one sort of knot and then another in order to form the web. Whereas naked humans can easily feel chilly, other species sport many different styles of outer clothing. They come equipped even with armament and weaponry. Nature "has armed them with claws, teeth, or horns for attack and defense; and has herself instructed them in what is fit for them—to swim, to run, to fly, to sing—whereas man can neither walk, nor speak, nor eat, nor do anything but cry, without apprenticeship." And "as for speech, it is certain that if it is not natural, it is not necessary." In any case, nature has given to other species too a faculty of "complaining, rejoicing, calling to each other for help, inviting each other to love, as they do by the use of their voice" (332–35/432–36 A). He concludes by observing that people like to reserve to themselves fanciful capacities for "reason, knowledge, and honor," but in truth the capacities for good that we concede to animals, such as "peace, repose, security, innocence, and health," are far more real (357/464 A). Further on in the essay (with more tips from Cicero) Montaigne asks the reader to consider a barnyard gosling who, like a vain Homo sapiens, imagines himself to be the center of the universe. The humans who feed and care for him are his gods even though, as he expects, they intend to eat him one day (397/514 B). This parable also operates on the animal–human continuum, but with the gosling representing the folly of both species of believers.

Que sais-je? Montaigne prefers to leave divinity in the dark rather than guess or surmise. "The least-known things are the fittest to be deified. . . . I would even rather have followed those who worshipped the serpent, the dog, and the ox; inasmuch as their nature and being is less known to us, and we have more chance to imagine what we please about those animals and attribute extraordinary faculties to them" (383/497 A). Rather, that is, than project our own imperfection and needs, which we know all too well, upon God. But to set off religion and package it strictly with the unknown seems foolish. How would that help with real-life experiences, animal-like or not, of which we do have a limited understanding? Montaigne's insistence on the point seems useless, unless he means it to score again for comic effect: "To Christians it is an occasion for belief to encounter something incredible. It is the more according to reason as it is contrary to human reason." That sounds like one of his send-ups of pagan anthropomorphic extravagance. He subsequently qualifies the second sentence, "If it were according to reason, it would no longer be a miracle; and if it were according to some example, it would no longer be singular" (368–69/478 A, B). But Montaigne is not notably into miracles, and no writer is fonder of multiplying examples when in the mood to make fun.

Moving on in a more serious vein, he seems to treat his "Que sais-je?" as a rhetorical question, with the implied answer, Nothing. Here the confession of ignorance in regard to divinity occurs in the midst of a statement of faith—and this in the first person, note:

> Our faith is not of our own acquiring, it is a pure present of
> another's liberality. It is not by reasoning or by our
> understanding that we have received our religion; it is by
> external authority and command. The weakness of our
> judgment helps us more in this than its strength, and our
> blindness more than our clear-sightedness. It is by the
> mediation of our ignorance more than of our knowledge that we
> are learned with that divine learning. It is no wonder if our
> natural and earthly powers cannot conceive that supernatural
> and heavenly knowledge; let us bring to it nothing of our own
> but obedience and submission. (369–70/479–80 A)

And, uncharacteristically, to conclude this paragraph Montaigne quotes scripture: namely, 1 Corinthians 1.19–21, where Paul himself quotes Isaiah 29.14 and then asks, "Where is the wise man? . . . Has not God made foolish the wisdom of the world? For since, in the wisdom of God, the world did not know God through wisdom, it pleased God through the folly of what we preach to save those who believe." This was a favorite with Erasmus too, but the writer of the *Essais* does not stop to fill in the substance of that which is believed, as with concrete applications.

In the judgment of Hugo Friedrich, "What Montaigne has to say about faith always ends up back in the disempowerment of reason, and thus in man's abased position. He does not intend to harm faith. . . . But his fideism has neither pathos nor a significant trace of mystical longing. . . . His fideism is negative in nature: the certainty of uncertainty." Thus Friedrich believes that Montaigne's stance is more rooted in skepticism of old than "specifically Christian."[18] He may be right as far as the "Apology" is concerned. The default conclusion from most of the reasoning in the "Apology for Raymond Sebond" may well be that the very existence of the deity is unproven. Yet Montaigne has not likely surrendered his faith in God and the specific teaching of his Christian background. He has emphasized more than once that we tend to believe what were brought up to believe. Meanwhile the comedy affords him leeway. The sifting through classical lore brings him freedom, as it does for other humanists.

Montaigne can be moved by Lucretius's brief account of the troubling sacrifice of Iphigenia, but neither he nor other early moderns wish to compare this to the sacrifice of Jephthah's daughter because that is told in holy scripture (Judges 11). It's telling sport to rehearse the troubles of the Olympian gods of old. Aristophanes and Lucian were master players at this centuries earlier. Here is Montaigne: "How many cuckoldries are there in the histories, procured by the gods at the expense of the poor humans! And husbands unjustly decried in favor of the children!" It would be blasphemy to take this tone with the story of Joseph of Galilee in the city of Nazareth, and Montaigne would never dream of doing so. His next sentence reads, "In the religion of Mohammed, according to popular belief, plenty of Merlins are found: to wit, children without fathers, spiritual, divinely born in the wombs of virgins; and they bear a name which signifies this in their language" (397/513 C). Nothing here about the cult of the Virgin Mary, whatever Montaigne's personal beliefs may have been. But there is no denying that the so-called "Apology for Raymond Sebond," as it played off divinity in general, became a comedic as well as a thoughtful apology for humanism.

3. HOBBES'S BRAVING OF THE DARK

Thomas Hobbes is famous—or infamous, in radical circles—as a political theorist. His weighty *Leviathan* (1651) evolved from earlier drafts, *Elements of Law*, composed in 1640, and *De Cive*, published in Latin in 1642. These were turbulent times of civil war, and Hobbes fled to Paris in 1640, returning to England in 1652. Today only the first two parts of the *Leviathan*, "Of Man" and "Of Commonwealth," are widely studied. The title of the book itself derived from the triumphant verses spoken by God at the end of the book of Job. With considerable temerity Hobbes specified in the opening chapter of part 2 that his Leviathan denoted in effect the sovereign, the *"one person"* who represented and held sway over the commonwealth (17.13).[19] But there were four parts of the *Leviathan* in all, the last two, "Of a Christian Commonwealth" and "Of the Kingdom of Darkness," occupying as many pages as the first two. The apportionment of space reflects Hobbes's commitment to topical issues of seventeenth-century Britain. But however much he disagreed with parliamentarians and presbyterians, the darkness assailed and ridiculed in the last part chiefly referred to Roman Catholicism.

If anything, Hobbes rates a more influential position in Western philosophy than is sometimes accorded him. His careful attention to the definition of words anticipates the ordinary language philosophy taught at Oxford and Cambridge in the twentieth century.[20] In a number of places he warns against the selective use of isolated passages from the Bible. Unlike Montaigne he does dwell on scripture at length but not without examining the context and different usages of key words. In noting what is meant by "the *Word of God* or of *man*," Hobbes could be said to anticipate the speech-act theories of J. L. Austin and John Searle. This is not a question of grammar or vocabulary but of "a perfect speech or discourse whereby the speaker *affirmeth, denieth, commandeth, promiseth, threateneth, wisheth,* or *interrogateth*" (36.1). He is as capable of mocking "metaphysics," Aristotelian or Aquinist metaphysics in particular, as a logical positivist would be. And Hobbes certainly indulges in the timeless philosophical pleasure of calling others' reasoning absurd. He even goes out of his way to explain what it means to call something absurd—the "canting of schoolmen," for example (5.5–16). In chapter 16, the other transitional chapter between parts 1 and 2 of *Leviathan*, he delivers an account of political representation essential to lawful exercising of power that does not omit the theatrical significance of *personation*.²¹ In Latin the original meaning of *persona* was a mask. Hobbes's political theory allows that a commonwealth may be governed as a monarchy, a democracy (the assembly of all), or an aristocracy (the assembly of a part); but it is no accident that the legal fiction he insists on is singular. The representative of the people must be a person.

Hobbes was a humanist in the sense that the word is commonly used for thinkers of his time. In the first part of *Leviathan*, "Of Man," he included a chapter on religion.²² Merely to name his chapter with the general term acknowledged the notion of comparative religions. He discourses briefly in Hobbesian fashion on the human needs for religion, such as to assign causes and origins in the past or to assuage fear and ignorance in the present. Then he distinguishes, perhaps defensively here, between religions invented by men and the true religion, established by men but under "God's commandment and direction." The former he proceeds to satirize: "Men, women, a bird, a crocodile, a calf, a dog, a snake, an onion, a leek deified. Besides that, they filled almost all places with spirits called *demons* . . . and built temples to mere accidents and qualities, such as are time, night, day, peace, concord, love, contention, virtue, honour, health, rust, fever, and the like." Thereby leeks and onions are juxtaposed with men and women, rust with peace and virtue. He is a master of the satiric catalogue, obviously, and has his own style of reckoning with the anthropomorphism of the ancients: "They invoked also their own wit, by the name of *Muses*; their own ignorance, by the name of *Fortune*; their own lust, by the name of *Cupid*; their own rage, by the name *Furies*; their own privy members, by the name of *Priapus*; and attributed their pollutions to *Incubi* and *Succubae*" (12.12, 16). When it comes to ancient practices of divination, Hobbes can sustain the laughter even longer (another satiric catalogue stretches a single sentence to about 350 words). The rest of the chapter "Of Religion" reads more soberly, touching on the Reformation and some historical alterations in Christendom itself.

"Of the Kingdom of Darkness," the last and shortest part of *Leviathan*, concerns this history and mainly purposes to fault Catholicism. Three chapters serve to review beliefs and rituals, to relate some of these to pagan customs, and to strip them of rational or scriptural justification. A final chapter, "Of the Benefit that proceedeth from such Darkness and to whom it accrueth" (47), rehearses one of Hobbes's typical political arguments: by focusing on the likely motives of leaders who frighten laymen with the unknown or who preach untruths outright, he can hope to cure superstitious beliefs by placing the blame for them on human agency, notably "the Roman and the presbyterian clergy" (47.4). A side effect can be that of darkness made more ominous, superstition commingled with paranoia.

But these were bad times. Hobbes was well aware that the civil war, no more than the religious wars on the Continent, hardly augured well for Christianity as a whole. His contribution to peace would be to explain how doctrinal differences arose and to sort out correct interpretations of scripture from incorrect. In the end his emphasis will be overwhelmingly political—the commonwealth, the civil state is that which matters most. Even these last chapters, however, begin with orderly exposition and analysis. The humanist in Hobbes does not believe in immortal souls. It is not just purgatory, an invention of the Roman church, that is wrong, but the popular notion of eternal torment awaiting the wicked. Yet he apparently accepts the idea of immortality confined to a few. The elect shall enjoy bliss in heaven, though not until resurrected on Judgment Day. As he has argued earlier, the Kingdom of God lies in the indefinite future.

Hobbes reminds his readers of what he has written earlier in *Leviathan* of dreams and imagination, out of which primitive beliefs arise. Myths about the unknown tend to be tenacious and do not respond readily to advances in knowledge. He analyzes what is meant by worshipping God. To be sure, he has to begin by comparing this to honoring a person. In the absence of the god, person, or thing worshipped, images of the same are called for; and in ancient times the images were like as not worshipped independently of what they stood for. That resulted in idolatry, a danger that persists even in the history of Christianity. It is important to worship only what the image signifies. Much as ancient peoples elevated certain heroes to be gods, the church has taken to canonizing saints. For Hobbes, honoring such persons as saints after their deaths would be fine, but praying to them is mistaken. Catholics' idolatry and canonizing of saints, he suggests, are practices inherited from the days of the Roman empire. Meanwhile the church resists true philosophy, otherwise known as science, and a Kingdom of Darkness still threatens. Mostly, things brighten only with laughter at the same.

Let there be light! In his penultimate chapter, "Of Darkness from Vain Philosophy and Fabulous Traditions" (46), Hobbes shines his light mercilessly on Aristotle, Aquinas, and the schoolmen. Rather like Lucretius and Epicurus, he insists that the universe is body—that is, matter—in every part. There are no such things as Aristotelian essences, which can be thrown about "as men fright birds from the corn with an empty doublet, a hat, and a crooked stick." The assumption of such essences fuels ghost stories, "for it is upon this ground that, when a man is dead and buried, they say his soul (that is his life) can walk separated from his body, and is seen by night amongst the graves." And, without a break, he moves on to supposed sacraments: "Upon the same ground they say that the figure, and colour, and taste of a piece of bread has a being there, where they say there is no bread." Hobbes contends, indeed, that such unreason or vain philosophy can be used to weaken the authority of the sovereign power, but more about that below. Turning to Aquinas, he dismisses some of the language used to explain what essences can be, then continues ridiculing the whole idea—or nonidea, as he might say: "And in particular, of the essence of a man, which (they say) is his soul, they affirm it, to be all of it in his little finger, and all of it in every other part (how small soever) of his body; and yet no more soul in the whole body than in any one of those parts. Can any man think that God is served with such absurdities?" (46.18–19). Besides, how can incorporeal essences be tormented in hell by fire? And in the next breath Hobbes is back to ghosts walking in the night, and wondering how they manage to keep the same old clothes on.

The targets Hobbes keeps returning to are Catholic beliefs and practices that have been left behind by Protestantism—or at least by the reestablished Church of England he adheres to—and a good many of the jokes strike one as original. The celibacy of the clergy, for example. What does that say about marriage? and does it say all that needs to be said of the clergy? Here is Hobbes (in part) on forbidding priests to marry, in "the name of continual chastity, continence, and purity":

Therefore, they call the lawful use of wives, want of chastity and continence; and so make marriage a sin (or at least a thing so

impure and unclean as to render a man unfit for the altar). If the
law were made because the use of wives is incontinence, and
contrary to chastity, then all marriage is vice; if because it is a
thing too impure and unclean for a man consecrated to God,
much more should other natural, necessary, and daily works,
which all men do, render men unworthy to be priests, because
they are more unclean. (46.33)

The repetition and slowing down enable his readers to get the point
without his having to spell it out. Alternatively, when summarizing other
predicaments, such as how in the sacrament "one body may be at one and
the same time in many places (and many bodies at one and the same time
in one place)," Hobbes gives up and compares his adversaries to clowns:

These are but a small part of the incongruities they are forced
to from their disputing philosophically, instead of admiring and
adoring of the divine and incomprehensible nature, whose
attributes cannot signify what he is, but ought to signify our
desire to honour him with the best appellations we can think
on. But they that venture to reason of his nature from these
attributes of honour, losing their understanding in the very first
attempt, fall from one inconvenience into another, without end
and without number—in the same manner as when a man
ignorant of the ceremonies of court, coming into the presence
of a greater person than he is used to speak to, and stumbling
at his entrance, to save himself from falling, lets slip his cloak;
to recover his cloak, lets fall his hat; and with one disorder after
another, discovers [i.e., discloses] his astonishment and
rusticity. (46.23)

In chapter 47 Hobbes devotes the very last pages of *Leviathan* to a
comparison of the Catholic hierarchy and a kingdom of fairies: "Their
whole hierarchy (or kingdom of darkness) may be compared not unfitly to
the kingdom of fairies (that is, to the old wives' fables in England,
concerning ghosts and spirits and the feats they play in the night). And if
a man consider the original of this great ecclesiastical dominion, he will
easily perceive that the Papacy is no other than the ghost of the deceased
Roman empire, sitting crowned upon the grave thereof." Do they not use

Latin in their churches? "What is it but the ghost of the old Roman language?" Hobbes proceeds to run through all similarities he can think of between fairies and these holy men. The fairies have a king, called Oberon or perhaps Beelzebub; the ecclesiastics have their pope. "Fairies and ghosts inhabit darkness . . . ecclesiastics walk in obscurity of doctrine, in monasteries, churches, and church-yards." The latter may have cathedrals, but "fairies also have their enchanted castles." Both are said to take young men and deprive them of their senses: "In what shop or operatory the fairies make their enchantment, the old wives have not determined. But the operatories of the clergy are well enough known to be the universities, that received their discipline from authority pontifical." And so he goes on, good-naturedly enough, shedding light on the darkness. Yet,

> to this and such like resemblances between the papacy and the kingdom of fairies may be added this: that as the fairies have no existence but in the fancies of ignorant people, rising from the traditions of old wives or old poets, so the spiritual power of the Pope (without the bounds of his own civil dominion) consisteth only in the fear that seduced people stand in of their excommunications, upon hearing of false miracles, false traditions, and false interpretations of the Scripture.

Hobbes then credits by name the sovereigns who put a stop to this religion in England: "It was not, therefore, a very difficult matter for Henry VIII by his exorcism, nor for queen Elizabeth by hers, to cast them out" (47.21–34).

Hobbes famously defined laughter as *"sudden glory,"* an emotion allied with *"joy* arising from imagination of a man's own power and ability" (6.42, 39). Laughter is more complicated and various than this allows, but without question the definition applies fairly widely.[23] The joke is usually on someone else, and the laugh signals a boast—or sigh of relief—that one is superior. The social circumstances count; it matters who shares the laugh, in this case Hobbes's readers, who are hardly all of one stripe and no longer even his contemporaries. Presumably in part 4, then, Hobbes is glorying in his mastery and possession of the true religion. Ridicule and laughter are scarcely characteristic of part 3, "Of a Christian Commonwealth," however, where he devotes far more space to a positive assessment of a reformed established church as he sees it.

There is a real question of what Hobbes's idea of true Christian faith comes down to. And to arrive at the answer, it is necessary to review this less witty and entertaining part of the *Leviathan*.

With the principal part devoted to political theory behind him—"Of Commonwealth": that is, any commonwealth—Hobbes is riding high in setting forth the rules for any Christian commonwealth. He sometimes seems quite carried away, as if he were prepared to preach sermons or dictate liturgy without stop. His ready recall of the Bible enables him to cite text after text in support of an argument. It is possible to come away feeling that Hobbes is one of those Christians who believes everything in the scriptures is true, and nothing else is needed to guide one. But that is far from the case. In fact he got in trouble for pointing out that much received wisdom about scripture, such as the idea that Moses authored the Pentateuch, was contradicted by the texts themselves. His brief chapter "Of the Number, Antiquity, Scope, Authority, and Interpreters of the Books of Holy Scripture" (33) remarkably anticipates the so-called Higher Criticism of the nineteenth century. He rapidly runs through the internal evidence as to authorship, time of the writing, and so on of each book. Or, in the following chapter, he analyzes occurrences of the word *spirit* in the Bible and comes up with seven distinct usages. Hobbes is obviously able to stand back from the text, in a manner foreign to most exegetes committed to the truth of scripture.

This higher criticism poses problems for Hobbes. On the one hand, he relies on scripture to speak the truth of divine revelation; on the other, passages of scripture often signal that they are not reliable. The Bible narrative itself treats of false prophets, and one sign of a true prophet was when God allowed him to perform a miracle or two. Still, Jesus himself warned against "false Christs and false prophets" who nonetheless "show great signs and wonders" that fool people (Matthew 24.24). "Seeing therefore miracles now cease," Hobbes concludes, "we have no sign left whereby to acknowledge the pretended revelations or inspirations of any private man"; yet in the same sentence he writes confidently of knowing what is "conformable to the Holy Scriptures" (32.7–9). The combination of skepticism and submission to bare scripture has long caused readers to question where he stands. Near the end of part 3 Hobbes will emphasize once more that the vast number of Christian faithful have never personally heard God or the Savior speak. Therefore, "it cannot be said that the person whom they believed was God. They believed the Apostles, and after them the pastors and doctors of the Church, that recommended to their faith the history of the Old and New Testament." He makes a stab at claiming that Paul, in Romans 10.17, remarked the same reduction of divine revelation to hearsay. But the upshot of this tends to be that we mostly believe what parents and pastors teach us. Almost as if he had been reading Montaigne, he asks, "What other cause can there be assigned why, in Christian commonwealths, all men (either) believe (or at least profess) the Scripture to be the word of God, and in other commonwealths scarce any, but that in Christian commonwealths they are taught it from their infancy, and in other places they are taught otherwise?" (43.6–8). Nor is it enough, Hobbes's critics may protest, for the citizens merely to "profess" what they believe.

Nothing was easier for humanists to laugh at than the patent anthropomorphism of archaic Greek gods or, for that matter, the gods of any distant peoples. But on religious concerns nearer home, there was also the temptation for the humanist to project on divinity his own understanding of social and political relations. Hobbes, with his felt need for the definition of terms, repeatedly appeals to analogy in this field. Thus he tries to be helpful by defining *holy* as a quality corresponding to "*public, or the king's,*" in the affairs of men (35.14). In the last, transitional chapter of part 2 he defines the purpose of worshipping God by analogy to the obeisance paid "by the weak to the more potent men, in hope of benefit, for fear of damage, or in thankfulness for good already received from them." Hobbes then numbers the attributes of God—in the singular here but not necessarily the Christian God—before concluding that there is "but one name of his relation to us, and that is God, in which is contained Father, King, and Lord" (31.13, 28). Again, he feels he needs to familiarize the relation—father, king, lord—in order to make himself understood. Fencing with darkness in part 4, he still defines *worship* as follows: "To pray to, to swear by, to obey, to be diligent and officious in serving—in sum, all words and actions that betoken fear to offend or desire to please—is *worship*, whether those words and actions be sincere or feigned; and because they appear as signs of honouring, are ordinarily also called honour" (45.12).

The stress that Hobbes places on *personation* in order to construct his political theory reflects this same concentration and reliance on a (male) human authority. Also the word *rights* in *Leviathan* regularly, if not exclusively, denotes the sovereign's rights, which in present-day political discourse would be translated *powers*. Law is usually conflated with lawful power, the power both to make laws and to interpret them. On nearly every page, it sometimes seems, Hobbes calls for obedience. In *De Cive*'s chapters on religion, for example, he quoted Jesus's reply to the lawyer (Matthew 22.37–40) in order to assert that just two commandments sum up all laws: "*You shall love your God,*" and "*You shall love your neighbour as yourself.*" Then he glossed the scripture this way: "For he who loves God and his neighbour has a heart of obedience to the laws of God and man. And God requires no more than an obedient heart" (*De Cive*, 17.8).[24] In *Leviathan* he devoted relentless definition and much thought to the nature of a Christian commonwealth. His chapter "Of Power Ecclesiastical" alone is by far the longest in the book. Ironically, the chapter mainly rehearses the limitations of ecclesiastical power; but this is essentially Hobbes's position throughout. The deep, dark comedy of *Leviathan* is that God himself has no practical power over the affairs of men. He "requires no more than an obedient *heart*" because he cannot, or cannot any longer, enforce his will or properly lay down any law. For every practical move among humankind God requires the (nearly unlimited) power of a human sovereign.

One can understand where Hobbes is coming from, defending the monarchy in a time of revolution. There was the possibility of a return of Roman Catholicism in England. But if that threat were all that likely, Hobbes would probably not have indulged in so much anti-Roman laughter. The civil war already under way, on the other hand, both pretended to a religious cause and promoted parliamentary rule. In theory Hobbes's philosophy would allow for a sovereign assembly as an alternative to a monarch. But his temperament, not to say his place in the world, deeply committed him to the status quo ante, for fear of the breakdown of the compact that establishes a commonwealth in the first place. At the end of the last chapter of *Leviathan* Hobbes warns of "an assembly of spirits" worse than popes: "For it is not the Roman clergy only that pretends the kingdom of God to be of this world, and thereby to have a power therein distinct from that of the civil state" (47.34). True (and thanks to the Reformation), an insistence on civil power clears a space for religious toleration. Because there is no universal state, he observes at one point, "there is on earth no such universal Church as all Christians are bound to obey" (39.5). But Christians, ecclesiastics, and everyone else *are* bound to obey a human sovereign, and that sovereignty trumps religious commitment every time. The sovereign has the right to appoint pastors of the church and is himself "the supreme pastor" of a commonwealth. There can be "nothing in men's manners that makes them righteous or unrighteous but their conformity with the law of the sovereign" (42.70, 96). There are strictly "no other laws divine" than the laws of nature and of the commonwealth (43.22). Those who are saved may get to heaven on the last day, but meanwhile "the Kingdom of God is a civil kingdom" (35.13).

Leviathan puts that human sovereign in charge every time. At least twice Hobbes underlines his point by writing that the sovereign must be obeyed even if he is an infidel. In *De Cive* he firmly sorted through the Mosaic law and took the position that the Savior did not attempt to establish or to interfere with civil law; and "in the *Kingdom of God* after this life there are to be *no laws*." The sovereign has an absolute right to administer capital punishment when he sees fit. Clearly the second commandment did not prohibit all killing. Hobbes explicitly cites Exodus 35.2, which penalizes working on the Sabbath with death, and Exodus 32.27, where Moses orders the deaths of thousands of rebellious followers—and easily could have cited other capital offenses proscribed by Moses. "Similarly," the commandment against adultery does not prohibit all extramarital sex, only sex "with *another man's* woman; but who is *another man's* woman, is for the commonwealth to say." Here the modern reader may have to suppress a laugh at such insistence on favoring the secular arm. Not so, perhaps, when Hobbes goes on to instance a case of infanticide: "For example, suppose a woman gives birth to a deformed figure, and the law forbids killing a human being, the question arises whether the new-born is a human being. The question then is, what is a human being? No one doubts that the commonwealth will decide—and without taking account of the Aristotelian definition, that a Man is a rational Animal" (*De Cive*, 17.8–12). Whatever Hobbes finally believes about the authority of scripture, he seems deliberately and selectively to cite it in order to support his position. Yet that hit on Aristotle and human rationality also gives one pause.

Hobbes does not shirk even the case of Jephtha's daughter. He hardly needs to bring this forward, to be sure. Nevertheless, the commandment against killing does not forbid a sovereign's killing, not even the killing of the innocent: he cites Jephtha's pledge of *"a burnt-offering"* in Judges 11 and observes that "God accepted his vow" (*De Cive*, 17.10). From comedy this dark it is instructive to turn to John Locke's Second Treatise of Government (1690), where the death penalty is asserted as inherent to political power but not insisted upon this wantonly or graphically. Here is Locke: "Political power, then, I take to be a right of making laws, with penalties of death, and consequently all less penalties for the regulating and preserving of property, and of employing the force of the community in the execution of such laws, and in the defence of the commonwealth from foreign injury, and all this only for the public good."[25] Yes, Locke also invokes capital punishment but mainly to expose the ultimate basis of government's lesser powers over the bodies of citizens and to distinguish political power from patriarchal power, which his opponent Robert Filmer used to defend royal sovereignty. Governments do have powers to limit certain activities of their citizens and to reward others. Incarceration and worse punishments await capital offenses. Locke's implicit reasoning was that since fathers do not and may not exercise capital punishment in the family, a family is precisely the wrong model for inheriting and passing on political power. In the Britain and America of the century to follow, history was on Locke's side.

4. SPINOZA'S DEIFICATION OF THE WHOLE LOT

Spinoza never cites Hobbes in his *Theological-Political Treatise*, though one of his notes implies that his readers are familiar with Hobbes's political theory. Moreover, in the preface to his *Treatise* he unmistakably, even sarcastically, repudiates the ways of monarchy: "It may indeed be the highest secret of monarchical government and utterly essential to it, to keep men deceived, and to disguise the fear that sways them with the specious name of religion, so that they will fight for their servitude as if they were fighting for their own deliverance, and will not think it humiliating but supremely glorious to spill their blood and sacrifice their lives for the glorification of a single man."[26] So much for monarchs. The Latin *Tractatus theologico-politicus* was published anonymously in Amsterdam in 1670 under a fictitious Hamburg imprint. Although it is often consulted today for Spinoza's political ideas, strictly speaking these occupy only the last fourth of the book.

Yet the primacy Spinoza grants to civil power is one measure of Hobbes's influence. Religion may inspire but has no political power whatsoever. Churches or synagogues do not make law and should not attempt to enforce judgments on anyone. That Spinoza was excluded from the Sephardic synagogue in Amsterdam and forbidden communication with any of its congregation at the age of twenty-three no doubt confirmed this position, but he also adopts a fixed paradigm of Hobbesian thinking. For all we know, the precocious young Spinoza was cursed and excommunicated because of his independent ideas.[27] On the priority of civil rule he was as stubborn as Hobbes himself—and far more vulnerable. In the *Treatise* he concludes that "religion, whether revealed by the natural light of reason or by prophetic light, receives the force of a commandment solely from the decree of those who have authority to govern, and that God has no special kingdom over men except through those who hold power" (19.7). His historical take on the matter is the same as Hobbes's. They both understand that the role of Moses was to bring law and order, to establish a covenant with the Hebrew people, and to rule over them accordingly. But this new state broke apart and took several other forms, as biblical history attests. Jesus made no laws, nor did the apostles. As the Christ, Jesus indeed spoke the word of God; the apostles were altogether human and basically teachers. But governing they left to the state.

Spinoza was more alert than Hobbes to the use and abuse of religion by the state. When piety becomes associated with patriotism or with allegiance to a particular tribe or people, hatred of others' religion takes over, "the most intense kind of hatred . . . as theological hatred tends to be." The Jews, ancient and modern, suffered accordingly. Their worship was consciously different and contrary to that of other peoples'. Such "daily expressions of reproach were bound to generate a ceaseless hatred" among those targeted, and a hatred "more firmly entrenched in their minds than any other, given that such a detestation born of great devotion and piety, was itself viewed as pious." Not surprisingly, "reciprocal abhorrence [became] more and more inflamed, because other nations were bound to react by developing an extreme hatred for them" (17.17, 23). Such manifestations of hatred are not planned but arise from a combination of the defensiveness and hope of religious beliefs, factors exaggerated by the herd mentality of the common people. But their beliefs can also be stirred up deliberately, and then they become truly insidious. Hobbes's apprehensions centered on the fragility of the original social covenant and the danger of reverting to a state of war. Therefore just do as the sovereign orders, and that's that.

Although Spinoza's strict subordination of church to state partly reckons with some of the same dangers, he is far more sensitive to mob psychology and political manipulation of religious differences:

> Pilate knew that Christ was innocent but ordered him to be crucified so as to appease the fury of the Pharisees. In order to strip those who were richer than themselves of their offices, the Pharisees aimed to stir up controversies about religion and accuse the Sadducees of impiety. Following the example of the Pharisees, all the worst hypocrites everywhere have been driven by the same frenzy (which they call zeal for God's law), to persecute men of outstanding probity and known virtue, resented by the common people for precisely these qualities, by publicly reviling their opinions, and inflaming the anger of the barbarous majority against them. This aggressive license cannot easily be checked because it hides itself under the cloak of religion, especially when the sovereign authorities have introduced a cult of which they themselves are not the heads.

Spinoza's evident disgust with all this is not wasted, for he draws an appealing conclusion. It might be better "to regard piety and the practice of religion as a question of works alone, that is, as simply the practice of charity and justice, and to leave everyone to his own free judgment about everything else" (18.6).

Spinoza weighs in with the word *obedience* almost as often as Hobbes does, but again with a difference. To call for obedience is one way to stress behavior rather than beliefs. Actions speak louder than beliefs, even tell more of where the believer stands. For example, consider merely the title of chapter 13 of the *Treatise*: "Where it is shown that the teachings of Scripture are very simple, and aim only to promote obedience, and tell us nothing about the divine nature beyond what men may emulate by a certain manner of life." This sounds almost sacrilegious in what it denies to scripture—nothing specific here about divine nature—and at the same time empowering to (at least male) believers, who may emulate scripture's representation of charity and adopt this as a way of life. And in this context obedience will be not to the sovereign but to scripture. In this same short chapter Spinoza spells out what he means in this fashion: "It was not the purpose of the Bible to teach any branch of knowledge . . . it requires nothing of men other than obedience," and then "obedience to God consists solely in love of our neighbour." He cites Romans 13.8, from which this last clause is almost a direct quotation. "All other philosophical concerns that do not directly lead to this goal, whether concerned with knowledge of God or of natural things, are irrelevant to Scripture and must therefore be set aside from revealed religion" (13.3). Compare Hobbes's use of Matthew 22.37–40.

It seems amazing to claim that the message of scripture is simple—"very simple," "extremely simple." Spinoza had a thorough knowledge of ancient Hebrew; he knows that the text of the Bible is anything but simple. But he wants the meaning to be clear to anyone who believes in the Bible, even illiterate believers. The phrase "the common people" occurs so often in his writing that he may seem condescending, if not class-biased. But he made a thing of living on very little means, and after his reputation was secure more than once refused the kind of aristocratic patronage Hobbes enjoyed. The common people were ignorant, yes, and Spinoza was a self-made member of an elite whom he characterizes as "the learned."[28] Like other humanists he could conveniently associate the common people with ancient gentiles who believed in the gods and attributed to them whatever powers they wished—and whatever they could not understand. Spinoza made that comparison to the ancients explicit in his chapter on miracles. In any event, there are no miracles, if such are supposed to be contrary to nature.

On the interpretation of scripture Spinoza carried on from where Hobbes left off. He too frankly declared that Moses could not have authored most of the Pentateuch, though he credited that particular observation to Abraham Ibn Ezra in twelfth-century Spain, whose commentary had been printed in the fifteenth century (a credit extended not because Ibn Ezra was another Sephardic Jew, for in the *Treatise* Spinoza took vigorous issue with Maimonides' reading of scripture). With greater care and authority Spinoza pursues such Hobbesian concerns with the Bible as the authorship, time of writing, apparent contradictions, and the provenance of each book. He calls for constructing a "natural history" of the Bible text, an analogy which may suggest the additional influence of Francis Bacon.[29] "The [correct] method of interpreting nature consists above all in constructing a natural history, from which we derive the definitions of natural things, as from certain data. Likewise, to interpret Scripture, we need to assemble a genuine history of it and to deduce the thinking of the Bible's authors by valid inferences from this history, as from certain data and principles" (7.2). In this chapter Spinoza distinguishes three requisites for confident interpretation. The first is studying the languages in which the scripture was set down and which the authors probably spoke. An interpreter pretty certainly needs to have Hebrew, and a historical knowledge of Hebrew at that. The second is sorting out the problems posed by the particular text: contradictions obviously, inconsistencies, metaphoric usages, tone and point of view, in order to grasp the possible meaning of the whole. The third and most important requisite is what Spinoza means by a natural history:

> the circumstances . . . the life, character and particular interests
> of the author of each individual book, who exactly he was, on
> what occasion he wrote, for whom and in what language. Then
> the fate of each book: namely how it was first received and
> whose hands it came into, how many variant readings there
> have been of its text, by whose decision it was received among
> the sacred books, and finally how all the books which are now
> accepted as sacred came to form a single corpus. (7.5)

Not a small order by any means. Spinoza illustrates the problem in one place, with good humor enough, by comparing a couple of supernatural happenings from Ariosto's *Orlando Furioso* and Ovid's *Metamorphoses*—Ruggiero using a magic bridle to guide his winged horse through the air, and Perseus tying wings to his feet before taking off to rescue Andromeda—to Judges 15.9–16 and 2 Kings 2.11 in the Bible, where Samson slays a thousand Philistines with the jawbone of an ass, and Elijah travels to heaven in a chariot of fire drawn by horses of fire. Again, one has to figure out what kinds of stories these might be, learn what one can about the writers, and deduce what they were up to: "We persuade ourselves that the first writer intended to write only fables, the second poetical [or political?] themes, and the third sacred matters, and the only reason for such [differentiation] is the opinion we have about the writers" (7.15).³⁰ The familiar examples are reassuring but don't go very far to privilege the sacred or to explain the grounds for that opinion.

Much worship and belief in God obviously depended on how and when the books of the Bible were assembled and made canonical while others were deemed apocryphal. The Reformation assured that some of these human decisions were still controversial and hence familiar, at least in outline, to many churchgoers. Now there was not only a Hebrew Bible and a New Testament to comprehend but more obtrusive differences among Christians. In subsequent chapters of his *Treatise*, as he runs through his considerable contributions to what would become the higher criticism, Spinoza returns to problems of the canon; and he does know more than most about the history of its formation. He is not always happy about what occurred. He depreciates 1 and 2 Chronicles, for example, and professes to be "extremely surprised that they were admitted among the sacred books by the same men who excluded the Book of Wisdom, Tobias and the other so-called apocryphal books." He admires Proverbs and Ecclesiastes but here "cannot remain silent about the audacity of those rabbis who wanted to exclude" these too from the canon. And he waxes sarcastic about the rabbis' judgment: "I congratulate them for their being willing to let us have these books, but cannot help doubting whether they passed them on to us in good faith" (10.1, 3). Spinoza drops the matter there, he says, because the canon has been accepted; but several times over, at the end of the same chapter, he reminds his reader that the authority of the Bible can be justified only by examining the credibility and provenance of each book. He remarks the amount of controversy over the book of Job and notes that Ibn Ezra believed it was translated into Hebrew from another language. That is something close to the consensus about Job today. Spinoza wishes Ibn Ezra "had demonstrated this for us more conclusively, since we could deduce from it that the gentiles too possessed sacred books" (10.8). He argues that people who worship every word of the Bible as true or attempt to reconcile all the contradictions and errors accumulated in transcribing them over time not only fail to understand the Bible but make its authors seem ridiculous.

But notice where such arguments tend. The common people love marvelous stories of any kind. Unscrupulous leaders or bishops and rabbis selectively interpret scripture for their own ends. Many more are well intentioned, no doubt, but seldom get it right without help. Perhaps only a few learned scholars are truly capable of reading—that is, collecting, comparing, and comprehending—ancient texts, and they must be able to communicate their findings to others. What it comes down to in each case is that the texts in question are holy scriptures, yet they must be legible to human eyes. Spinoza weighs the evidence and appeals to human reason at every turn. Take his deconstruction of prophecy, which is the very first move in the *Theological-Political Treatise*. Since as far as he knows there are no prophets at present, this inquiry concerns the Bible, which strictly construes prophecy as the word of God. But precisely, "owing to religion and piety," the ancient Jews scanted proximate causes for what happened to them or what they prayed would happen next and made a habit of invoking God. So there is the problem of sifting out whatever words or images "Scripture expressly designates as prophecy or revelation." Because "the words, and the images too, were either true and independent of the imagination of the prophet who heard or saw them, or else imaginary, that is the prophet's imagination, even when he was awake, was so disposed that it seemed to him that he was clearly hearing words or seeing something" (1.6–7).

Spinoza agrees that God spoke directly to Moses, though he observes that the ten commandments in Exodus differ verbally from those in Deuteronomy. But then he raises more difficulties of how it would be possible for their encounter literally to be true. In spite of the language of Exodus 33.11, God could not have spoken to Moses face to face. Just because he can find nowhere in the New Testament "that God appeared to Christ or spoke with him," Spinoza infers that the second pair communicated "mind to mind" and concludes that, "apart from Christ, no one has received revelations from God except by means of the imagination, namely by means of words or visions, and therefore prophecy does not require a more perfect mind but a more vivid imagination" (1.17–20). He devotes his next two chapters to combing the Hebrew Bible for more evidence of the same. Complimenting prophets in this manner has to be a greater tribute to the human imagination than to God.

Spinoza's final position is that philosophy and faith do not mix, nor do reason and theology. His advice is simply to accept both sides of these mental exercises and to keep them separate. Yet throughout the *Treatise* he advocates and demonstrates the use of human reasoning to ascertain the truth value of scripture and to recognize the work of others' human imagination. His own reasons are decisively set forth, and he impatiently dismisses alternatives as nonsense or absurd. He is not like Erasmus or More, translating Lucian on the side; his faith and moment in history were even less secure. Spinoza is not laughing, even to himself, but he does enjoy the game whenever some superstition falls within his sights. Where the *Treatise* bears down on the formation of the biblical canon and on theology, as distinct from the far fewer pages on politics, the production earns its place in the humanist comedy.

As to what Spinoza actually believed about God—what he wanted to believe and also what he did not believe—the *Treatise* is not the best guide. The beliefs expressed are appealing and can be made out, but a better text for this question is Spinoza's *Ethics*, in which all of part 1, "Of God," and much of part 5, "Of the Power of the Intellect, *or on Human Freedom*," are especially relevant. He began writing the *Ethics* and may have almost completed it before he thought to write the anonymous *Treatise*; but then he prudently put off publishing the *Ethics* and instead arranged for it to be published after his death (1677). The closest models for the *Ethics*, with its geometric logic, were Descartes's *Principles* and *Meditations*. As in the case of Hobbes's influence, however, Spinoza radically disagreed with some of Descartes's conclusions, even such a basic principle as the difference between mind and body.[31]

In that era there was nothing like mathematical proof to inspire a philosopher's confidence, especially since rules for numbers and triangles appear to be fixed in realms of pure thought, without commitment to hard substance. With at least this much certainty in mind, the philosopher can also safely commit, at the start, to doubting everything else, thereby holding at bay any prejudices of his or her upbringing. Demonstrations begin by putting one's definitions and axioms on the table and taking off from there. This ancient method worked very well for Euclid and his followers. For philosophers with different ambitions, the initial definitions and axioms they ask their readers to accept regularly anticipate the proofs to follow, and the propositions set forth thereby may seem redundant. Descartes began by doubting everything but his consciousness of doubting. He deduced from his thinking, his existence; from his thinking of God, the existence of God; from the perfection of God, the certainty that God does not deceive us—a proposition he repeated over and over, as if to reassure himself. But in his third

Meditation most of what he proves about God and more resides in the definition of the same: "By the name God I understand a substance that is infinite, independent, all-knowing, all-powerful, and by which I myself and everything else, if anything else does exist, have been created. . . . hence, from what has already been said, we must conclude that God necessarily exists." A remarkable egocentrism pervades and directs this meditation. Man thinks, therefore God exists, with all the perfections this particular man approves, perfections that include creating humankind. Here as elsewhere Descartes raises all the objections to his proofs that he can think of and then disposes of these. Thus it might appear that the boy's parents created René Descartes? Well, his parents may have shaped his body perhaps but not his mind, not the thinking man: "And thus there can be no difficulty in their regard, but we must of necessity conclude from the fact alone that I exist, or that the idea of a Being supremely perfect—that is of God—is in me, that the proof of God's existence is grounded on the highest evidence."[32] Le dieu, c'est moi! This looks like humanist usurpation.

In truth Spinoza may be the better geometrician, but his proof of the existence of God suffers from similar problems. In *Ethics* part 1, his initial definitions (D) are more succinct and well chosen, but the most frequently cited thereafter, D6, goes like this: "By God I understand a being absolutely infinite, that is, a substance consisting of an infinity of attributes, of which each one expresses an eternal and infinite essence." Implicit in this definition alone are a good many of the thirty-six propositions (P) and corollaries Spinoza lines up to be proved in this part of the *Ethics* devoted to God. His carefully ordered definitions include substance, attribute, and essence, so as to prepare for D6, and they too can be fairly potent in the argument to follow. D1 reads, "By cause of itself I understand that whose essence involves existence, *or* that whose nature cannot be conceived except as existing." The definitions anticipate an argument to be conducted in the abstract, on a purely conceptual level as in Descartes, but Spinoza is a materialist. D8 reads, "By eternity I understand existence itself, insofar as it is conceived to follow necessarily from the definition alone of the eternal thing." That definition, the last, virtually wraps up in advance a pair of subsequent propositions: P19, "*God is eternal, or all God's attributes are eternal*"; then P20, "*God's existence and his essence are one and the same*," which he proves by P19 and D8 together with his definition of attribute. As in Descartes, there is a good deal of redundancy. The two philosophers strain to prove what they have already set their minds on, though they by no means go after the same thing.[33]

Although Spinoza's proofs may depend too much on the foregoing definitions, a look at more of the key propositions will show where his thoughts are directed. The part of the *Ethics* devoted explicitly to God arrives at a climax with propositions P11 through P15. Indeed, P11 by itself must strike any reader brought up within a Judaic or Christian tradition as ungainly: "*God, or a substance consisting of infinite attributes, each of which expresses eternal and infinite essence, necessarily exists.*" Nor is Spinoza's demonstration of the proposition all that persuasive, since he cites one very circular axiom (A7) in regard to essence and existence and one proposition (P7) that is little more than another definition ("*It pertains to the nature of a substance to exist*"). But the point is that, for Spinoza, God and nature—that is, the entire universe—are the same: hence P15, "*Whatever is, is in God, and nothing can be or can be conceived without God.*" No wonder many of his critics and some of his supporters label him a pantheist; but this is not the sort of pantheism that altogether eliminates divine personhood. For all his mocking of anthropomorphism, Spinoza himself intermittently employs the third person masculine pronoun with reference to God. He does not write "it" or "substance."

From this principled, if not fully proven, coincidence of God and nature, God being equivalent to everything that exists, some remarkable conclusions logically follow. If God is the creator, for one thing he is not a creator who is positioned outside creation. In a scholium to P15, Spinoza dismisses out of hand those who imagine God has an anthropoid body plus mind or is "subject to passions." The favorite idea of God is that of some incorporeal being, and he goes to some length to demonstrate that this too is nonsense. "Absurd," he keeps calling this. How could an incorporeal being have the power to shape extended, corporeal substance? "All things, I say, are in God, and all things that happen, happen only through the laws of God's infinite nature." In a scholium to P17 he contends that intellect and will, as we understand these human capacities, simply do not apply to God. Or if we suppose they do, the divine and human kinds "would not agree with one another any more than do the dog that is a heavenly constellation and the dog that is a barking animal." From here to the end of part 1 of *Ethics*, Spinoza characterizes conclusions that differ from these as absurd, so much so that readers may begin to feel he is anxious for his proofs. Sheer perfection of God-and-nature-in-one can be as baffling as competing theologies that wrestle with attributes like omniscience and omnipotence. According to the scholia for P33, God's perfection entails that the universe could have been created in no other way and also entails constancy. Therefore God "can never decree anything different" from what he has already caused to be set in motion, otherwise known as nature. Spinoza disagrees with those who believe God always acts for the good, if that implies that he aims at a goal outside himself. That would be "simply to subject God to fate," another absurdity.

Part I, "Of God," swiftly draws to a conclusion with three brief propositions that essentially refer the ongoing power of God to ongoing cause and effect evident in nature. The debater in Spinoza, however, was apparently not satisfied with this Euclidian style of argument, since he introduced a more readable appendix to this part of his *Ethics* in order to rebut the "prejudices" he has been trying to expose. Those prejudices can be summarized this way: "Men commonly suppose that all natural things act, as men do, on account of an end; indeed, they maintain as certain that God himself directs all things to some certain end, for they say that God has made all things for man, and man that he might worship God." First he asks *why*, why did people react this way and frame such superstition? Basically, his answers amount to charging them with anthropomorphism again: "While they sought to show that Nature does nothing in vain (i.e., nothing not of use to men), they seem to have shown only that Nature and the gods are as mad as men. . . . Among so many conveniences in Nature they had to find many inconveniences: storms, earthquakes, diseases, and the like. These, they maintain, happen because the gods are angry." Here we are back with Epicurean Lucretius once more. It is curious how Spinoza, contending with adversaries within the Judeo-Christian tradition, falls back on gods in the plural, as if he were backdating their differences by a couple of millennia. Of course early modern humanists right along found such a move enabling because they felt freer to debate theology in the classical mode.

The discursive appendix chides people for being uncomfortable with natural phenomena divorced from God. This is due to their sheer ignorance or longing for narratives with a purpose, however, and has nothing to do with Spinoza's idea of God's immanence. In a diversion that goes on a bit long, he rather enjoys mocking people who cannot accept the role of accidents in life: "For example, if a stone has fallen from a roof onto someone's head and killed him, they will show . . . that the stone fell in order to kill the man. For if it did not fall to that end, God willing it, how could so many circumstances have concurred by chance . . . ? Perhaps you will answer that it happened because the wind was blowing hard," and so on, with similar questions and answers. "And so they will not stop asking for the causes of causes until you take refuge in the will of God, that is, the sanctuary of ignorance." A lovely phrase, the sanctuary of ignorance, with its unholy sarcasm. Spinoza does not pause to think of the possible resemblance to his own assimilation of God to nature. Won't nature by itself suffice to explain chance and circumstance? According to P36, the last proposition in part 1, "*Nothing exists from whose nature some effect does not follow.*" Yet Spinoza's nature includes God, even though here and elsewhere he rules out any day-to-day *will* of God.

For all his modernity and attraction to science, in broad terms Spinoza's thinking harks back to the Stoics of old. Those who took up Stoicism in the period of the Roman revolution believed in a unitary god, associated that god with nature and perfection, and urged the study of nature. Their moral code was also similar to Spinoza's.[34] Cicero, in his dialogues of the same era, moved back and forth from gods plural to god in the singular without being troubled by the difference. Cicero's dialogues and his allegiance to the new Academy's ideal of cross-examining every theory were far more familiar to Spinoza's time than to our own. Epicurus's and Lucretius's conviction that if there were still gods they had retired and were not at all concerned with humanity anticipated Spinoza's proofs that God did not and could not intervene in human life or change the course of nature. Besides classical precursors there were present in Amsterdam early modern religious reformers who undoubtedly attracted Spinoza's interest, such as the Socinians, who influenced the Quakers and Unitarians. They were followers of a sixteenth-century uncle and nephew from Siena, Laelius and Faustus Socinus—Faustus fled north to escape the Inquisition—who believed in applying reason to interpret the Bible and held that Jesus was not divine but human.

To grasp the positive *idea* of the meaning of God to Spinoza one has to turn to part 5 of the *Ethics*, which primarily celebrates the promise and freedom of human thought. Even here God's limitations are proven once more. A corollary to P17 ("*God is without passions . . .*"), for example, states that "strictly speaking," because God is not affected with joy or sadness, he "loves no one and hates no one." And what follows from this, P19, reads, "*He who loves God cannot strive that God should love him in return.*" But note that irrepressible personal pronoun for God: regardless of his consubstantiality with nature, *he* neither loves nor hates anyone. Also, the human mind is fully capable of attributing love to God. A preface (mainly devoted to disposing of Descartes's pineal gland) to this last part of his *Ethics* identifies blessedness with "freedom of mind." Spinoza hints that everyone knows this from experience in any case, but as customary he will proceed logically to "*deduce all those things which concern the mind's blessedness.*" That aim reflects his confidence in his reasoning powers and rings true to his given name, Baruch or Benedict, either of which translates as blessed.

Part 5 has more to do with what is usually called ethics than part 1, since Spinoza gets the argument under way by promoting mind over matter, and more especially mind over the body and its affects. Passions he singles out that need to be overcome include hatred and anger and obviously fear. But he does not favor the sheer willpower or self-control associated with Stoicism; rather, he promises a gladness that comes with hard-won knowledge and practice of virtue. Beginning with P14 (and this move has been anticipated in *Ethics* part 2), Spinoza brings in the role of God by way of the idea of God: "*The mind can bring it about that all the body's affections, or images of things, are related to the idea of God.*" It is as if the materiality of God and humanity alike can combine to add weight to the scale on the side of virtue. This introduces a series of propositions in which Spinoza's uplifting theory—and it is a theory, finally unproven—becomes almost lyrical. Successive propositions will concern this "*intellectual love of God.*" The theory need not be untrue because it is based on the mind's idea of God and a critically redacted version, as in the *Theological-Political Treatise*, of the God of scripture. Each mortal being is part of the created universe, which is also God's. The individual can thus relate to God; and (P15), "*He who understands himself and his affects clearly and distinctly loves God, and does so the more, the more he understands himself and his affects.*" God cannot be expected to return the love in the same way, and he certainly does not hate humans, who are a part of creation;

conversely (P18), "*No one can hate God*"—at least no thinking man who understands his own feelings. Then with P20 and a scholium Spinoza ventures how love of God enhances virtue in a community because it is not mixed with passions like envy or jealousy that afflict love among humans. Love for God can thus grow greater and greater without delimiting side effects.

Such might be called pragmatic reasons for believing in God. They may even supply a rationale for feeling that one is immortal. After cautioning (P21) that the mind cannot imagine or remember anything except while the body is alive, Spinoza almost sentimentally declares (P22), "*Nevertheless, in God there is necessarily an idea that expresses the essence of this or that human body, under a species of eternity.*" The emphasis has to be on an *idea* again; and in P23, on *mind* and *absolutely*: "*The human mind cannot be absolutely destroyed with the body, but something of it remains which is eternal.*" His scholium concludes that we "feel that our mind . . . is eternal. . . . Our mind, therefore, can be said to endure, and its existence can be defined by a certain time, only insofar as it involves the actual existence of the body, and to that extent only does it have the power of determining the existence of things by time." We feel, therefore something *is* eternal? No. But clearly humankind read and debate the thoughts of individuals who are no longer among us. In any event, Spinoza did not need this concept of individuals' share of eternity in order to ratify his idea of God as long as his readers were content with that idea.

True to the spirit of this ending of his *Ethics* is the invocation of a "*third kind of knowledge*" from P25 and on to P38.[35] "The third kind of knowledge proceeds from an adequate idea of certain attributes of God to an adequate idea of the essence of things." Here Spinoza explicitly returns to part 4, on coping with human affects or passions. He cites his definition of virtue there as a power to bring things about, and his proposition 28, that "*Knowledge of God is the mind's greatest good; its greatest virtue is to know God.*" (Propositions 40 and 45–49 of part 2, on the mind, also anticipate these ending thoughts.) Let's face it, even Spinoza is capable of reasoning in circles, but his third kind of knowledge that commits him only to an adequate idea is meant to inspire and to save God, the biblical God as well, for humanity. And it is contagious. After one of the most patently circular of propositions, P36, his scholium reads, in part, "From this we clearly understand wherein our salvation, *or* blessedness, *or* freedom, consists, namely in a constant and eternal love of God, *or* in God's love for men. And this love, *or* blessedness, is called glory in the Sacred Scriptures—not without reason. For whether this love is related to God or to the mind, it can rightly be called satisfaction of mind, which is really not distinguished from glory." How's that again? God's love for men? Although we have been shown that God cannot love individual human beings, he can love humans as a species. The moral for individuals seems obvious enough, however. Famously, the last proposition of all (P42) states, *"Blessedness is not the reward of virtue, but virtue itself."*

Compared to Descartes's unpersuasive proof of the existence of God, Spinoza's hopeful preserving of the *idea* of God has everything in its favor, even the geometrics. It is hard to see how his intentions could have been mistaken, but they were, and for about a hundred years Spinoza was maligned from every conceivable point of view. Pierre Bayle, in by far the longest and most annotated entry of his *Dictionnaire historique et critique* at the end of the seventeenth century, simply couldn't let up on him; it is as if Bayle never read part 5 of *Ethics*. The grimmest joke of all—a practical joke, as it were, certainly deliberate—was the wholesale plagiarizing of Spinoza's appendix to part 1 for the second chapter of the notorious *Traité des trois imposteurs*, also known as *L'Esprit de Spinosa*. This atheist pastiche of free thinking, perhaps compiled around 1690, circulated widely in manuscript in the early decades of the eighteenth century. The first published version, in French, appeared in 1719. There were other borrowings, from Hobbes and from Spinoza's *Treatise*. No doubt it was regarded as a serious missive by the radical underground of the time, but it was a travesty of Spinoza and blasphemous from almost any point of view: the three impostors of the title were Moses, Jesus, and Mohammed, all supposedly working up revealed religion for their own purposes. Ironically, the compilers of the *Treatise of the Three Impostors* seem to have been responsible for the first printing of any portion of the *Ethics* in French.[36]

Stuart Hampshire published a book on the philosophy of Spinoza in 1951. A half century later, at the end of his long life, Hampshire drafted a fresh summary of his thoughts, a moving testimony to the philosopher who died at the age of forty-four. Hampshire had come to scorn the Christian notion of life after death: "For centuries the lives of individuals had been both planned and assessed against the dark background of the Christian story with its stern tariff of rewards and punishments." But

Spinoza, he felt, threw light on this dark doctrine and above all exalted reason and freedom: "'Free' is the only normative term which Spinoza uses without restriction and without apology." The twentieth-century British philosopher informally situates Spinoza's naturalism, as he calls it, in the long tradition of Western humanism: "Spinoza shows how we may in our thinking rise above our immediate reactions and thereby liberate ourselves from the negative and more destructive passions. Reflecting on true and probable, as opposed to illusory, causal beliefs, we may overcome the fears that engender false but comforting supernatural beliefs. This is the path of enlightenment marked out by Epicurus and Lucretius, and Spinoza follows this path, implicitly criticizing Descartes' account of the passions of the soul and of the dominance of the will over the passions."[37] In this twenty-first century Spinoza thus still comes out ahead of the game. He is no impostor, nor can his detractors very well charge him with atheism, when he deified everything there is. He remains one of the most attractive figures in the history of philosophy and a subtle performer of the humanist comedy.

5. BAYLE'S SEND-UP OF A COMET

Pierre Bayle (1647–1706) may have been wrong about Spinoza, but he was a shrewd observer of human behavior. His widely read *Dictionnaire historique et critique*, which accumulated enough so-called remarks to fill four volumes in its second edition, offers countless observations that bemuse and then impress a reader as being probably quite true. He was a master at uncovering the other side of any issue and coming at it again and again, a writer so unstoppable in his tangential thought processes that he can easily irritate as well as reward the reader.

Here is a good example, abridged from his article on Faustus Socinus in the *Dictionnaire*, remark H, which takes off from a consideration of motives behind human ambition. People do not necessarily want to exercise reason. Christians might prefer to be relieved of the burden of trying to understand such abstruse doctrines as original sin, predestination, transubstantiation, and so forth. In truth "the speculative mysteries of religion trouble hardly anyone, though they may indeed exhaust a professor of theology who contemplates them with intensity, whether to explain them or to respond to the objections of heretics." And most people are not professors:

They feel far more at ease with a doctrine that is mysterious, incomprehensible, and above reason. They suppose that one is more apt to admire what one does not understand; since one thereby creates for oneself an idea more sublime and more consoling. In consequence all the ends of religion are better sought in objects that one does not understand: they inspire more admiration, more respect, more awe, and more confidence. If false religions have had their mysteries it is because they have been forged in imitation of the true one. Thus God, through an infinite wisdom, has accommodated himself to the human condition by mixing darkness with light in his revelation. In a word, we must admit that incomprehensibility in certain matters is agreeable to us.[38]

Bayle cannot help putting things a little differently from what his compeers might write. Is he trying to be funny? mischievous? Not necessarily, since the gesture at comparative religion here is a humanist commonplace. And how does God come into the picture, with his infinite wisdom, hereby accommodating himself to *l'état de l'homme?*

Bayle was the second of three sons of a Calvinist pastor. They were poor, lived in the foothills of the Pyrenees, and badly wanted schooling. Pierre attended a Jesuit school in Toulouse for more than a year and while there converted to Catholicism. He received his degree in 1670 but then privately converted back to Calvinism and had to flee to Geneva to avoid the consequences. In France, under the Edict of Nantes, Protestant families had limited freedom to pursue their faith, but recusancy was not tolerated. The edict was revoked altogether by Louis XIV in 1685. Bayle next held a chair in philosophy at Sedan, a Protestant community in the Ardennes, but by 1681 had arrived as an exile in Rotterdam, where he remained for the rest of his life.

The only publication to which he put his name was the ample *Dictionnaire historique et critique*, in which brief, mostly biographical articles were accompanied by more or less limitless footnotes, or remarks, of which he was justifiably proud. The format allowed Bayle to follow his own thoughts on his reading wherever they led; but the results could be controversial. Many objected to the article on David in particular, whom Bayle criticized relentlessly for his sexual aggrandizements and merciless massacres, as undeniably told in the Bible. He drew attention to David's deceitfulness and the political liability this posed. For instance, the murderous escapades of the hero in the service of Achish of Gath, as narrated in 1 Samuel 27, when David took no prisoners and put both men and women to the sword: "The secret that he did not want to have discovered was that these ravages were committed not on the lands of the Israelites, as he made the king of Gath believe, but on the lands of the ancient inhabitants of Palestine. . . . To hide one fault he committed a greater one. He deceived a king to whom he had obligations; and to conceal this deceit he exercised extreme cruelty" (remark D).[39] So many readers protested that in the edition of 1702 the article on David was radically revised, and several of the objectionable remarks were dropped entirely.

More characteristically, Bayle augmented his *Dictionnaire*, indulging the same crotchety license with which he began it. That spirit included composing dialogues, as in the wonderful dialogue of the two abbés in the article on Pyrrho, remark B. In the end "a learned theologian who was present" takes over, and he has to be a stand-in for Bayle himself.[40] A nice summary of the total contents of the *Dictionnaire* is that of Elisabeth Labrousse, Bayle's twentieth-century biographer, in her short introduction to his career and accomplishments: "Bayle's *Dictionary* is a graveyard of ideological systems. . . . He dismantles totems, treats heterodox notions with impartiality, ridicules theologians and their anathemas, reveals the bankruptcy of received ideas, and yet leaves the foundations of morality intact." Bayle was a congenital pessimist who as a writer could be flippant and cheerful, "life being much too tragic to be taken seriously."[41]

Bayle's first book, however, was the one on the comet, specifically a comet of 1680 that spawned a terrific number of dire prophecies and presages of things to come. The book that appeared two years later, *Pensées diverses sur la comète*, did not bear the author's name, but he made little show of denying he had written it. Robert C. Bartlett has translated the second edition, of 1683, as *Various Thoughts on the Occasion of a Comet*.[42] The book takes the form of a series of letters to an imaginary theologian at the Sorbonne, addressed throughout as Monsieur. The original title gives an idea of the organization, or lack of the same: *Letter to M.L.A.D.C., Doctor of the Sorbonne, In Which It Is Proved by Several Reasons Drawn from Philosophy and Theology That Comets Are Not the Presage of Any Misfortune,*

With Several Moral and Political Reflections and Several Historical Observations and the Refutation of Certain Popular Errors. Numbered and titled sections, 263 in all, are unevenly distributed among eleven so-called letters, each dated with a specific day of the year 1681, which may register the time of their original composition. Bayle also enumerates his reasons (eight in all) against the presages of comets as well as his responses (ten) to three objections, which are then further subdivided. Nevertheless, the objections and hence his responses all concern his "Seventh Reason, Drawn from Theology: That if Comets Were a Presage of Misfortune, God Would have Performed Miracles in Order to Confirm Idolatry in the World" (57). A good point, but as a result well over half of the book is supposedly devoted to this seventh reason or argument based on theology. That seems a very arbitrary organization of the whole, but not to worry. The author of *Pensées diverses* warns Monsieur in advance that "I wander very frequently from my subject" (1), and in the end he in effect apologizes: "Here I come to a stop, Monsieur, amazed at myself when I cast my eyes over the enormous length of this writing, but still more so when I think of the strange mix of things running throughout it. For of what have I not spoken?" (262).

An obvious inspiration for this book that seems to have written itself as it came along—and was reverted to again in subsequent publications, *Addition* (1694) and *Continuation* (1704)—was Cicero's *De divinatione*. In general Bayle took a very positive attitude to the works of Cicero, even identifying with the Roman as one who thought through and debated matters at hand. In his *Pensées diverses* on comets, he quotes from *De divinatione*, borrows from it, and shares its high spirits. Cicero kept his dialogue more in control than Bayle's digressive, pretended correspondence with a theologian, but both operations invite laughter and comic release. There can be little danger of confusing divination with the deity; prodigies and presages can be assailed without necessarily bringing in the gods or God. If comets occur less frequently than thunderbolts, Bayle can handle that. They afford the same kind of disconnect from historical happenings on the planet as pig entrails or bird flights do. Cicero, remember, felt so sure of the silliness of divinations that in book 2 of his dialogue he counterattacked in his own persona.

Bayle similarly feels that this is a subject on which he can let himself go. Reading the signs of comets can be thought of as a branch of astrology;

and as for astrology, nothing could be "more impertinent . . . chimerical . . . ignominious . . . deceitful." It is a disgrace to humanity that people are so stupid as to believe in astrologers. According to such confidence men, "Saturn, for example, dominates Bavaria, Saxony, and Spain, a part of Italy, Ravenna and Ingolstad, the Moors and the Jews, ponds, cesspools, cemeteries, old age, the spleen, the black, the tan, and the sour; for there is nothing, right down to colors and flavors, that they do not share in." Among the signs of the Zodiac, the Ram "dominates all things subject to the planet Mars . . . which are the north, a part of Italy and Germany, England and the capital of Poland, the liver, bile, soldiers, butchers, sergeants, executioners, the red, the bitter, and the prickly." Obviously the inhabitants of still other lands, with bakers and so forth, might have a *good* horoscope. Bayle forgoes further satiric catalogues and, returning to comets, speaks deadpan: "Rarely are comets made to signify any good fortune" (17).

As recently as 1667 the king of Persia despaired of help from his physicians and ordered them to consult with astrologers: Bayle remarks that this would have been a fine subject for a comedy by Molière (19). A certain bishop and a cardinal, however, "had the temerity to do the horoscope of Jesus Christ"; they surrendered the planets to false religions and reserved the sun to Christianity, "and it is for this reason we hold Sunday in singular esteem" (20). Monsieur must be aware that men of his profession argue over just about anything: "A book costs them nothing to write on such occasions, and nothing is as difficult for them as to lay down their arms. This is why the pacification of theologians is regarded as a very difficult task." Bayle instances the quarrel between Jesuits and Jansenists. This quarrel lasted more than twenty years and was settled by the court of Rome and an edict of 23 October 1668. Therefore the comets of 1665 should have been regarded as a good omen rather than a bad omen (42).

More than once Bayle points out that the vicissitudes of human affairs may result from a great many causes, some major perhaps but even more minor. Chance enters into the causation of events, at different times and places; the passions that drive people to act are legendary, yet some perhaps are never registered. Shouldn't this call for multiple smaller presages before soothsayers can speak with authority of the outcome—say, victory or defeat? He cites the Persian wars of ancient time and the

Crusades in order to illustrate the difficulty. Then he amusingly applies this reasoning to the first and foremost war of Western epic:

> For if one supposes that a comet formed all the passions that produced the Trojan War, one must suppose also that some of its atoms were charged with the not so difficult task of making Paris fall in love with Helen and Helen with Paris; that other atoms took it as their business to animate the good man Menelaus and to persuade him, though there was nothing in it, that his dear wife longed for him in the extreme because she saw him no more and was inexorably cruel to her lover; that others received the order to suggest to Agamemnon that this stain upon his family should not be endured, and to flatter him with the hope of becoming commander general, while innumerable other atoms would go throughout the villages, cities, and towns of Greece to cause everyone to take up arms; that others were transported to the court of King Priam to make him resolve not to give up Helen, and so on with the rest. . . .
>
> I am persuaded also, by the aid of this little bit of good sense that nature has given me, that even if a comet were never to shine in the heaven, there would not fail to be here on earth much coquetry, jealousy, ambition, envy, love, and hatred. (237)

It so happens that human passions and how they play out in individual and collective lives are one of Bayle's principal concerns in this book. But to the very end he concludes some digressions by sending up one or more comets again. This rhetorical turn not only signals that he is a winner by raising a laugh each time but also helps to render acceptable—or perhaps to hide somewhat—more serious purposes.

One very prominent theme is Bayle's contempt for idolatry. He was on pretty much safe ground here, since the Bible itself attacked the worship of false idols. In this book his formal argument about idolatry, which he characterized as a theological argument, commences with that Seventh Reason against the presages of comets (57). But his reasoning is hardly simple or direct. Bayle assumes and believes his readers will agree that if comets are indeed presages of misfortune, then God must go out of nature's way to set the comet in motion and follow through with the event or events in question. That is to say, God would be performing a miracle.

Performing very many such miracles would certainly feed human superstition and perhaps make idols of comets themselves. But God no more
approves idolatry than Bayle does. Therefore comets do not presage future
events. Idolatry is an embrace of false religion—worse, it turns out, than
no religion at all. This constant theme owes much of its inspiration to an
essay by Plutarch, "Of Superstition," which Bayle proceeds to quote.
Plutarch claimed to be astonished that atheism was said to be impious:
"What! He who does not believe that there are Gods is impious, and he
who believes they are such as the superstitious depict them—does he not
have an opinion whose impiety surpasses by much that of the atheist?"
Plutarch cheerfully went on to say that he personally would rather posterity
forgot *his* existence than have any grounds to fault his character (115).

After the Reformation it was common for Protestants to charge
Catholics with idolatry because of their church's prescribed sacraments
and relics, paintings and sculptures of the Virgin and of the saints. Thus
Pensées diverses sur la comète has sometimes been read as a veiled attack on
Catholicism. Catholics are not the only sinners Bayle has in his sights,
however, and there is nothing secret about his view of the persecution of
the Calvinists during the reigns of François I and Henri II. When persecution failed, the state found it "preferable to plunge the kingdom into the
terrible devastation of a civil war than to allow there to be a new religion
in France." Extermination of Huguenots became a means to this end; and
because they were armed their leaders "were brought to the court on the
finest pretext in the world, and they were cruelly massacred there" (155).
This is outspoken and the tone unmistakable. No question Bayle the
Protestant frowned on, and may have personally disliked, Catholic ways.
But to read this book as a coded attack on the Church does not allow for a
deeper-lying understanding and reprobation of humanity in general. As
he would argue in the *Dictionnaire* also, most people are all too ready to go
in for mystery. When the causes operating in nature are difficult to make
out, people make a cult of unknowns rather than investigate them. Their
own everyday affairs are driven by passions, not reason, and their credu-
lity about higher matters knows no limits. In short, idolatry comes naturally to most people; few are truly religious or blessed by grace, and few
are learned.

That comet of 1680 is merely the occasion of Bayle's book. The
contents pour forth as an outing of superstitions of many kinds. The

author rebuts these again and again, often by examples drawn from a ready store of analogies that make all seem ridiculous. Pagan beliefs especially are fair game, and these are treated as representative of human weakness. Bayle is very respectful of the writings of Cicero, Seneca, and Plutarch, but he has it in for worshippers of the ancient Greek and Roman gods, whose trust in ceremonial correctness went so far as practicing human sacrifice: those "who built temples and ordered feasts and sacrifices . . . to Jupiter as the husband of his sister Juno . . . to say nothing of Romulus, founder of the city of Rome and one of its principal gods, who was acknowledged to be the son of the god Mars and Rhea Sylvia, descended from the shameless loves of the goddess Venus . . . [who] had debauched the good man Anchises, to make him sleep with her," and so on (197). In those times, poets wrote of gods who hovered about "a flagrant crime, in which one among them had surprised his wife, the goddess, and on which some offered extremely roguish reflections." Bayle adroitly manages to link that epic occasion in the *Odyssey* to another embarrassing moment from Lucian's "Zeus Tragoedus" (125). Such was the mischief concocted by poets of old, and unfortunately this aspect of the classical past has become a part of Christians' heritage.

Bayle contends that by the conversion of gentiles God clearly did not purpose to make them better philosophers or scientists. Experience belies that "the persons to whom God communicates the richest treasures of his grace, whom he fills with the firmest faith and the most ardent charity, are the most penetrating geniuses, reason with the greatest force, and put themselves above a thousand false judgments that are of no consequence as regards the salvation of the soul." Most pagans who converted to Christianity brought many of their prejudices along with them, since "few people bother to examine whether widespread opinions are true or false" (84). If by grace some found God and the means to salvation, that was the significant payoff. Like Spinoza, Bayle seems to feel that philosophy and religion are two separate matters.

Subsequently he argues that pagan beliefs about the gods were so outrageous that they helped bring about atheism. Like Montaigne, he finds Plutarch useful, and now quotes the essay "Of Superstition" at greater length. "It is superstition . . . that gave birth to atheism and that every day gives to it resources to justify and defend itself, if not justly, at least with much more pretext and plausibility." Plutarch's overview of the

question was both contemptuous and comprehensive. At fault are superstition's "strange actions, its ridiculous passions, its utterances, its move-
ments, its sorceries, its enchantments, its twists and turns, its impure
and abominable purifications, its drums, its villainous and filthy continence, its barbarous mortifications, and the outrages it itself performs in
the temples." One thing Plutarch explicitly had in mind was the practice
of human sacrifice and the notion that gods "took pleasure in the effusion
of human blood with which their altars were bathed." Bayle anticipates
that point in this long quotation by providing, in a footnote of his own, the
familiar line of Lucretius, "Tantum religio potuit suadere malorum."
Such was the contribution of the sacrifice of Iphigenia to atheism (188).[43]

By a remarkable process comets and divinations give way in this book
to the subject of religious belief versus the absence of belief. The inspiration for this move is most likely the same essay from Plutarch's *Moralia*,
as Bayle's attempt to distance himself from the essay a few sections on
may suggest (193). To a substantial degree atheism becomes *the* theme of
Pensées diverses sur la comète. Granted that Bayle's argument does not
usually come across as highly organized but as thoughts, pensées
diverses. (Their spontaneity is all in their favor, except on the few occasions when they fail to hold a reader's interest.) The ostensible logical
ordering of the book also singles out atheism, however, since about one-
third of its pages—including, to be sure, digressions—are subordinate to
Bayle's Fourth Response to objections to his Seventh Reason (see above).
And this Response formally contends, "That Atheism Is Not a Greater
Evil than Idolatry" (114). But whose atheism? Bayle names very few
names. And why argue this at all? The response is couched as the negation of a given comparative—that atheism is not a greater evil than idolatry. That could be Bayle's favorite kind of locution, judging from how
often he resorts to it. It is not the same as saying idolatry *is* a greater evil
than atheism or even that atheism is a lesser evil. He presumes that his
readers, including idolaters, believe atheism to be the greatest evil of all,
and he begs to differ. In the First Clarification appended to his *Dictionnaire
historique et critique* he at least distinguished between practical atheists
and theoretical atheists. Practical atheists are "persons who have stifled
the explicit faith in the existence of God by their debauchery and by long
criminal habits." They far outnumber theoretical atheists but are not the
ones Bayle has been referring to as atheists on their good behavior leading

moral lives. Such are "theoretical atheists, as, for example, Diagoras, Vanini, Spinoza, and their sort—people whose atheism is attested to either by the historians or by their own writings."[44]

Diagoras was a Greek poet from Milos who settled in Athens in the late fifth century BC. Almost nothing is known of him except his reputation for atheism. The Athenians condemned him to death for sacrilege, and he fled for his life. Giulio Cesare Vanini (1584–1619) was a radical philosopher and critic of revealed religion who taught medicine in Toulouse in his last days of freedom. Although he professed Christianity, he was tortured by the Inquisition before being burned to death. That leaves Spinoza, who managed to escape this fate. In his article on Spinoza in the *Dictionnaire*, Bayle clearly assumed his readers had all heard that this extraordinary philosopher was an atheist. Bayle himself was partly depending on hearsay: "He died, they say, completely convinced of his atheism, and took precautions to keep any last-minute lapse from his principles from being found out, should it occur." But he acknowledged that Spinoza lived modestly apart from the world in order to pursue his studies; and observed that "those who were acquainted with him, and the peasants of the villages where he had lived in retirement for some time, all agree in saying that he was sociable, affable, honest, obliging, and of a well-ordered morality." Bayle was utterly put off by Spinoza's metaphysics, especially that "God is the only substance in the universe and that all other beings are only modifications of that substance."[45] The sheer length of the article and attached remarks, however, was something of a compliment.

It is tempting, therefore, to declare Spinoza the atheist Bayle had in mind for the thesis he keeps returning to at the center of *Pensées diverses*: namely, that so-called theoretical atheism, at least, is perfectly compatible with morality. But this is a notion partly inspired by Plutarch, and in this earlier book Bayle mentions Spinoza by name only twice in passing, the second time to scold him for his deathbed "vanity" (181)—hearsay this time treated as authoritative. Half a dozen more candidates are named, but all are pagans with the exception of Vanini once again, to whom Bayle devotes a separate section weighing whether such a holdout might be thought of as a "martyr" to atheism (182). Among the ancients were some, including Cicero, who conceived of the "unity of God" and were not repudiated on that score by a polytheistic society. Very little is known about the opinions of some whom Bayle mentions; he puts in a good word for Epicurus, however, and observes that most who later came to be called epicureans did not adopt lascivious ways from the master: "Epicurus, who denied providence and the immortality of the soul, lived in as exemplary a way as any of the ancient philosophers; and although his sect was subsequently decried, it is nonetheless certain that it was made up of a number of persons of honor and probity" (174). He reminds his readers that St. Jerome compared the character of Epicurus favorably to that of some Christians.

Bayle's instinct is to argue his case the other way around—and in the negative. There are far more pagan or Christian believers than atheists to begin with, and among that population numberless instances of immorality or downright criminality come to hand. To a great extent human behavior is driven by a herd mentality, and religious beliefs whether true or false tend to enhance that. Thus in ancient times idolatrous nations fiercely defended their homelands when the cry went out to protect temples and shrines and likewise more readily killed and risked lives by attacking neighbors who worshipped different gods. Bayle takes note of the behavior of soldiers in particular. Trained to fight, they wreck havoc anywhere unless severely disciplined. Killing is certainly not part of the Christian creed, yet the Crusaders fancied "they saw angels and saints at the head of their armies." Imagined prodigies and miracles justified whatever they chose to take on: "The Christians whom they went to defend had as much hatred of them as of the Turks and Saracens." Moreover, the resident Christians "made use of the blackest and most disloyal betrayal there can be to destroy the Christians of the West," while the latter "committed horrible excesses of every kind." Warriors boast a kind of courage, Bayle argues, different from that taught by the Gospels and held to by Christian martyrs: that is, "suffering insults, being humble, loving our neighbor, seeking peace, returning good for evil, abstaining from all that smacks of violence. . . . I leave it at saying that if the principles of Christianity were well followed, we would never see a conqueror among Christians, nor offensive war, and we would be content to defend ourselves against the invasions of infidels." But he does not leave it there. No people on earth are more bellicose than Christians, and those that get in their way are seldom as good fighters: "I find here a very convincing reason to prove that one does not follow the principles of one's religion in the world, since I have shown that Christians use all their intellect and all their passions to perfect themselves in the art of war without the knowledge of the Gospel crossing the path of this cruel design in the least" (139–41).

The courtesans and prostitutes of Paris, Venice, and Rome regularly say their litany and other prayers, Bayle claims. What he terms shamelessness denotes any kind of sexual congress outside marriage, and there appears to be a lot of shamelessness in this world. Not only sex workers, however, but out-and-out scoundrels pray to the Blessed Virgin for her protection. At the highest level of society, the royal court is fraught with superstition. Courtiers are not atheists, as some people presume, yet many of high birth are taken in by magicians and sorcerers. Indeed, "nobles make clear that when they are on their death bed, they believe in the mysteries of the Gospel." When it comes to naming names, Bayle zeroes in on Louis XI, who "professed the whole of his life to a duplicity of the heart so opposed to the spirit of the Christian religion that there is scarcely any king whom one could suspect of irreligion with less temerity than he." Yet Louis XI did think of himself as a Christian, believed in the efficacy of prayer, and sent out for holy men who might be able to prolong his life. The story of his last days is told by Philippe de Commines. Bayle concludes that in Louis XI we have "the example of a perfect agreement between an altogether nasty soul and a conviction of the existence of God, which extends to the most extreme zealotry" (152). His candidate for an equally ruthless ruler and consulter of celestial signs and presages is Alexander the Great. And somewhere between streetwalkers at one end of the social scale and royalty at the other, among the middling classes, are "people who hardly say three words without taking the name of God in vain"—the same "people who steal with both hands." Stealing with both hands suggests devotees of the cult of Hermes come home again: "Are they at war? They fleece the peasant mercilessly, and they profit as much as they can from the pay of their soldiers. Are they in command somewhere? They have a thousand oblique or violent ways to enrich themselves. Are they in business, the great theater of rapine and extortion? They enrage everyone with their chicanery and tricks" (148).

Sometimes it seems as if Bayle were haranguing his readers from a pulpit, rubbing noses into "the distressing depravity of morals that has descended upon the whole of Christianity for a thousand years" and sparing none (160), comparing the majority unfavorably to atheists for not having followed the Bible. But he is more philosophical than that and more focused on human behavior in general. As for morals, people are governed "by the inclinations of their temperament and by the weight of the habits they have contracted" (144). Most seek pleasure and do very much what they want to do. Human greed is almost as compelling as thoughts of vengeance, for people are certain it is pleasant to be rich and to get back at those who offend them. Neither estimating "the greater or lesser malice of certain vices" nor "having fine declamations made from the pulpit" interferes with "the direction of our taste for pleasures." Atheists are no worse in this respect than idolaters (171).

Bayle does put forward the idea that for two sorts of moral concern, decency and honor, a society of atheists would work as well as any other. Christians may have the same values, but not because these are taught in the Gospels:

> Whoever would like to be fully convinced that a people destitute
> of the knowledge of God would make for itself rules of honor
> and show great delicacy in the observance of them, has only to
> note that there is among Christians a certain worldly honor that
> is directly contrary to the spirit of the Gospel. . . . One may run
> through all the ideas of decency there are among Christians;
> scarcely two will be found that are taken from the religion. And
> when things become decent from having been indecent, it is in
> no way because the morality of the Gospel has been better
> consulted. . . . Let us therefore admit that there are ideas of
> honor among men that are purely a work of nature, that is, of
> general providence. Let us admit it above all of that honor of
> which our brave men are so jealous and which is opposed to the
> law of God.

Nor do these codes of behavior depend on belief in the next world, in landing in heaven or in hell: "It is therefore not the belief in the immortality of the soul that causes the love of glory; and as a consequence, atheists are very capable of wishing for an eternal reputation" (172–73). In fact, earning and keeping the day-to-day respect of fellow mortals sufficiently motivates decent behavior. A reputation for virtues like honesty and trustworthiness, generosity and gratitude, consideration for others, is worth the occasional material cost to oneself and does not require religion, "for it is to the inward esteem of other men that we aspire above all" (179). The adjective *inward* gives Bayle's meaning: *l'estime interieure* refers to what others truly think of one, not necessarily what they speak aloud and certainly not their flattery or passing favor.

Bayle comes back to his main point again and again. Here concertedly and there incidentally, but persistently, he argues that morality is largely independent of beliefs. He would like to suppose we are rational beings who thoughtfully weigh our immediate interests and long-term happiness or indeed are "convinced that there is a Providence governing the world . . . which rewards with an infinite happiness those who love virtue, [and] which chastises with an eternal punishment those who give themselves over to vice." He illustrates his point with several examples from classical times and then tentatively hypothesizes that in that case, if one were an atheist, "being untouched by all these considerations, he must necessarily be the greatest and most incorrigible scoundrel in the universe" (133). Then Bayle takes this back because it "does not conform to experience." Perhaps if some visitants from outer space heard about Christianity, they would expect to meet people committed to mercy and forgiveness, careful not to harm or offend their neighbors, and dwelling on the life to come—for that is what Christians are like, in the abstract. But "they would not have lived for two weeks among us before announcing that in this world we do not guide ourselves by the lights of the conscience" (134). Why is this so? why do our beliefs correspond so remotely, if at all, to our actions? Sometimes the particular choices we make conform to our wider knowledge of what we should do, but mostly they do not. The action "almost always accommodates itself to the dominant passion of the heart, to the inclination of the temperament, to the force of adopted habits, and to the taste for or sensitivity to certain objects." Here Bayle's authority is no other than Medea as her desire for Jason begins to overcome her reason, in Ovid's account of that affair: "*I see and I approve the good, but I do the evil*" (135).[46] Given Medea's subsequent actions, the example could not be better chosen.

Since there is hardly any limit to what people can do while knowing it is wrong, it is a mistake to suppose their behavior can be judged from what they believe. To do so makes even less sense than "to judge [a man's] actions by his books or his harangues," as Bayle apparently never would (135). It makes little difference if the moral agent is eminently reasonable and not subject to false principles: he or she regularly succumbs to "unregulated desires." Human passions are remarkably constant throughout history and in widely disparate cultures. The proximate causes of actions tend to be "nothing other than the temperament, the natural inclination toward pleasure, the taste one contracts for certain objects, the desire to please someone, a habit gained in the commerce with one's friends, or some other disposition that results from the ground of our nature, in whatever country one may be born, and from whatever knowledge our mind may be filled with." This was true of the ancients with their many imagined gods, and it is true of Christians, who have both much stronger reasons to believe in God and eternity and "so many excellent preachers . . . so many zealous and learned directors of conscience and so many devotional books" (136).

Finally, neither wholehearted nor fulsome commitments to religious ritual and ceremony have any bearing on morality. Jews keep the Sabbath, for example, and practice circumcision (Bayle notes that circumcision is not painful for the parents), but these customs do not affect moral behavior or business deals. Basically we participate in religious holidays and dress appropriately for church for the same reason we do so many other things: namely, in order to keep the respect of the community. "What is nicer than a holiday? We do not work, we put on our finest clothes, we dance, play, drink, the two sexes find themselves together; for the hour or two we give to God, we give ten or twelve to our entertainment. No doubt this is an important victory that religion gains over the passions, to make one observe either circumcisions or holidays." Worshipping in style can also serve as a distraction: "We abstain the whole of Lent from eating meat, yes; but do we abstain from speaking ill of our neighbor? Do we abstain from enriching ourselves by fraudulent means? Do we abstain from women of ill repute? Do we renounce vengeance? Not at all." Once he gets going in this vein, it is hard for Bayle to let up. "For as things stand, I do not see that one should have merit before God because one does not marry one's sister. . . . If civil law and canon law were to leave the matter at our liberty, it is very likely that one would have no greater scruples in this respect than as regards adultery" (137).

These sections reveal Bayle at his best, and he is sending up far more than that foolish comet. Here as elsewhere he occasionally inserts a pro forma exception to the targets of his satire—"those in whom the grace of the Holy Spirit is deployed with all its efficacy" (136)—but such an aside never slows him down. He is fully persuaded, as Hobbes and Spinoza were persuaded, that human law and human justice offer the only effective check on the passions. One reason he despairs over human "shamelessness" (162–68) is that the law doesn't concern itself very much with sex. The skepticism about religious beliefs links his humanism to that of Erasmus and Montaigne. They each in their own way eschewed the quarrels of theologians, differences over doctrine and dogma, and rigid interpretations of scripture. Erasmus himself had taken orders but understood that theology could serve as aggressive priming for wars of religion. Pierre Bayle, in the course of writing this funny yet serious book, convinced himself that people's beliefs had little to do with how they behaved. He too judged that the Church cared far more about policing correct dogmas than about people's conduct or well-being. He instanced the Inquisition's treatment of Galileo, who seconded Copernicus's finding that the earth travels around the sun. Scripture told of the sun circling the earth, so Galileo was imprisoned and then sentenced to house arrest for the rest of his life. Bayle speculates that "Galileo would never have been bothered if, instead of being a Copernican, he had undertaken to support several concubines" (199–200).

This humanist comedy repeatedly stages a chorus of nonbelievers. These are people with *no* religious beliefs, ancient or modern—a society of atheists, as Bayle likes to call it. To test empirically that "a simple knowledge of the truth of the Gospel" is not enough to cure "the inclination to evil that is found in the heart of man" (156), for example, a protosociologist would merely need to record enough cases to make his point. First determine that each subject of the experiment is a believer who acknowledges the truth of the Gospel and then examine the subject's behavior past and present. That would take work, and there would be quicker and sloppier ways to go about this, such as lining up as many bad guys and gals as are conveniently at hand and asking them whether they believe in God. In truth, Bayle himself heaps up so many case studies of this sort that in the end he apologizes to his supposed theological correspondent. The rhetorical gambit he most favors, however, is to ask his reader to contemplate one very mischievous negative universal: that no believer is ipso facto morally superior to an atheist. Every time the lengthy chain gang of historical believers comes up against the hypothetical nonbelievers, they either break even or lose as moral agents. Believers, be they pagans or Christians, can't win. So the question arises whether this comedy is for real. For if the negative universal proposition is true, why not start over again clean, as real historical atheists with a better chance at being good? Bayle's view of human nature does not allow for that outcome; but his skepticism about the efficacy of belief does, and on margin atheism wins.

Bayle the Calvinist, to be sure, leaves a way out. From cover to cover the comedy can be said to prove the necessity of grace. Clearly men do not "bring us to love the truths of the Gospel; and as a consequence it is God who brings us to love them by adding to the illumination of our mind a disposition of the heart that makes us find more joy in the exercise of virtue than in the practice of vice" (157). That reads almost as if Bayle had registered the fifth part of Spinoza's *Ethics* after all, where the last proposition (P42) states, "*Blessedness is not the reward of virtue, but virtue itself.*" Bayle and Spinoza remained true to the faith in their own ways, though both grace and the idea of God in their respective works are very tenuous concepts. That society of atheists, however—the manipulated but stout chorus of Bayle's comedy—demonstrably resonated in the thinking of Voltaire and Hume.[47]

6. HUME'S JESTING WITH NATURAL RELIGION

By natural religion David Hume (1711–76) understood deism, a widespread movement in eighteenth-century Britain among divines as well as philosophers and the literati. Deists reasoned that the evident order and design in nature could have been brought about only by God, the creator of the universe as we know it. Thus theoretically no scriptural revelation is involved, and deists need not be Christians. Hume's *Dialogues concerning Natural Religion*, unlike so many humanist works, never cites or interprets scripture. Adhering closely to his Ciceronian model, Hume refrained from identifying any one speaker with the author. He composed his *Dialogues* very ingeniously, revised it several times, but held it back from publication in his lifetime. Perhaps he was wary that his sheer force of argument and sense of humor would not be appreciated. The book was seen through the press by his nephew David in 1779.

Hume came from Berwick, Scotland, and was sent by his family to Edinburgh to study law. He left the university at the age of fifteen, however, and set off on his own to become a philosopher. The evidence suggests that while he was still a teenager he conceived of writing the book that would be published anonymously in three volumes titled *A Treatise of Human Nature* before he was thirty. Without question this was an astonishing achievement, though Hume was utterly disappointed with its reception. Needless to say, that reception has radically improved over time. The *Treatise* is an ambitious empiricist study of what we know and how we know it, and it contains the groundbreaking arguments for which the author is famous—his analysis of causation, of human motivations, of moral philosophy—and his skepticism. Apart from the six-volume *History of England from the Invasion of Julius Caesar to the Revolution in 1688* (1754–61), this was surely Hume's greatest achievement.

The *Treatise* owed a good deal to Bayle, especially in book 1, part 3, on the influence of beliefs, and in book 2, part 4, on the will and the passions. Just as Bayle argued that people are fond of believing one thing or another but that beliefs do not much affect their behavior, Hume contended that abstract reasoning does not drive the will to action. He can be said to take Bayle's pessimism one step further: "Nothing is more usual in philosophy, and even in common life, than to talk of the combat of passion and reason, to give the preference to reason, and to assert that men are only so far virtuous as they conform themselves to its dictates. . . . In order to shew the fallacy of all this philosophy, I shall endeavour to prove *first*, that reason alone can never be a motive to any action of the will; and *secondly*, that it can never oppose passion in the direction of the will." Famously— and provocatively, for sure—Hume concluded, "Reason is, and ought only to be the slave of the passions, and can never pretend to any other office than to serve and obey them."[48] And there are a good many other general and specific echoes of Bayle's writings. Although the *Treatise* rarely touches on topical matters, for example, Hume also writes from a Protestant point of view and equates Catholic rituals with superstition.

Hume's singular passion, it soon appeared, was to acquire fame as a writer. His disappointment with the reception of the *Treatise* led quickly to the first printing of *Essays Moral and Political* in a style aimed at a wider readership. Also in a livelier manner, he prepared *An Enquiry concerning Human Understanding*, first published in 1748. The *Enquiry* at once managed to summarize much of the *Treatise* and add to it, all in the space of twelve essays, some very short. The new material mostly concerns religion, and Hume the philosopher now writes in the humanist vein. A longer essay "Of miracles" does away with miracles altogether in effect. Lucian and Lucretius are invoked. Christians who try to rationalize the fabulous happenings recorded in the Pentateuch are ridiculed and dismissed outright. Another essay, "Of a particular providence and of a future state," takes the form of a conversation with a friend that the author recalls. Hume speaks in the first person and begins by remarking the freedom of speech and toleration of diverse beliefs in ancient Athens as contrasted to "this bigoted jealousy, with which the present age is so much infested." This observation echoes the thinking of Bacon and other humanists in early modern Europe but may have been triggered by the recent denial, apparently on religious grounds, of Hume's candidacy for the chair of ethics at Edinburgh University. To illustrate the point, he urges his friend "to try [his] eloquence upon so extraordinary a topic" by showing how Epicurus might have defended himself and his philosophy. So within this imaginary conversation the reader is treated to an imaginary speech from ancient times—the speaking parts all scripted by David Hume. Before the end of the conversation, its author deploys his famous analysis of what can be meant by causation in order to refute so-called deism or natural religion.[49]

As an empiricist Hume taught that all we could be sure about cause and effect ultimately derived from experience. No a priori certainty applied, only the repeated observation of a certain effect following a given cause established the relation, and by analogy this expected cause and effect might then be recognized in other phenomena. In the conversation conducted in the *Enquiry*, Hume's friend examines the essentially anthropomorphic notion of a designer of the universe and finds it wanting. From a clock we can infer a clock maker because we know that clocks and other machines are made by skilled mechanics. We have plenty of experience with human intentions and can make intelligent guesses even if we have never met the person in question. But we have nothing with which to compare a remote Being at work, no experience to go on, in order to infer cause and effect: "All the philosophy, therefore, in the world, and all the religion, which is nothing but a species of philosophy, will never be able to carry us beyond the usual course of experience, or give us measures of conduct and behaviour different from those which are furnished by reflections on common life. No new fact can ever be inferred from the religious hypothesis; no event foreseen or foretold; no reward or punishment expected or dreaded, beyond what is already known by practice and observation."[50] At least that is what my friend said, and I have just shared with you his dramatic imitation of Epicurus.

The last section of the *Enquiry* takes the measure of skepticism in philosophy. There are more echoes of Bayle and a couple of explicit references to the *Dictionnaire*. An excursus on ancient Pyrrhonians and the Academic school provides some, but not much, historical background. Hume is willing to accept what he calls "*mitigated* skepticism," perhaps with Cicero in mind. The answer to Pyrrhonism "is action, and employment, and the occupations of common life." The only ground for belief in the existence of God and immortality of the soul "is *faith* and divine revelation." Morality and beauty are properly objects "of taste and sentiment." And Hume brought his *Enquiry concerning Human Understanding* to a close with an invitation to a book burning. The two questions return to the heart of his philosophy and were not meant to be quixotic: "When we run over libraries, persuaded of these principles, what havoc must we make? If we take in our hand any volume; of divinity or school metaphysics, for instance; let us ask, *Does it contain any abstract reasoning concerning quantity or number?* No. *Does it contain any experimental reasoning concerning matter of fact and existence?* No. Commit it then to the flames: For it can contain nothing but sophistry and illusion."[51]

Hume also wrote a number of independent essays bearing on religion, one titled "The Sceptic" that engages some of the same issues. Two more, "Of Suicide" and "Of the Immortality of the Soul," he withheld from publication, and these had to wait to be printed anonymously in 1777 after his death. It is hard to measure Hume's hesitancy about going public with these and with his *Dialogues*, since in 1757 he produced a longer essay, *The Natural History of Religion*, which he then revised and reprinted a good many times. This longer essay is uneven, but it endorses the usual humanist distinctions between the polytheism of ancient times and the monotheism of subsequent Western civilization. Hume can hardly be said to favor the latter, which he declares notorious for its intolerance. He compares the "traditional" religions of the past with the "scriptural" concerns of modern times that invite still finer differences of dogma. He gets in a few jokes, but the tone of the whole might be called cool. *The Natural History of Religion* seems far from the mischievous spirit of the *Dialogues concerning Natural Religion* twenty years later.

Although Hume's *Dialogues* would have been unthinkable without the example of Cicero, they are livelier than Cicero's and crafted more like a work of dramatic art. There is more spontaneity and give-and-take but also development. The fairly short parts (twelve in number again) are not designed to package competing philosophical schools and often keep the conversation in suspense. Three speakers with suggestive names—Philo, Cleanthes, and Demea—form shifting alliances, so that the debate can sometimes be two against one. Philo, the skeptic, takes up the most positions and easily outtalks the others. His name suggests Philon of Larissa, the last head of the Academy, who was Cicero's teacher. Cleanthes, the deist, suggests Cleanthes of Assos, a fourth-century-BC student of Zeno and head of the Stoa. Demea, the Christian, speaks his mind but has the fewest lines of the three (the subject, of course, is natural religion). Perhaps his name suggests *demos*, or the common people. The conversation takes place at Cleanthes' home and is written down from memory by one Pamphilus, meaning beloved of all, a young man and sometime pupil of Cleanthes. He ostensibly sends the script off with a letter to one Hermippus, as if the prizewinning fifth-century-BC comedian by that name (none of his plays survive) were still alive and awaiting fresh material in Athens.

So Hume's project gestures toward ancient Greek drama that, both in its tragic and comic modes, allowed for quite marvelous supernatural turns of plot—usually beholden to myth in tragedy and more inventive with comedy. But this project, though it enjoys the freedom permitted to dialogue, undergoes the wider constraints of the author's express modern philosophy: unless he can come up with some *"abstract reasoning concerning quantity and number"* he had better limit the discussion to *"experimental reasoning concerning matter of fact and existence."* That is the point of addressing natural religion, and the plan also affords an escape hatch: Hume need not risk making fun of God, only of the deity that others infer from the evidence of the surrounding world. Even so he opted for posthumous publication of his comedy.

An invitation to laughter and anticipation of the same are present from the start. In his cover letter to Hermippus that serves as a frame to the *Dialogues*, Pamphilus registers his appreciation of the form it will take, since "opposite sentiments, even without any decision, afford an agreeable amusement." As the dialogue gets under way in part i, he watches Demea and Cleanthes smiling, and in Cleanthes' expression he fancies "an air of finesse; as if he perceived some raillery or artificial malice in the reasonings of *Philo*" (1.4).[52] Cleanthes himself, as the proponent of deism and wary of Philo's wit and quickness in debate, remarks a couple of times that he can put up with skepticism as long as the skeptics are only jesting. He finds the teaching of the ancient Pyrrhonians ridiculous, stops short of Antoine Arnauld's opinion that skeptics are not philosophers, but calls them liars. "I may, however, affirm (I hope without offence), that they are a sect of jesters or railers. . . . A comedy, a novel, or at most a history, seems a more natural recreation than such metaphysical subtleties and abstractions" (1.15). Backing off from You lie to You jest may or may not get Cleanthes off the hook, but at least it is more in the spirit of the present conversation.

Initially Demea and Philo seem to be allied. Both the religionist and the skeptic start from the limitations of human reason and perception, and Philo somewhat patronizingly comes to the defense of Demea. All three participants ostensibly agree that the nature, not the existence, of the deity is at issue. Philo takes the Humean position that human experience can tell us nothing about all that. Need he add that he finds it "a pleasure" to say that "just reasoning and sound piety here concur . . . and both of them establish the adorably mysterious and incomprehensible nature of the supreme being"? The man's irony is not easy for the others—and perhaps the reader—to cope with. But Cleanthes brushes this aside and delivers in uncompromising terms the deist argument from design, as follows:

> Look round the world: Contemplate the whole and every part of it: You will find it to be nothing but one great machine, subdivided into an infinite number of lesser machines, which again admit of subdivisions, to a degree beyond what human senses and faculties can trace and explain. All these various machines, and even their most minute parts, are adjusted to each other with an accuracy, which ravishes into admiration all men, who have ever contemplated them. The curious adapting

of means to ends, throughout all nature, resembles exactly, though it much exceeds, the productions of human contrivance; of human design, thought, wisdom, and intelligence. Since therefore the effects resemble each other, we are led to infer, by all the rules of analogy, that the causes also resemble; and that the author of nature is somewhat similar to the mind of man; though possessed of much larger faculties, proportioned to the grandeur of the work, which he has executed. (2.4–5)

This is the kind of argument often directed to the existence of a divine being, though strictly speaking, Cleanthes here addresses the nature of his author of nature. Demea immediately protests the matching of divine nature to human nature and the proof a posteriori; Philo also dismisses the analogy and reiterates the difficulty of reasoning about cause and effect except empirically.

"Good God! . . . where are we?" That's Demea, complaining that Philo has deserted him and distressed that this dispute is taking place "before so young a man as *Pamphilus*." Philo more or less takes over at this point and, with the consent of both his listeners, expounds what Cleanthes is trying to argue—and then proceeds to refute it. For the first time in the *Dialogues* he introduces a different aspect of the history of the universe as we know it: a universe evolving over time. Much like Lucretius expounding the ideas of Epicurus, Philo invokes an analogy very different from that of a completed machine. (What sort of great machine is subdivided into an infinity of lesser machines?) He shifts the metaphors toward biology and suggests thinking about an "embryo-state" of things: "By observation, we know somewhat of the economy, action, and nourishment of a finished animal; but we must transfer with great caution that observation to the growth of a foetus in the womb, and still more, to the formation of an animalcule in the loins of its male parent." The discussion turns to outer space when Cleanthes protests that Philo objects to his position much as a caviler might object to Copernicus's. But Philo breaks in and tops this with praise of Galileo, calling the latter's discoveries to his side. And he gets the last word:

In this cautious proceeding of the astronomers, you may read your own condemnation, *Cleanthes*; or rather may see, that the subject in which you are engaged exceeds all human reason and

enquiry. Can you pretend to show any such similarity between
the fabric of a house, and the generation of a universe? Have
you ever seen nature in any such situation as resembles the first
arrangement of the elements? Have worlds ever been formed
under your eye? And have you had leisure to observe the whole
progress of the phenomenon, from the first appearance of order
to its final consummation? If you have, then cite your
experience, and deliver your theory. (2.10, 21, 28)

Unquestionably Philo has won round 2. So is Cleanthes or Cleanthes'
intelligent designer the loser? Formulations like *generation, first* arrangement, worlds *formed*, whole *progress* open the field to developmental ideas.
Nature has ways of changing by itself, and little more will be heard of
clockwork machinery. Cleanthes is not silenced, of course, not this early
in the *Dialogues*. Other human achievements besides machinery are analogies that can be trusted to throw light on the workings of a deity.

Demea once again comes to the aid of Philo and presents readers
with something like the resolution of Montaigne's doubts: skepticism has
to fall back on faith rather than reason. The point is not lost on Cleanthes,
who starts referring to his two friends collectively as *mystics*; Demea
objects to this name-calling and rejoins with *anthropomorphite*. His adversary charges that mystics, since they do not think, are atheists "without
knowing it" and seem to fancy a deity without a mind (4.1–3). This time
Philo intervenes and is soon back in form, quoting Lucretius's *De rerum
natura* (2.1095–99) and Velleius in Cicero's *De natura deorum* (1.19). If
the ancients knew this much, he says, how much more we know since the
invention of microscopes. He easily nails down Cleanthes' conviction that
the mind of the deity is like that of a human. No other, Cleanthes admits—
what other sort of mind could one have in mind? Then Philo pounces. He
argues, first, that Cleanthes thereby has no basis for claiming infinity as
an attribute of his deity. Second, his kind of reasoning will not support the
perfection of the deity either. To rub in this point Philo notes that we have
no experience of human craftsmanship that achieves perfection all at
once. On the contrary, often it takes successive attempts over the ages by
different craftsmen to achieve perfection in the arts. Third—and this
seems to follow from the last—Cleanthes has no grounds for establishing
the unity of his creator: "A great number of men join in building a house

or ship, in rearing a city, in framing a commonwealth: Why may not several deities combine in contriving and framing a world?" (5.5–8). An argument for polydeism, this.

When, now on the march, Philo proposes that the universe resembles a human body more than a human artwork, and Cleanthes responds that the universe is more like a vegetable, both are evidently fencing ironically. But Philo then begins to dish out some evidence of the changing surface of the earth. He refers to familiar relocations of fauna and flora, some of these due to human discovery and trafficking about the world. At some point in time it seems the planet may have been entirely covered by the seas. He speculates about "convulsions," "general transformations," and "matter . . . susceptible of many and great revolutions" as a challenge to deism's notion of order and design (6.12). This would seem to be an allusion to volcanic upheavals and changes in the terrain. Geological time is in the air, though the scientific commitment to that concept as contrary to biblical time did not begin to go fully public before the end of the eighteenth century. Not surprisingly, Demea wants to know where their conversation is heading: "How is it conceivable . . . that the world can arise from anything similar to vegetation or generation?" Philo doesn't have an answer, but his sense of humor is always obliging and capable, like Bayle's, of various thoughts:

> A comet, for instance, is the seed of a world; and after it has
> been fully ripened, by passing from sun to sun, and star to star,
> it is at last tossed into the unformed elements, which
> everywhere surround this universe, and immediately sprouts up
> into a new system.
>
> Or if, for the sake of variety (for I see no other advantage) we
> should suppose this world to be an animal; a comet is the egg
> of this animal; and in like manner as an ostrich lays its egg in
> the sand, which, without any farther care, hatches the egg, and
> produces a new animal; so . . . (7.4–6; Hume's ellipsis)

Demea has heard enough of this now to come right back with what Philo himself would say to it: we have no *data*. Philo replies, that's what he's been saying all along. He does pause to make explicit the contrast between Cleanthes' recourse to the analogy of the universe to a machine and his sporting embrace of generation or vegetation. Both he and Cleanthes are devoted to reason, however: "Reason, in innumerable instances, is observed to arise from the principle of generation, and never to arise from any other principle" (7.15). Get it? In order to have reason, the reasoning being must first be conceived and born, even educated a little. At this point Cleanthes throws in the towel—or half a towel. Philo is too fast for him.

Still, the skeptic's musings can be fruitful and forward looking. He contemplates reviving Epicurean particle physics, but with a difference: namely, that the matter of the universe is finite rather than infinite. Everything is in motion and consequently coming together and falling apart, tending to order or to chaos. No imposed order here; whatever works works. This also seems to anticipate nineteenth-century conceptions of the history of the world and life on earth: "Thus the universe goes on for many ages in a continued succession of chaos and disorder. But is it not possible that it may settle at last, so as not to lose its motion and active force . . .? This we find to be the case with the universe at present. Every individual is perpetually changing, and every part of every individual, and yet the whole remains, in appearance, the same. . . . and may not this account for all the appearing wisdom and contrivance, which is in the universe?" (8.8). He goes on to discuss with Cleanthes what human systems of cosmogony entail. Demea's reaction is to suggest that they reach instead for some a priori proofs of infinity and divine attributes.

From here on in the conversation Demea's significant move is to propose that human ills and shortcomings explain the need of religion and divine truths. Instead of being struck by wonder at the design of the universe, people more likely feel helpless and afraid before so much suffering and wickedness, their own and that of others. Their faith and prayers give them hope. Demea now does seem to represent the people, as his name suggests. Philo immediately concurs. It is as if he were silently picking up on Bayle's worldview and perhaps going Bayle one better. The evidence for unhappiness and evildoing abounds; moreover, on this "the learned are perfectly agreed with the vulgar." The poets too, "from Homer down to Dr. [Edward] Young," have most eloquently treated of human pathos (10.1–4). Demea quotes ten lines from *Paradise Lost*— the angel Michael displaying to Adam a video of the hideous diseases, besides death, brought about by Eve's "inabstinence" (Milton's word) in the Garden of Eden. When Philo places in evidence nature red in tooth and claw, so to speak, Demea tentatively exempts humans, because of their capacity for "combination in society." But Philo simply redoubles his bid. Society brings more problems: "Man is the greatest enemy of man. Oppression, injustice, contempt, contumely, violence, sedition, war, calumny, treachery, fraud; by these they mutually torment each other" (10.10–13). This back and forth begins to invest Demea, of all people, with the role of a satirist. "Were a stranger to drop, on a sudden, into this world," he says, adopting a favorite trope of satire, "I would show him, as a specimen of its ills, a hospital full of diseases, a prison crowded with malefactors and debtors, a field of battle strewed with carcasses, a fleet foundering in the ocean, a nation languishing under tyranny, famine, or pestilence. To turn the gay side of life to him, and give him a notion of its pleasures; whither should I conduct him? To a ball, to an opera, to court?" (10.15). Cleanthes, who has sat by listening to all this, is unmoved. His silence is telling. *He* doesn't feel this way about the world.

Because Cleanthes has hardly said a word and has more or less just shrugged at this testimony of the wrongdoing and victimhood of humanity, Philo turns on him afresh by throwing the human condition at deism. The old, old questions return about evil and the purpose of creating this world. Epicurus's questions about god, indeed, "are yet unanswered. Is he willing to prevent evil, but not able? then he is impotent. Is he able, but not willing? then is he malevolent. Is he both able and willing? Whence then is evil?" (10.25).[53] The votaries of natural religion believe the deity must be at least as rational as they are. Whatever the pleasures of life, they also are acquainted with life's wretchedness to all people some of the time, to many people most of the time. "How then does the divine benevolence display itself, in the sense of you anthropomorphites?" asks Philo. "None but we mystics, as you were pleased to call us, can account for this strange mixture of phenomena, by deriving it from attributes, infinitely perfect, but incomprehensible." Can one account for anything by declaring it incomprehensible? Philo's arm-in-arm linking up with Demea may be charming but is a joke as far as he is concerned; and Cleanthes calls attention to the "concealed battery" lined up against him (10.27–28).

His recourse is to concede Philo's logic about the proof of divine benevolence but to dismiss the supposed evidence against it. He proceeds "to deny absolutely the misery and wickedness of man" by abruptly indicating, though hardly delivering, a sort of utilitarian calculus. His adversaries' representations of the facts "are exaggerated." "Health is more common than sickness: Pleasure than pain: Happiness than misery. And for one vexation which we meet with, we attain, upon computation, a hundred enjoyments." That answer almost sets Philo chortling: "I must use the freedom to admonish you, *Cleanthes* . . . [for] unawares introducing a total scepticism into the most essential articles of natural and revealed theology. What! no method of fixing a just foundation for religion, unless we allow the happiness of human life" (10.31, 33). But Philo has contrived this trap for Cleanthes by siding with Demea's genuine concerns about human wretchedness and driving the argument home. Philo generally does get the last word.

It seems that both his interlocutors onstage by now respect Philo's superior debating powers. Cleanthes invites him to spell out his position at greater length; he obliges, and they both listen without interrupting. Philo patiently replies with four sets of circumstances in the world as we know it that together discourage inferring the existence of a perfect and benevolent creator: the introduction of pain as well as pleasure as a motive to action; the operation of general laws in nature, with which the lawmaker does not interfere; the evident frugality with which individuals have been endowed with powers (he singles out idleness: a creator could have fashioned far more industrious and mindful human beings); the vast machinery of nature that is too poorly adjusted to negate either large or petty disasters. That is a very compressed summary of his talk; to be on safe ground Philo concedes that such circumstances might be "compatible" with perfection and benevolence of the deity: "But surely they can never prove these attributes" (11.12). Without pause or interruption he then suggests that Manichaeism might be a more defensible doctrine. This maneuver is typical of Philo: he introduces Manichaeism to diminish once again the likelihood of benevolent creation. Instead of four bundles of circumstantial evidence, he uses logic to dispose of four hypotheses: "There may *four* hypotheses be framed concerning the first causes of the universe; *that* they are endowed with perfect goodness, *that* they have perfect malice, *that* they are opposite and have both goodness and malice, *that* they have neither goodness nor malice. Mixed phenomena can never prove the two former unmixed principles. And the uniformity and steadiness of general laws seem to oppose the third. The fourth, therefore seem by far the most probable" (11.15). So Manichaeism won't help, but more important, no moral purpose whatever lurks in the first cause of the universe.

"Hold! Hold!" Demea cries. What of their alliance to defend "the incomprehensible nature of the divine being. . . . Are you secretly, then, a more dangerous enemy than *Cleanthes* himself?" And Cleanthes too chimes in: "Believe me, *Demea*; your friend *Philo*, from the beginning, has been amusing himself at both our expense." But he adds, "It must be confessed, that the injudicious reasoning of our vulgar theology has given him but too just a handle of ridicule." Pamphilus reports that Demea was not pleased and "took occasion soon after, on some pretence or other, to leave the company" (11.18–19, 21).

It is certainly not hard to understand why Demea excuses himself from the party. This last real or imagined shift in alliances figuratively leaves him out in the cold. He has held a minor role in the argument right along, and he may very well now feel offended. There is some truth in Cleanthes' thrust that Philo has been amusing himself at their expense. At the less personal level, they have both offended Demea's Christian faith. When he calls Philo a more dangerous enemy than Cleanthes, he does not imply a threat to his person but a threat to the faith he shares with many others. All this is dramatically understandable. But Demea never returns. His stage exit at the end of part 11 is the last we ever hear of him, so the larger question is how to interpret his role in Hume's *Dialogues*. His departure might be supposed to signal an end to religion based purely on faith and revelation. Or, defensively, Hume may have wished to fend against the impression that his other two characters would never stop talking down to the one professed Christian on the scene. Or if Demea represents the voice of the common people, that is no longer the issue. Presumably the more learned Philo and Cleanthes will continue to thrash out their differences in part 12; neither of those two is personally concerned with revealed truth or with reward and punishment in the next world. But these are, to be sure, *Dialogues concerning Natural Religion*, not concerning Christian faith or revealed truth.

Cleanthes suggests that it is just as well Demea has departed since Philo's "spirit of controversy" and "abhorrence of vulgar superstition" often spares no one. Philo in turn admits that he often gets carried away on the subject of natural religion. But he and Cleanthes come together with "unreserved intimacy," and his friend must know that in spite of his outspokenness "no one has a deeper sense of religion impressed on his mind, or pays more profound adoration to the divine being, as he discovers himself to reason, in the inexplicable contrivance and artifice of nature" (12.1–2). It would seem as if these intimate friends were both deists all along, and an unaccustomed sanctimoniousness has crept into Philo's voice. He is certainly in a very conciliatory mood. Cleanthes puts in another word for comparing the universe to a machine, neither advancing nor retreating from anything he has said earlier. At considerably greater length Philo concocts imaginary cross-examinations, first of a theist and then of an atheist, to demonstrate how little both really have to go on. It may all boil down to differences about the meaning of words. "Will you quarrel, Gentlemen," Philo addresses his imaginary theist and atheist, "about the degrees, and enter into a controversy, which admits not of any precise meaning, nor consequently of any determination?" For if it is a gentlemanly disagreement, let there at least be no animosity (12.7).

Their dialogue is splendidly scripted but still somewhat of a tease: "These, *Cleanthes*, are my unfeigned sentiments on this subject." Why unfeigned? No one has claimed the sentiments were feigned, so perhaps Philo is confessing that they might be. The speech is often cited as a summary of the position Hume finally adopts in this posthumous work, but the conversation is far from finished yet. Philo does acknowledge that, "in proportion to my veneration for true religion, is my abhorrence of vulgar superstitions"; and that reminder triggers one last intervention by Cleanthes, who replies, "Religion, however corrupted, is still better than no religion at all. The doctrine of a future state is so strong and necessary a security to morals, that we never ought to abandon or neglect it" (12.9–10). Two things need to be said about this lingering thought of Cleanthes. First, the prospect of salvation or damnation has not hitherto been discussed in the *Dialogues*, and Philo will forthwith deliver some original thoughts on that score. Second, the declaration of intimacy between these two friends, the referral of the deist cause to a gentlemen's disagreement, the deference rendered to divine being do not constitute the end of the play. One might question whether part 12, the final and longest part, should even be called a dialogue. The actor playing Cleanthes has little to say, and the only new matter he introduces is this of the afterlife. The rest is Philo.

Philo, who immediately takes exception to the notion that superstition can be salutary, sounds more and more like Pierre Bayle. History tells us that when the religious spirit prevails, misery follows. Obviously "finite and temporary rewards" move people to act, but supposed "infinite and eternal" rewards move very little. People's actions are rarely influenced by distant and uncertain matters. Experience shows that "the smallest grain of natural honesty and benevolence has more effect on men's conduct than the most pompous views, suggested by theological theories and systems" (12.13). As for anticipating life in the hereafter, "the steady attention alone to so important an interest as that of eternal salvation is apt to extinguish the benevolent affections, and beget a narrow, contracted selfishness" (12.19). Curiously, "we ourselves, after having employed the most exalted expression in our descriptions of the deity, fall into the flattest contradiction, in affirming, that the damned are infinitely superior in number to the elect" (12.27). The put downs of this one-man conversation—and these are only a small selection of the total—provide a comedy in solo. Cleanthes need never say another word. Even if the order evident in nature bore some (very) remote resemblance to human intelligence, that would have no bearing on human affairs and human actions in the here and now. It is still more absurd to imagine an intelligent designer subject to human passions, or for that matter caring about inferior beings.

After similarly dominating part 8 of the *Dialogues*, Philo had generalized boldly there on the improbabilities embraced by all religions, then focused on the disputatiousness of Christian theologians and, rather like Cicero's Cotta, savored his own role as that of a skeptic:

> All religious systems, it is confessed, are subject to great and
> insuperable difficulties. Each disputant triumphs in his turn;
> while he carries on an offensive war, and exposes the
> absurdities, barbarities, and pernicious tenets of his antagonist.
> But all of them, on the whole, prepare a complete triumph for
> the sceptic, who tells them, that no system ought ever to be
> embraced with regard to such subjects: For this plain reason,
> that no absurdity ought ever to be assented to with regard to any
> subject. A total suspense of judgement is here our only
> reasonable resource. And if every attack, as is commonly

observed, and no defence, among theologians, is successful;
how complete must be *his* victory, who . . . has himself no fixed
station or abiding city, which he is ever, on any occasion, obliged
to defend? (8.12)

Regardless of occasional kind allusions to the "true religion" of persons
he respects, there can be no way to conclude that Philo is a believer. Here,
pursuing the metaphor of warfare he has resolved to stay clear of, he
wickedly observes that *every* attack against another religion but *no* defense
of the same by partisan theologians is successful. That pairing of universal
propositions calls any believer foolish and a loser.

In the end Philo turns toward Cleanthes' pupil, Pamphilus, and
suggests he adopt a philosophical skepticism. Then the last joke of all
comes directly from Hume's hand, though indirectly from Cicero's at the
conclusion of *De natura deorum*. Pamphilus once more addresses the
reader and opines that "*Philo*'s principles are more probable than
Demea's, but that those of *Cleanthes* approach still nearer to the
truth." Even should Hume's reader not recall the Ciceronian precedent
for this turn, Pamphilus's opinion draws a smile. Notwithstanding
the young man's loyalty to his tutor, Philo has been the winner all along.[54]
Also, in the initial pleasing conversation among the speakers in *De natura
deorum*, remember, Velleius smiled at Cicero and Cotta and declared that
both were "disciples of Philo, and have learned from him to know
nothing" (1.17). That jest can be reduced to, You two are skeptics, trained
in the new Academy to suspend judgment. Hume's principal character in
the *Dialogues concerning Natural Religion* descends from the same school
of thought and displays appreciable humor and irony. An ironist mocks
and regularly conveys opposite meanings at the same time, and thus
irony suspends judgment—or appears to suspend judgment.

David Hume was demonstrably alert to the wit of Cicero, then, as
well as an unabashed borrower from Bayle. Hume the comedian? The
late Dwight Culler put it this way:

With his elegant sense of form, his exquisite style and delicious
irony, he is not only conscious that he has produced a revolution
in philosophy but also that this revolution is rather funny. It is
in the nature of a sly retort or witty repartee. It is a kind of comic
reversal in which the tables are turned upon an opponent to his

intense discomfiture and the delight and satisfaction of his enemies. It is no accident that some of Hume's finest works are cast in the form of a dialogue, for his thought would lose half its savour if there were no antagonist to express the overblown, a priori point of view which is then deflated by a sly, insinuating wit.[55]

Culler complimented the philosopher's sense of humor in the course of pointing out that Hume's approach to causation anticipated Darwin's empiricism. Besides an awareness of the universe changing over time, what the two thinkers had in common was a skeptical approach to teleology. Reminds one of Lucretius's expositions of Epicurean science long ago.[56]

7. WHOSE *ABERGLAUBE?*

Nineteenth-century intellectuals in the West to a great extent accepted that divinity was a human idea after all and came to terms with it in their own scholarly ways. For them the nineteenth century became the age of the higher criticism, when the scriptures were to be scrutinized with the same attention to source and provenance as classical texts. A search for the historical Jesus was under way and resulted in a good number of serious, readable biographies of the man. Above all there was a widespread post-Enlightenment anxiety among thinking persons for the fate of Jesus's teachings and Christian morality should the masses also cease believing in an independent divinity.

With his wicked sense of humor and satiric bent, Matthew Arnold belongs in the ranks of humanist comedians. Arnold was a believer in the sense that Cicero was a believer, however: they both valued religion for societal reasons, Cicero's leaning toward the preservation of the state and Arnold's toward keeping the peace and good behavior at home. Arnold thought he just might help shape a Christianity impervious to the advance of science, which would inevitably filter down to unbelief among the uneducated if religion were not prepared for it. Revelation could not prevail against science, perhaps not even against ordinary experience and working common sense. But the Bible might be read as literature, morality preserved in the teachings of Jesus or conveyed elsewhere in the familiar texts as metaphor.

In German, *Aberglaube* is the ordinary word for superstition. But why would Arnold need to resort to the German when framing a sweeping criticism of his fellow Britons' professed Christianity? How many of his readers did he suppose knew German? In the essays collected as *Literature and Dogma*, Arnold persistently introduced *Aberglaube* and defined it as *extra-belief*. In German, as he certainly knew, *Glaube* without the prefix could mean either belief in general or faith—religious faith. He also admired the Germans' higher criticism of the Bible and some of their up-front anthropological analyses of religious faith. The notion of extra-belief accommodated a singular tactic of Arnold's own solution to the post-Enlightenment anxiety about preserving Christian morality: to be rid of the unverifiable extra-beliefs and to get down to basics. But Arnold, to put it mildly, had an aggressive streak of humor that he could scarcely contain, and the word *Aberglaube* had the metrics of a sporting jab. Its two trochees of derision were almost as neat as *mumbo jumbo*, Victorian slang for meaningless worship that originated from colonial Africa. (The *OED* gave the white man's meaning of *mumbo jumbo* as "an object of senseless veneration" and dated it from 1847.)

Matthew Arnold (1822–88) behaved like an outsider in his own land, but a privileged outsider. He was the eldest child of Thomas Arnold, the outstanding headmaster of Rugby; and he attended Rugby and Oxford himself but did not remain a don. Instead he turned to poetry, married before he was thirty, and became an inspector of schools as a means of securing an income. Like David Hume, Arnold was essentially self-taught and extremely well read, but he had to master that learning in his off-hours, while traveling about England and also to the Continent to visit schools and keep up on different styles of education. By the 1860s he was writing mainly prose, criticism not only of literature but of the cultural scene in nineteenth-century England. He rather enjoyed calling people names. In the essays collected in *Culture and Anarchy* (1869) he named the aristocratic, middle, and working classes of England the Barbarians, the Philistines, and the Populace, respectively. Note the relative tact when it came to the working classes.

Arnold the outsider proceeded to satirize the surrounding lack of culture. Chapter 4 of *Culture and Anarchy*, titled "Hebraism and Hellenism," set forth his position in broad historical perspective. As the terms suggest, this was a humanist stance. Arnold divided the influences on human development in the West between thinking and doing, between seeing things as they really are and obedience. Just when classical culture held out hopes of the former, the rise of Christianity favored the latter; then the fifteenth century began a renaissance of Hellenism, after which the progress of modern science was off and running. The Reformation benefited to some degree from Hellenism, but in England Puritanism's concern over sin and obedience scored for Hebraism. Arnold was persuaded that Victorian England continued to feature doing rather than thinking. Probably his thirty-five years as inspector of schools didn't help. But he possessed a ready recall of the Bible, too, and a sharp eye for nonsense reported in the daily newspapers. The back and forth between his own periodical essays and the press at large seems to have made his days. And then there was that complacent sense of humor. For example, a couple of sentences from Arnold's introduction to *Culture and Anarchy*:

> Now for my part I do not wish to see men of culture asking to be
> entrusted with power; and, indeed, I have freely said, that in my
> opinion the speech most proper, at present, for a man of culture
> to make to a body of his fellow-countrymen who get him into a
> committee-room, is Socrates's: *Know thyself!* and this is not a
> speech to be made by men wanting to be entrusted with power.
> For this very indifference to direct political action I have been
> taken to task by the *Daily Telegraph*, coupled, by a strange
> perversity of fate, with just that very one of the Hebrew prophets
> whose style I admire the least, and called "an elegant Jeremiah."
> (5:88)[57]

In the last two decades of his life Arnold churned out more than four volumes of articles on religion. This was understandable: like other intellectuals of the period he felt that the advance of science might surpass the Christian faith and make it seem a fairy tale. Darwin's *Origin of Species* appeared in 1859, and Arnold's contemporaries fretted over the diminishing numbers of attendance at church services by nearly all social classes. (The age of statistics was also under way.) Arnold did not make much of either Darwinism or church attendance, and on the positive side he thought literature might save the day. For the poet, naturally, culture was mainly literature. Humanity's stories and poems had long exploited the freedom of fiction, meaningful representations of life that no one proposed to check against historical records or submit to laboratories for verification. Reading the Bible as literature might very well save the lessons it held for posterity, and most especially the teachings of Jesus. One positive aspect of *Aberglaube*, or extra-belief, could be this tolerance for valuable fiction. But in Arnold's hands the concept quickly becomes pejorative and may as well frankly be termed superstition. He refers to this extra-belief as dogma and occasionally as theology. Much like Erasmus and other Christian humanists, Arnold thought quarrels over theology and demands in the parish or the episcopate to get the words right counterproductive or useless at best.

Therefore *Literature and Dogma* (1873) is not about two ingredients of Western civilization like Hellenism and Hebraism, but more like two distinct curricula of study, the first worthwhile and the second a waste of time. The inspector of schools contentedly steps back and adopts a sarcastic stance, and he can be very entertaining—up to a point. Two of the victims of these essays (assays) on contemporary culture were bishops, one deceased. "Everyone, again, remembers"—this in the introduction to the book—"the Bishops of Winchester and Gloucester making in Convocation their remarkable effort 'to do something,' as they said, 'for the honour of Our Lord's Godhead,' and to mark their sense of 'that infinite separation for time and for eternity which is involved in rejecting the Godhead of the Eternal Son.'" That counts as dogma or theology, but each time he brings it up Arnold ridicules rather than analyzes the bishops' phrasing. Rhetorically he expects the reader to side with the critic rather than with those who are being laughed at, and typically he nails the target with his proper name or title so that there can be no mistake—no very pleasing tactic if you should happen to be a friend of the bishop in question. In the essays gathered in this volume, commencing with "that tenet of the Godhead of the Eternal Son, for which the Bishops of Winchester and Gloucester are so anxious to do something," Arnold repeats variations of the bishops' lines with or without quotation marks at least nine times. Thus everyone now "remembers" the foolish bishops' lines because the satirist has rung so many changes on them. They speak indeed a "false dogmatic theology" (6:166, 234, 310). Such nonsense, Arnold would argue, reflects the negative aspect of *Aberglaube* and regularly interferes with the proper study of the Bible.

Rather maddeningly Arnold also used insistent repetition to convey his own message. He would settle on a certain phrasing of a position he wished to take and then repeat it, with slight variations, over and over again. He even counted on readers' familiarity with the terms of a position spelled out on earlier occasions, as if he were addressing his fan club. For example, the campaign for a larger measure of Hellenism might be said to have commenced with the influential essay "The Function of Criticism" (1864). There he cited the same passage from Goethe that he would appeal to at the end of *Culture and Anarchy*: "To act is so easy, as Goethe says; to think is so hard!" Then he settled on the word *disinterestedness* before proceeding to work out, and to repeat, a definition of criticism as *"a disinterested endeavour to learn and propagate the best that is known and thought in the world"* (3:276, 283). In *Literature and Dogma* Arnold over and over again defines divinity as *"the not ourselves that makes for righteousness."* First he introduces "the *not ourselves*" and explains that for the Hebrews this not ourselves became *"a power which makes for righteousness."* In the same key passage he suggests translating Jehovah or Yahweh (usually translated as "the Lord" in English Bibles) as "the Eternal" (6:182–83). Thus he constructs a definition of God that he repeats, with variations, literally dozens of times—such as *the Eternal not ourselves that makes for righteousness*, or the Power, or the enduring power.

Sometimes only the words *not ourselves* are italicized. One can understand the attraction of the negation, starting with its open-endedness. There is a lot out there that we know very little about and that Arnold does not pretend to know: call it nature, if you will. Second, it is not human nature we are talking about. *We* are not gods—something, to be sure, that should be kept in mind when assigning humans political power. Third, even without the *righteousness* (which Arnold does not closely define), his *not ourselves* implies a connection between the religious belief and morality, as in heeding the Golden Rule. Fourth, the concept reflects the psychological insight of Jesus's teachings about selflessness and giving up one's life in order to find it. Toward the end of *Literature and Dogma* the clauses about eternal righteousness and the not ourselves come thicker and faster. Arnold penned what the twenty-first century calls sound bites, except that in that earlier information age dominated by rotary presses and steam power his were more like type clusters. He chose the words, whether clusters of his own composition or those of would-be theologians. He invites the reader to choose between "an enduring Power, not ourselves, that makes for righteousness" and, for example, "A Great Personal First Cause, who thinks and loves, the moral and intelligent Governor of the Universe." The first can be verified, he dares assert, but never the second. "But if . . . they ask: 'How are we to *verify* that there rules an enduring Power, not ourselves, which makes for righteousness?'—we may answer at once: 'How? why as you verify that fire burns,—by experience!' " (6:374, 370). Besides, Arnold claims we can learn about the not ourselves which makes for righteousness by critically, thoughtfully reading the Bible. And Arnold knows his Bible. When he first conceived of the not ourselves, in *St. Paul and Protestantism* (1870), he offered these lines of the Bible: "I know . . . that the way of man is not in himself; it is not in man that walketh to direct his steps" (6:37). Alas, without apology Arnold's footnote identifies this as Jeremiah 10.23, words of the prophet whose style he admires least!

Arnold does enjoy himself and invites the reader to come along, even if the tools of his rhetoric sometimes clatter as they drop to the floor. Consistency and more precise definition often float away on the breeze. Another lifeline strung out in *Literature and Dogma* is conduct—"conduct as three-fourths of human life." This fraction too is repeated, with variations, again and again. Arnold genially settles on three-fourths in chapter 1, after putting forward four-fifths or five-sixths, but never qualifies what he means by conduct: "And so, when we are asked, what is the object of religion?—let us reply: *Conduct*. And when we are asked further, what is conduct?—let us answer: *Three-fourths of life*." That's no more than the proportion he has asked us to agree on. If conduct is the object of religion (not what Bayle or Hume concluded), then the behavior in question has to be good conduct, and that makes the proportion doubtful. People are good three-fourths of the time and bad the other fourth? But the sentence is repeated like a handy maxim, until in chapter 11 we get, "But conduct, plain matter as it is, is sixth-eighths of life, while art and science are only two-eighths" (6:173–75, 388). Arnold is not just being cute but finally filling in what pastimes might be assigned to the remaining fourth. This seems very perverse, on two grounds. First, life has so much more to it than conduct plus art and science. We sleep, eat, play, work, read, talk, wed, give birth, and so on. "Three-fourths of life" makes no sense unless one specifies what is meant by the whole of life being divided. Second, overall Arnold judged that in the nineteenth century doing and thinking, Hebraism and Hellenism, were out of balance; not more conduct but more culture, science, and art would restore the balance. The style of Arnold's rhetoric carries him away and if anything obscures his meaning.

His penchant for satire and polemic nevertheless did stand him in good stead. Readers were entertained or annoyed enough to respond, and the back and forth may actually have helped clarify Arnold's thinking. Thus *God and the Bible* (1875), a more systematic response to critics of *Literature and Dogma*, devoted the first three chapters to "The God of Miracles," "The God of Metaphysics," and "The God of Experience." Arnold reintroduced the not ourselves and acknowledged that "in the language of common speech and of poetry" it was natural to personify this superior power: "So we construct a magnified and non-natural man, by dropping out all that in man seems a source of weakness, and by heightening to the very utmost all that in man seems a source of strength, such as his thought and his love." When storied miracles and etherealized angels are added to the picture, this popular supposition about God becomes "credible, probable, and even almost necessary" (7:162–63). But stories of miracles no longer suit the zeitgeist in any case.

When he turns to metaphysics, Arnold picks on Descartes, "who is said to have founded the independence of modern philosophy and to have founded its spiritualism." Descartes, who began with doubting absolutely everything, ended by assuring us that everything followed from our distinct certitude about God. Arnold's protest that he himself is not a philosopher gives his readers a nudge and becomes something of a clown act: "It is true, the doubts which troubled Descartes and which have troubled so many philosophers . . . are not exactly the doubts by which we ourselves have been most plagued." He confesses that he has never really understood the axiom *Cogito, ergo sum*. Arnold has experienced thinking, that is to say; but "Descartes does not tell us what those other terms *be* and *exist* mean. . . . Philosophers know, of course, for they are always using the terms" (7:174–77). He mischievously plays with the problem of definition a bit, then claims he has found the work of a certain German professor helpful.

"But not a professor of logic and metaphysics. No, not Hegel, not one of those great men, those masters of abstruse reasoning," but "a mere professor of words," the philologist Georg Curtius. And he proceeds to use Curtius's *Grundzüge der Griechischen Etymologie* (Arnold's footnote) to provide an account, in considerable detail, of the verb *to be* in three or four ancient languages. To the devil with all those abstractions of metaphysics. Originally to *be* meant something like to *breathe*:

> *Cogito, ergo sum*, will then be: "I think, therefore I breathe."
> A true deduction certainly; but *Comedo, ergo sum*, "I eat,
> therefore I breathe," would be nearly as much to the purpose!
> Metaphysics, the science treating of *être* and its conditions, will
> be the science of treating breathing and its conditions. But
> surely the right science to treat of breathing and its conditions is
> not metaphysics, but physiology! "God *is*," will be, God *breathes*;
> exactly that old anthropomorphic account of him which our
> dogmatic theology, by declaring him to be without body, parts,
> or passions, has sought to banish! (7:182–89)

Arnold is a handy parodist, and he can go on and on with the parody like a stand-up comic, while still presenting an argument and hinting to the reader pretty much where he stands. It is better to laugh a little about serious differences of opinion, though facetiousness perhaps ought to be the last resort of a humanist comedy.

Arnold too puts in play comparisons between the ancient Greeks' polytheism and the Judeo-Christian God. But he suggests that, contemplated aright, *both* Apollo and Jehovah are anthropomorphic. They are the not ourselves, but it is natural to see them as superior thinking and loving beings. The ancients saw it so, and we "can well understand, how by a natural impulse men were moved to represent in a human form like their own, the powers that attracted their hope, fear, and worship. . . . And even when men did not represent their gods in human form, they still supposed in them human thoughts and passions" (7:217). As he had asserted repeatedly in *Literature and Dogma*, the language of the Bible as well as the language of the Greeks was literary, language "*thrown out*" at objects of consciousness not scientifically comprehended. In post-Enlightenment times he believed it crucial to interpret scripture figuratively rather than to persist in theological or metaphysical *Aberglaube*. "With much of the current theology our unpretending account of God will indeed make havoc," the author modestly approves of his efforts; "but it will enable a man, we believe, to use and enjoy the Bible in security.

Only he must always remember that the language of the Bible is to be treated as the language of letters, not science, language approximative and full of figure, not language exact" (7:201). After all, Arnold was one of a half dozen prose artists who used to be called the Victorian prophets.

The second half of *God and the Bible* consists of practical criticism to help the reader. A chapter mostly on the New Testament canon precedes two long chapters of close reading of the fourth gospel. Arnold corrects the mistaken assumption that the biblical canon was determined in heaven by pointing out that St. Jerome had to decide what books it should consist of when he created the Latin Vulgate in the fifth century. Although "all Jerome's sympathies were with what was orthodox, ecclesiastical, regular," he set forth "without the least concealment, the essential difference in authority between some documents in our New Testament and others." Yet the late Dean of Carlisle and by implication other clergymen contend that everything in the Bible is the Word of God. This doctrine Arnold compares to "the Bishop of Lincoln's allegation that 'episcopacy was an institution of God Himself'; an allegation which might make one suppose that in Genesis, directly after God had said *Let there be light* (or, perhaps, even before it), he had pronounced, *Let there be bishops!"* (7:255–57). Arnold seems to have a thing about bishops. But he sketches a pretty decent summary of the problems associated with the text of the Bible such as Jerome had to cope with, before he tries to help with the fourth gospel, where problems abound.

Even the authorship of the gospel according to John is doubtful. The amanuensis may have been a single hand, but if so he was gathering materials from several hands. The synoptic gospels are relatively free of theology, and they often support one another on the life and teachings of Jesus. The fourth gospel is a later compilation, not always consistent with itself, and emphatically messianic. Arnold finds himself fending off a too-dismissive higher criticism in order to save the teaching of Jesus that is recorded in John but not elsewhere. The source is not the question, but what Jesus said; and sometimes the only way to test that is by a kind of literary criticism. He reads the Old Testament as being about righteousness, the New "as an immense poetry growing round and investing an immortal truth, the secret of Jesus: *He that will save his life shall lose it, he that will lose his life shall save it.*" But said immortal truth is not to be confused with the possibility of personal immortality: "Our common materialistic notions about the resurrection of the body and the world to come are, no doubt, natural and attractive to ordinary human nature. But they are in direct conflict with the new and loftier conceptions of life and death which Jesus himself strove to establish" (7:370–72).[58]

In spirit, Arnold's reading of the Bible is surprisingly close to Spinoza's. He never cites Hobbes's sorting of biblical texts (or that philosopher's insistence on a considered choice and definition of words), but he did read Spinoza, probably because of Goethe's and Coleridge's appreciation of the latter. Moreover, Arnold read Latin: he dismissively reviewed a bad translation of the *Tractatus* in 1862 and announced that "whatever Spinoza was, he was not an Atheist" (3:57). In a more substantial essay he prefaced his own summary of what Spinoza was up to by putting himself in the writer's place: the Bible is not what people "imagine it to be. . . . I will show them what it really does say, and I will show them that they will do well to accept this real teaching of the Bible." Here Arnold came close to stating what the purpose of his own writing on religion would come down to a decade later. The essay, "Spinoza and the Bible," initially posts a lengthy translation of the visceral curse with which Spinoza was excommunicated, after which Arnold begins: "With these amenities, the current compliments of theological parting, the Jews of the Portuguese synagogue at Amsterdam took in 1656 . . . their leave of their erring brother, Baruch or Benedict Spinoza. They remained children of Israel, and he became a child of modern Europe" (3:160–61, 158). He then provides a remarkable summary, in ten pages or so, of the *Theological-Political Treatise*, except for Spinoza's last five chapters on the political side. It is quite possible that Arnold's not ourselves owes something to Spinoza's expansive deity of the *Ethics*. True, the not ourselves does not contain the persons contemplating it, but it would seem to include the rest of the universe.[59]

Much more significant for Arnold were the nineteenth century's higher criticism and quest for the historical Jesus. He was acquainted with a good deal of this, including two of the most influential books, the lives of Jesus by David Friedrich Strauss and by Ernest Renan. The former, *The Life of Jesus, Critically Examined* (1835–36), was an exhaustive analysis of the gospels and historical record in two volumes, the fourth edition of which was anonymously translated by Marian Evans in 1846. Strauss's project was to sort out the facts from the myth of Jesus; but he was a student of myth and did not treat it pejoratively. He tried to ascertain the intentions of the evangelist before interpreting each gospel. Many of the miraculous cures attributed to Jesus might be explained psychologically; but an instant cure of leprosy was not possible, nor did raising Lazarus from the dead have any historical foundation. Like other scholars and like Arnold, he was concerned with the differences between John and the synoptic gospels. When the evidence was debatable Strauss did not pretend to know the truth but gave his honest opinion. Any religious sect was of interest and could be studied objectively. Renan's *Life of Jesus* (1863) was written for a wider readership, was much more recent, and was closer in spirit to Arnold's writing on the subject. Renan too worried that the inroads of science in the culture could distract from the teaching of Jesus and defeat Christianity altogether, if theologians continued to scrap over meaningless dogma. Supposed miracles, which undoubtedly induced earlier generations to believe in Christ, would become its downfall. The Old Testament featured successive covenants of God with the Hebrew people, and for eighteen centuries Christian churches cultivated this plant of intolerance instead of uprooting it. The Bible needs to be read more thoughtfully, with the history of its composition in mind, and freely interpreted in a secular age. Neither Strauss nor Renan had Arnold's sense of humor and feistiness; the three were not personally acquainted, but they and other liberal thinkers of the time were engaged in a common enterprise.

That enterprise rehearsed a last act of humanist comedy itself. For in order to save God, the intelligentsia of the nineteenth century sought to demonstrate that gods, singular or plural, were purely a human invention. In order to save Christianity and Christian morality they had to recover and free from *Aberglaube* the historical Jesus, an extraordinary human being. Christ's mistaken beliefs were errors of his time—and of humanity. In order to keep the faith they tried to clear it of palpable falsehoods and attributed all of its worthy claims to humane needs. The writer who most forthrightly scripted such an act, partly in response to Strauss, was Ludwig Feuerbach in 1841. Marian Evans published her translation of *The Essence of Christianity* in 1854, and this time she put her name as translator on the title page. (She also completed a translation of Spinoza's *Ethics* on the side but that was not published until 1981).[60] By then she had moved to London, worked full-time at the *Westminster Review*, and written many articles of her own; a few years later she would take up her career as the novelist George Eliot. Feuerbach's contribution was thus available in English and well known to Victorian freethinkers.

There is no evidence that Arnold read Feuerbach, though as Lionel Trilling would point out, their two projects had something in common.[61] Both privileged experience over theology, reduced revelation to human desires, and sought to shelter religious feelings by arguing that they were intrinsically human. Feuerbach kept focusing and refocusing on the psychology of religion and could be merciless in exposing its wish fulfillment. Man projects his idea of God as an objective being and himself as an object of that being: "Man is an object to God. That man is good or evil is not indifferent to God; no! . . . Thus man, while he is apparently humiliated to the lowest degree, is in truth exalted to the highest. Thus, in and through God, man has in view himself alone." *The Essence of Christianity* came divided in two parts, "The True or Anthropological Essence of Religion" and a demolition entitled "The False or Theological Essence of Religion." Yet this approach leaves questions such as the existence of God crystal clear by the end of the first part: "We have reduced the supermundane, supernatural, and superhuman nature of God to the elements of human nature as its fundamental elements. Our process of analysis has brought us again to the position with which we set out. The beginning, middle and end of religion is MAN."[62] Compare Peter L. Berger a century later: "Religion is the audacious attempt to conceive of the entire universe as being humanly significant."[63] The comedy, in short, was all too human.

In a poem of the first decade of the twentieth century, Thomas Hardy imagined the voice of God uttering "A Plaint to Man" that began like this: "When you slowly emerged from the den of Time, / And gained percipience as you grew, / And fleshed you fair out of shapeless slime, / Wherefore, O Man, did there come to you / The unhappy need of creating me— / A form like your own—for praying to?" In "God's Funeral," a better-known poem published in the *Fortnightly Review* in 1912, Hardy complemented God's plaint with the voices of the crowd mourning the passing of the deity they had invented but still needed somehow to worship:

> "O man-projected Figure, of late
> Imaged as we, thy knell who shall survive?

Whence came it we were tempted to create
One whom we can no longer keep alive?

"Framing him jealous, fierce, at first,
We gave him justice as the ages rolled,
Will to bless those by circumstance accurst,
And longsuffering, and mercies manifold.

"And tricked by our own early dream
And need of solace, we grew self-deceived,
Our making soon our maker did we deem,
And what we had imagined we believed.

"Till, in Time's stayless stealthy swing,
Uncompromising rude reality
Mangled the Monarch of our fashioning,
Who quavered, sank; and now has ceased to be. . . ."

Like Arnold—or Cicero, for that matter—Hardy and his fellow mourners worry about what can substitute for the customary religion and serve to give their lives direction and cohesion. Indeed, a few stubborn onlookers, apart from the funeral crowd, protest and cry out, "Still he lives to us!" Considering the historical moment, or what Arnold would call the zeitgeist, Hardy the poet observes, "How to bear such loss I deemed / The insistent question for each animate mind."[64]

One wonders how Arnold would have reacted if he had read and studied Feuerbach. Or if he had taken natural history as seriously as many of his contemporaries did—George Eliot and her friend G. H. Lewes among them—so as to be prepared to understand Darwin. If Arnold ever read *On the Origin of Species by Means of Natural Selection*, it certainly did not make much of an impression. Dwight Culler, in "The Darwinian Revolution and Literary Form" again, linked the phenomenon of natural selection itself to comedy.[65] To support that association Culler appealed to an earlier work of German scholarship, August Wilhelm von Schlegel's *Course of Lectures on Dramatic Art and Literature* of 1808. The key passage there was one of Schlegel's shrewd comparisons of tragedy and comedy, more particularly so-called New Comedy. Whereas tragedy, a "struggle between the outward finite existence, and the inward infinite aspirations," appropriately appealed to Destiny, this comedy dealt with more common aspirations, "always within the sphere of experience." In New Comedy, it follows, "The place of Destiny is supplied by Chance."[66] Culler pointed out that Darwin's approach to natural history or evolution also put Destiny aside in order to focus on something more like Chance: that is, on the variation and adaptation over time that enable natural selection. Darwinism, like the Humean take on causation, would do away with the notion of intelligent design.

From Ernest Renan and others, Matthew Arnold picked up the secular target of metaphysics as well as strictly religious *Aberglaube*. During the Enlightenment metaphysics began to have unfavorable connotations for many intellectuals. By the twentieth century, for the Vienna Circle and logical positivism at least, the cry of Metaphysics! would become just another way of saying Nonsense! In the very last sentence of *Literature and Dogma* Arnold left the bishops of Winchester and Gloucester to posterity in similar terms: "our two bishops," as he fondly calls them, a "pair of distinguished metaphysicians." Still, every satirist's *Aberglaube* is bound to be someone else's *Glaube*.

ACT THREE

Laughter at the Passing Generations

The danger is in standing to it; that's the loss of men, though it be the getting of children.
—Clown, in Shakespeare's *All's Well That Ends Well*

For what could be more serious than the love of man for woman, what more commanding, more impressive, bearing in its bosom the seeds of death; at the same time these lovers, these people entering into illusion glittering eyed, must be danced round with mockery, decorated with garlands.
—Virginia Woolf, *To the Lighthouse*

Over the ages belief in divinity has most often been coupled with a hope of surviving death, whether such hope be knowing or wistful, worked out to the last detail or inchoate, confined to a privileged few or charitably extended to the many. People have plentiful experience of death and decay throughout the animal and plant kingdoms, not to say among their friends and families. Because humans—and not only humanists—are rational beings, they anticipate death and even have sophisticated means at hand, such as actuarial tables, to count the years; likewise records and memorials of past deaths. Animals too manifest an awareness of death; most know better than to chew on the same poisonous weed twice, for example, and others can be found mourning at times. Many plants as well as animals burst with seed before dying. Human consciousness, at least, can take consolation in the awareness of generations to come as well as generations past. Still, that human level of awareness takes in a great many deaths as well as births and stages of life.

One way to cope is to treat generation as the core matter of a human comedy, a comedy that makes room for at least two points of view, the younger and the older. Laughter very likely accommodates mortality more happily than preaching does. Such a secular comedy, with a laugh at each passing generation and without any essential invocations of divinity, long ago played in the theaters of the West and continues to this day, with muted philosophical commitment, if any, and regardless of disputation except when mocking philosophers along with priests, doctors, and lawyers. As early as the fourth century BC in Attica stage comedy had moved on, as Old Comedy gave way to New Comedy. The latter directed laughter not at the gods, not at rival playwrights or notorious politicians, but at commonplace human folly, typed and classified for easy recognition. Stock characters abounded and drew laughs in play after play, as if to document the all-too-human condition or reduce it to a statistic.

The sheer repetition of the same actions in New Comedy argued that, under the circumstances, such were very probable, hence predictable strivings. Typically young lovers seek to pair off; one or more parents have different ideas. Lost heirs and heiresses abound, their identities often in question. Yet it very likely takes impersonation and deception to put things right—joyful impersonations and deceptions, shared with the audience, that work like magic to make fools of elders and masters. No gods are called for in such comedy, unless it might be Hermes; no outstanding heroes, just people from the ordinary walks of life; and cosmopolitan rather than cosmic settings. The combat zone is not the space between humanity and divinity but that of everyday relationships, particularly that between generations. Therefore one implicit vector of the action is toward the death of parents. The comedy accedes to that inevitable passing but also alleviates it. In this regard New Comedy is essentially tragicomedy.

Plautus's *Amphitruo* might seem to be an exception, harking back to Old Comedy with its supernatural agenda and half its lines assigned to two Olympian gods. Jupiter and Mercury have the power to be wherever they wish to be and not merely to impersonate but transform themselves as the principals Amphitruo and his slave Sosia. But this is a comedy in which myth collides with everyday life in the intimate act of sexual reproduction. Also Sosia, for all his clownish cowardice, emerges as the human nature most consciously resistant to divine manipulation. Jupiter's power of making himself over as an identical twin of Amphitruo, in possession of the latter's very thoughts and memories, renders the wife, Alcumena, entirely innocent of the night of love with the god she is unable to distinguish from her husband. Sosia's wrestling with the similar powers of Mercury to impose himself as a second Sosia raises questions of whether anyone has a definitive personal identity. Who are you? and who am I? The bafflement anticipates the obsessions with identity of Luigi Pirandello a couple of millennia later, and the play *Amphitruo* itself would be adapted by other playwrights, most memorably by Molière and by Dryden.

Mercury is no other than our friend Hermes under his Roman calling, the god of thieves and tricksters, not to say small business, instant messaging, and comedy itself, as well as being the left-hand assistant of his father Jupiter. Plautus's comedy of deceiving Alcumena and cuckolding Amphitruo, a Theban general who has just fought victoriously in war, is introduced by the actor got up as the god Mercury posing as Sosia, who has the long prologue all to himself. Stepping in and out of his double role, the actor begins with a godlike reminder to the merchant class represented in the audience: "As you wish me to give you rich gain in the buying and selling of goods and to support you in everything, and as you wish me to advance the business matters and speculations of all of you abroad and at home and to prosper with good and large profit for ever what you have begun and what you will begin," and so forth and so on, then attend this play and judge the players accordingly (1–15).[1] He also points out that, in order to help the audience tell Mercury and Sosia apart, he, Mercury, has little wings on his hat; and Jupiter will wear a gold ribbon to distinguish him from the real Amphitruo.

Thus it is hard not to sympathize with St. Jerome's confessed struggle to put aside reading Cicero and Plautus, his indulgence in argumentative and entertaining pagan reading, and concentrate on his own past sins and penitence. Amid the selflessness and demands, promises, and threats of strict monotheism, even a saint might find relief in the easygoing mischief-ridden polytheism of old. Indeed most of what we know of classical New Comedy survives from the Roman stage: twenty-one plays by Plautus in the second half of the third century BC and six by Terence in the first half of the second. These were mostly, if not all, adaptations from Greek plays by Menander and others, some of them specifically alluded to in the prologues. Since these surviving play scripts were in Latin, they could readily be translated for early modern theater. Notwithstanding his story matter, Terence became a regular school text in the Renaissance as a model of style. Plautus could also be met with in school but continued to make headway on the stage as well.

The Comedy of Errors, likely the very first comedy by Shakespeare, was a close adaptation from Plautus, and it is fair to say that the courtship and marriage plot of almost all Shakespearean comedy was Plautine or new comedic in origin. Shakespeare's was the greater talent for sure, and his play scripts far richer; but he owed much of that richness to Renaissance humanism in general. Emrys Jones, in one of the more daring explorations of Shakespeare's heritage, sums up his opinion this way: "Without humanism, in short, there could have been no Elizabethan literature: without Erasmus, no Shakespeare."[2] Jones makes the case for the Elizabethans knowing something of classical Greek drama by pointing out, among other things, that Erasmus translated Euripides' Hecuba and Iphigenia in Aulis into Latin. No one doubts that Shakespeare was a voracious reader, whether acquainted with this particular reading or not. He was also a profound thinker, and the dramatic form invited suspension of judgment akin to philosophical skepticism.[3]

In All's Well That Ends Well and Measure for Measure, problem comedies, as they say, Shakespeare began to ponder the adverse side of marriage and raising children: the survival of the species, but the passing of the present generation. The heroines are willing to devote themselves to a new generation, but the husbands they seek turn away and awkwardly have to be tricked into consummating the marriage. Shakespeare partially resolved the problem in his upbeat romances—also known as his tragicomedies—by representing more than one mature generation onstage. In *Pericles, The Winter's Tale*, and *The Tempest*, the time of the dramatic action is extended so as to provide the male protagonists with daughters, and grown daughters at that, daughters old enough to mate and bear a third generation. Passing generations every time, but celebrated in marriage ceremonies for all time. Shakespeare scholars and playgoers have often asserted a connection between his romances and *King Lear*, the tragedy of a king in his eighties with no male heirs and three daughters. When his two older daughters begin to take over, Lear brutally curses them and their organs of increase, their ability to bear children in turn. His favorite, Cordelia, he rashly disowns, and in the end all three daughters predecease the old man. No wonder that the romances, with their daughters' pending marriages, seem to be Shakespeare's answer to the searing tragedy of Lear as well as to those baffling problem comedies crafted a few years earlier.

Even older than the institution of theaters in the ancient world were fondness for clowning and playful impersonations not only of people but of animals both real and make-believe. Such play mocked but also helped to type and mend assumed personal identity. In the West the sport caught on in ancient Greek narrative as well as drama, and in Latin literature was magically condensed and given a boost by Ovid's *Metamorphoses*, which recurrently entertained the Middle Ages and Renaissance as well.[4] Shakespeare made room for clowns and fools not only in his comedies but in *Hamlet* and *King Lear;* the legendary metamorphoses versified by Ovid enriched play after play. In the sixteenth century popular stage fools enjoyed considerable independence. But storied clowns were able to enjoy, if that's the word, more or less continuous careers in later times.

Consider the career of the Jongleur of Notre Dame, which stems not from folklore but from a poem in Old French dating possibly as far back as the twelfth century. The jongleur, or juggler clown, eventually broke into print in the late nineteenth century to live again in a short story by Anatole France, an opera by Jules Massenet, and numerous stage, motion picture, and cartoon adaptations.[5] There was a potential all along for even the lowliest to feature in comedy, and therefore a place for namelessness and mutable identity. In tragedy, the identity of a protagonist and key supporting characters seems crucial, as in honor codes real or imagined; in comedy, on the other hand, identity can be up for grabs, bait and switch, and ready disguise. Possibly the earliest doubling of personal identity, in most any culture, was that between body and soul, which enabled humanity to think beyond the manifest decay of its flesh and bones. If each person changes in size and shape and customarily plays more than one role in this lifetime, perhaps other transformations occur after death.

New Comedy and its inheritors and adaptors, particularly commedia dell'arte and Molière's company, regularly featured actors impersonating characters impersonating other characters, much to the delight of audiences in on the game. The dramatic irony that privileges the audience over one or more characters onstage typically invites us to identify with the impersonators and tricksters, mostly clever slaves and retainers. Even when distinctly different-looking actors play identical twins we suspend disbelief in order to share in the fun. Moreover, custom dictates and experience proves that personal identity changes over an individual's lifetime. Small boys and girls grow taller and cannier day by day. When they come of age different roles are expected of them. Families form over again as children become parents; aging takes its effects. The work—a means of living, as it has come to be called—defines the worker, and careers may set off in new directions. This is all perfectly commonplace, complete with closure and the promise of other generations to come.

As for the novel, Cervantes's astonishing and promptly translated achievement, *The Ingenious Gentleman Don Quixote de la Mancha*, gave a fresh impetus to the question and potential of creating a personal identity of soul and body both. Don Quixote himself argued quite reasonably that people do imitate, if not always impersonate, other individuals in order to find themselves and a career; and he included admittedly fictional models of male and female roles from epic and romance.[6] More generally, comedy that ends with marriage would become the principal plot of the novels that dominated the literary production of the long nineteenth century. Shakespeare was obviously an important inspiration here: British novelists as different as Austen and Scott, Fielding and Dickens were much indebted to Elizabethan and Jacobean theater. In the rise of the novel, a courtship-and-marriage plot tended to dominate; and that plot celebrated marriage as—depending on how one wants to put it—the end of life or a new generation. With a new generation on its way, the older was not destined to be mourned for long.[7]

Moreover, nineteenth-century multiplot novels could readily accommodate tragic actions within an overall comic framework. Allusions to Hamlet became something of a joke in the nineteenth century; more surprisingly perhaps, daughters afflicted with helpless Lear-like fathers would be destined for timeworn comedic outcomes. This is not the place to survey the history of the novel, but it is worth jumping ahead to the end of the twentieth century in order to examine one postmodern novel for its combination of the tragicomedy launched by New Comedy and an outlandish humanist comedy. Novels handily play with fact and fiction both. This one, *The Gospel According to Jesus Christ* by José Saramago, is a historical novel with the secular point of view to which modern historicism has accustomed us. Saramago nonetheless blithely narrates the divine powers and miracles attested to by the gospels composed closer to the events in question. It's a fine example of the way humanist comedians can juggle and keep their batons in the air.

In the aftermath of nineteenth-century anthropology, William James delivered his Gifford Lectures at the University of Edinburgh, published as *The Varieties of Religious Experience*. James's postscript to the lectures contained this sweeping reduction of contemporary Christians' belief in God to a compelling belief in immortality: "The difference in natural 'fact' which most of us would assign as the first difference which the existence of God ought to make would, I imagine, be personal immortality. Religion, in fact, for the great majority of our own race *means* immortality, and nothing else. God is the producer of immortality; and whoever has doubts of immortality is written down as an atheist without farther trial."[8] James places the natural "fact," that is, immortality, in scare quotes, but his lectures sincerely attempted to isolate and to confirm that there were such things as religious truths. Here we are—most of us—he claims, trusting that the existence of God guarantees life beyond the grave.

The philosopher and psychologist's opinion on this matter should be placed alongside St. Augustine's utter conviction about the same equation at the beginning of the fifth century AD. James quoted from Augustine's *Confessions* in his lectures and was familiar with *The City of*

God as well. In book 14 of the latter Augustine almost forcibly asserted that true happiness could not be achieved in the present life. In the midst of these assertions he oddly quotes a verse and a half from Terence's first comedy, *The Woman of Andros*, to help make his point, before concluding in his own words that "the man who so loves [life] cannot help but wish it to be eternal. Life therefore will be happy when it is eternal."[9] The words he has quoted, from the dialogue that commences act 2 of *Andria*, are these: "quoniam non potest id fieri quod vis, / id velis quod possit"(since you can't have what you want, want what you can have). Obviously Augustine repeats the saying, probably from memory, as an aphorism—testimony to how Terence's wisdom was cited even in antiquity, often lifted out of context. The dialogue in question is between the slave Byrria and his master Charinus, one of the two youthful lovers in this comedy. "Please, Charinus, for god's sake," Byrria says, "since you can't have what you want, want what you can have." And Augustine does well to omit—if he should have the context in mind—Charinus's reply, which completes the second verse: "The only thing I want is Philumena" (305–6).[10]

At the end of the play Charinus will get his wish, as will the principal young man, Pamphilus, after the fathers of the two youths quickly work out their difficulties and approve both marriages. Pamphilus is so delighted that he cannot believe his luck and says to himself, as if he were giving a different slant to Augustine's and James's words on immortality, "In my opinion what gives the gods eternal life is the fact that their pleasures are theirs to keep. *I'm* immortal, if no sorrow comes to spoil my joy" (959–61). Living happily ever after, as we say. Pamphilus's metaphor would also seem to link divine being with secular love and marriage; and if so, the joke is on St. Augustine and William James.

Remember, too, that in the universe contemplated by Lucretius "nature makes up again one thing from another, and does not permit anything to be born unless aided by another's death" (1.263–64).

1. NEW COMEDY IN THE HANDS OF PLAUTUS AND SHAKESPEARE

New Comedy could be said to be written by the people for the people. It need not assume literacy at all, let alone much book learning. The labored prologues and repeated expositions of the plot seem to imply that at least some in the audience need to have the action patiently explained to them regardless of its familiarity: family matters, money troubles, winking at crime and deception, love and sex, marriage and inheritance—mostly from a perspective favoring the young and the enslaved. Plautus's clever slaves manage the action, insofar as any characters do, and sometimes hold out for emancipation as their reward. Terence himself was a slave, from Carthage, and won his freedom from a Roman senator before dying in his twenties. "At the core of most Renaissance comedy, including Shakespeare's," Northrop Frye decreed half a century ago, "is the formula transmitted by the New Comedy pattern of Plautus and Terence."[11] In truth New Comedy outlasted and outlived Old Comedy for a couple of millennia, even as its young protagonists implicitly outlived their elders.

There is wide agreement that Shakespeare first approached comedy in the Plautine manner. He obviously knew a number of Plautus's plays at first hand, and he based *The Comedy of Errors* directly on the *Menaechmi*, except that Shakespeare twinned the slave characters as well as the principals. To do this he adopted a conventional back-action that implausibly bestows an identical name as well as appearance on the twins—both pairs of twins in this case. The twin Antipholuses are the last to realize they have been reunited; the audience knows from the start and has been waiting for them to stumble onstage together, face to face. When they finally do so, in the last scene, the duke remarks, "And so of these, which is the natural man, / And which the spirit?" (5.1.334–45).[12]

To find two actors who look so alike that their wives and acquaintances cannot tell them apart would seem to pose a headache for casting and wardrobe, yet to go along with the fun audiences willingly put up with even token resemblances. This comic tradition takes for granted the quite extraordinary powers of human recognition, the way we can tell one face from a thousand others and recognize an acquaintance from a hundred yards merely by the way she walks; but it also nervously calls into question these powers by bringing front stage clowns who cannot quite manage to achieve them. What would life be like if we couldn't so easily distinguish between the faces we know and those we don't know? Plautine comedy routinely delayed recognition by one character of another, or by both characters of each other, as a scene got under way. A character will enter from one of the doors at center stage and begin speaking, while another, often the person who is being spoken about, comes on stage left or right and may also speak. Then one character will peer in the appropriate direction and ask aloud, Isn't that so-and-so now? Partly this routine contributes to the dramatic exposition, but it can also instigate and begin to manage dramatic irony. Some characters in New Comedy, moreover, wore traditionally styled masks; they could be anyone of a certain type. Recognitions are thus doubly blurred. The routine of not noticing, then speculating, then confirming who is present unfolds as a kind of anticipation of the action to follow.

Compared to modern staging and lighting, let alone cinema, the sets for New Comedy were very rudimentary. Yet they persisted in commedia dell'arte and many seventeenth-century productions in Paris, where Molière's troupe competed with the Italian theater. From such later practices and the play scripts that survive by Plautus and Terence, we know that the standard set comprised the front of two houses center stage, each with a door, open or shut, on which much of the performance turns. Characters emerge from the door in the process of completing a conversation with others within; characters within are called to and may step out; characters enter stage left or right and pound on a locked door. The inhabitants of one house do not know what is going on at this moment in the other, though often what might be going on is said to be scandalous. Characters coming from outside report what they have seen in the harbor or marketplace—very likely that the master of one of those houses has unexpectedly returned from abroad. This narrowly confined setting, repeated from one script to another, endlessly dramatizes the difficulty of knowing what goes on behind the walls and doors across the street and by extension what goes on in someone else's mind.

The audience, however, usually knows more than the principals do since in Roman comedy the circumstances of the principal characters and a portion of the plot were often narrated in a prologue. Typed characters also helped one know what to expect. With knowing anticipation, we repeatedly find that a parasite is looking out for his dinner, that a soldier who boasts of unbelievable deeds is a coward, that the young man of the family is truly in love, that the old man is looking out for his money and wishing his wife had passed on, that young women are mostly agreeable (though sometimes mute or never even present onstage), and that a slave, who typically sides with youth against the master who owns him and sometimes complains of his lot or expects to earn his freedom, is the most enterprising and adroit of all these characters.[13] Italian commedia dell'arte of the sixteenth century inherited and stylized these familiar types: we know less about that because it was a theater of improvisation, without scripts for the most part. Two *vecchi*, or old men, and two *zanni*, or servants, wore half-masks covering the nose and cheeks and played variations on predictable roles. Of these, the zany and acrobatic Harlequin became the most recognizable and popular in centuries to come.[14]

The Taming of the Shrew, Shakespeare's other early play that owes most to Roman comedy, provides an excellent introduction to such types and their interactions. The very names of the servants Tranio and Grumio come out of Plautus, and when Grumio invites us to "see, to beguile the old folks, how the young folks lay their heads together" (1.2.138–39), it's as if the playwright himself were giving the wink to the audience and attesting his familiarity with the genre. Much of that beguiling is initiated by the servants, as by the slaves of old. Tranio, for example, in the first scene of the play reads his young master Lucentio's mind and articulates the first of a good many impersonations: namely, that Lucentio should disguise himself as a schoolmaster in order to gain access to Bianca, with whom he has fallen in love at first sight. Lucentio responds by directing Tranio to exchange clothes with him and perform *his* role. By the second scene a rival suitor, Hortensio, has also hit upon the idea of disguising himself as a schoolmaster. Still a third suitor, Gremio, is identified as "a pantaloon" in the stage direction—the older clown from commedia dell'arte and a sure loser here. In almost no time we have coming onstage together Lucentio as a schoolmaster, Hortensio as a music teacher, Tranio as Lucentio himself, along with Gremio and Petruchio, the self-announced wooer of Bianca's "curst" sister Katherina.

Thus *The Taming of the Shrew*, unlike *The Comedy of Errors*, makes sport with deliberate and motivated impersonation. And this is only the beginning. Petruchio, the comedy's protagonist and Katherina's antagonist, will perform in his own name and semblance, but what a performance it is: he shall lie to others about her and lie to her own face until he has her agreeing with everything he says. And he tells the audience so:

> Say that she rail, why then I'll tell her plain
> She sings as sweetly as a nightingale;
> Say that she frown, I'll say she looks as clear
> As morning roses newly wash'd with dew;
> Say she be mute, and will not speak a word,

Then I'll commend her volubility,
And say she uttereth piercing eloquence. (2.1.170–76)

This wholesale lying becomes an assault on the ordinary conventions we depend on in order to communicate, and many find Petruchio and the entire play hard to take. Katherina, it seems, becomes an entirely different person by the end.

Notice that because Petruchio confides in the audience here and elsewhere (as the shrew does not), the dramatic irony works in his favor. In the scenes with Katherina we know that Petruchio is putting on an act, but she can only guess what he is up to. Dramatic irony pleases by empowering the audience. It is the same technique that pleases in so many little ways in New Comedy whenever the audience recognizes someone before another character onstage makes out who it is. When the represented action consists of a deliberate disguise or deception, to be invited in this way to understand what is going on puts us in a position much closer to that of the deceiver than that of his victim. This is delightful when it is just clowning, as we say. In the last act of *The Taming of the Shrew* still another Plautine deception will be brought off. A so-called pedant will be instructed how to impersonate old Vicentio from Pisa in order to claim that Lucentio has his father's consent to marry Bianca. At the end of the same scene in which Petruchio signals to the audience his method of taming the shrew, the scheming Tranio, impersonating the actual Lucentio and supposedly paired against the pantaloon Gremio for the hand of Bianca, hints to the audience what will happen in this fashion:

'Tis in my head to do my master good.
I see no reason but suppos'd Lucentio [i.e., himself]
Must get a father, call'd suppos'd Vicentio;
And that's a wonder. Fathers commonly
Do get their children; but in this case of wooing,
A child shall get a sire, if I fail not of my cunning. (2.1.406–11)

Part of the fun comes from the highly implausible success of such disguises. Cunning they may be, but the characters onstage who are fooled are also very gullible. Shakespeare did not shy away from such willful impersonations in his later, more sophisticated comedies either. And think of the notorious, unconventional role of Edgar in *King Lear*, who takes the disguise of a Bedlam beggar: "Poor Turlygod! poor Tom! / That's something yet: Edgar I nothing am" (2.3.20–21).

The alliance between underdogs—a clownlike servant or slave and a young man courting a wife or even a prostitute—is virtually the rule in New Comedy. There is, if you will, an economic motive: the have-nots against the haves. A slave may be owned by the young man's father yet regularly conceive of a way of delivering needed money to the son, who seemingly cannot figure out what to do for himself. This pattern deflects most of the blame for what happens on the slave or servant, the cheerfully desperate operator rather than the helplessly desperate lover. Fathers are mostly looking out for their own interests or expecting their sons to marry money. They usually come around in the end, by remembering their own youth or sometimes by the revelation, as in a Greek romance ending, that the young woman in question is not who she was thought to be. In comedies scripted in classical times the slave had no civic identity to lose and was sometimes beaten about the stage for laughs. There is notably more slapping about in *The Comedy of Errors* and *The Taming of the Shrew* than in Shakespeare's other comedies of the time. Shakespeare scholars and directors seldom know quite what to make of the abortive theatrical frame for the *Shrew*, in which a practical joke is played by a nobleman on a tinker named Christopher Sly. As for mistaken identity and deception, this lord and his men come upon Sly asleep and contrive to make him believe when he awakes that *he* is a nobleman, surrounded by luxury and in the company of a young page dressed up as his wife. Sly is surprised but takes this all in stride, and it is a little unclear against which party the joke tells more. But the class difference evoked in this skit, like the play that follows, is also reminiscent of Roman comedy.

Shakespeareans often remark in passing that *The Taming of the Shrew* owes little more to Plautus than the names of a couple of slaves, Tranio and Grumio. That is true in a sense, and one has to look elsewhere for demonstrable borrowings and changes rung on the surviving play scripts of New Comedy.[15] Nevertheless, Shakespeare was clearly familiar with Plautus's *Mostellaria*, the play from which these two servants emerge. Grumio's voice is the appropriate one to announce the theme of young folks versus old folks, since in the original he chastises Tranio for helping to ruin their young master Philolaches while their old master Theopropides is abroad in Egypt. Of the two, Tranio has the much larger role in the original. He is the clever slave: contriver of most of the action when Theopropides unsurprisingly returns, confident of improvising as needed to conceal young Philolaches' sexual and financial mishaps from his father. The *Mostellaria* is most notable for an extended prologue, uttered by Philolaches himself, comparing parents' raising of their children to the architectural design of a particular desired home. The analogy rubs against the lies Tranio invents about the house next door in this play; but more important, it elaborates on the theme of two generations in New Comedy and underlines the changing grounds of personal identity. Philolaches' thoughts include the kind of education parents may design for their children, the behavior to be expected, and the choice of career. He is beginning to reflect that he needs to take more responsibility for his own life, the sort of reflection that would become commonplace in novelistic exploitations of New Comedy.

Frye explained what he meant by the formula of New Comedy in the following terms: "The normal action is the effort of a young man to get possession of a young woman who is kept from him by various social barriers: her low birth, his minority or shortage of funds, parental opposition, the prior claims of a rival. These are eventually circumvented, and the comedy ends when a new society is crystallized, usually by the marriage or betrothal of hero and heroine."[16] This is fair enough and adroitly put but slightly misleading in two respects. First, the young man's desire seldom results in a compelling effort on his own behalf. Instead, the action is determined and pursued by a clever slave. A typical case is the eponymous clever slave in Plautus's *Pseudolus*. Given the abrupt and curtailed prologue—"It's better to stretch your loins and get to your feet: a long play by Plautus is about to come onstage" (1–2)—this could easily be an original comedy rather than a translation from the Greek. Nothing fazes the impertinent Pseudolus, whose readiness to cheat and lie makes him useful when the family's credit is low. He sides with his young master Calidorus, naturally, over the head of the family, Simo, whom he refers to as "this old tomb" (412); but the adversary at hand is a pimp, one Ballio, who owns Calidorus's girlfriend and, not having received a promised down payment, is about to sell her elsewhere. Pseudolus has no idea how he will proceed, but something will occur to him: like a poet, he will look all about him and render "likely what is a lie" (403). And when a plan falls into place Pseudolus sees himself as a military campaigner:

"Whatever was uncertain or unclear in my heart before is clear now . . . the passage is easy now: I'll lead my troops in order under these standards, with the bird to the left, with positive auspices, and according to my own wish. I have confidence that I can annihilate my enemies" (759–63). Obviously he has been useful to this family before. When Pseudolus begins to move effectively against the pimp, the father Simo thinks of him as "my Ulysses." Simo has promised his slave a cash reward if he succeeds in trapping that pimp, and he will now deliver it: "He's a very smart, very clever, very wicked fellow; Pseudolus has surpassed the Trojan trick and Ulysses" (1063, 1243–44). In the end Ballio the pimp finds himself suffering double jeopardy, a bit like Shylock's fate in *The Merchant of Venice*. As in some other comedies of Plautus, the beautiful young woman in question has no speaking role and very likely never set foot on stage in original productions of the play.

So the clever slave is he who acts but also bides his time. Apparently much will depend on chance. Or, to put it another way, the realm of New Comedy is that of the everyday and represents the hope of manipulating ordinary, conceivable plights and motivations. This is the second respect in which Frye's account of the formula may be misleading. There is not strictly speaking a *new society* established at the end of the play. Rather, the restoration of usual social expectations marks the end—the passing of generations along with the passing of time but not a significantly different society. In the words of Robert Torrance, echoing Schlegel, "The true divinity of New Comedy is *Tychê:* Luck or Chance." Furthermore (and Torrance has *Pseudolus* specifically in mind), "a fundamental limitation of perspective seems implicit in a form of comedy that never calls into question—even in its bolder Plautine variation—the adequacy of existing society as the framework for any possible human self-realization."[17] One thing Shakespeare will notably contribute is a degree of self-realization, and more especially the self-realization of highly articulate heroines like Rosalind in *As You Like It* and Viola in *Twelfth Night*.

In the last century C. L. Barber's *Shakespeare's Festive Comedy* established a position that was quickly adopted by other critics of Shakespeare and might seem to contravene the influence of Plautine comedy. Barber purposed to show "how art develops underlying configurations in the social life of a culture,"[18] but that was true also of New Comedy in a broader sense. The social life Barber had particularly in mind was comprised of folk festivals in the English countryside, especially local celebration of Saturnalia and mock rule. He might easily have stepped further back and shown how New Comedy depicted mating and sexual reproduction, the raising and financing of families, the coming and passing of generations, all at the heart of social life. Barber's first chapters detailed festive holidays and saturnalian folkways, and unquestionably Shakespeare put these to good use; but he was inspired by literary sources as well. The earliest play Barber treats in detail is *Love's Labor's Lost*, from which he quotes the following lines by Berowne:

> Then fools you were these women to forswear,
> Or keeping what is sworn, you will prove fools.
> For wisdom's sake, a word that all men love,
> Or for love's sake, a word that loves all men,
> Or for men's sake, the [authors] of these women,
> Or women's sake, by whom we men are men,
> [Let] us once lose our oaths to find ourselves,
> Or else we lose ourselves to keep our oaths.
> It is religion to be thus forsworn:
> For charity itself fulfills the law,
> And who can sever love from charity? (4.3.352–62)

Barber himself notes Berowne's indebtedness here to "the classic manner of Erasmus in his *Praise of Folly*" and the "overtones of Christian folly in proclaiming the logic of their losing themselves to find themselves and in appealing from the law to charity."[19] Berowne manifestly alludes to Matthew 16:25, Luke 9:24, and Romans 13:8. One might also note his rhythmic insistence on sexual reproduction, the biological origin of both the speaker and those who attend him. Berowne has the leading role in *Love's Labor's Lost*, in which the principals are of royal and aristocratic rank, not of the folk. Of all Shakespeare's productions, *Love's Labor's Lost* is most like those of the coterie and court theater of the time, typically enacted by choirboys from the Chapel Royal or St. Paul's; for this is his one comedy that does not certainly promise marriage. With the exception of a few plays which may have initially been designated for a private performance, Shakespeare wrote for the public and professional theater, where love and marriage were conspicuously valued.[20] This play ends with delightful song, except that winter follows spring, and the first refrain, "Cuckoo,

cuckoo," sounds "unpleasing to a married ear." The exit line pronounces, "The words of Mercury are harsh after the songs of Apollo."

Barber turns next to *A Midsummer Night's Dream*, a comedy that he understands to have originated as a private performance celebrating the marriage of a noble couple, represented on the stage by Theseus, the Duke of Athens, and his bride, Hippolyta. He does not fail to note Theseus's warning Hermia against the life of a nun, should she fail to accept her father's choice of a husband for her. And besides the star-crossed engagements of two young couples and Theseus and Hippolyta themselves, the *Dream* has a play within the play out of Ovid, oddly chosen by the mechanicals to celebrate the noble wedding, along with Puck, or Robin Goodfellow, to create mischief as well as the fairies of the wood. Oberon and Titania, king and queen of the fairies, are already married and quarreling over a changeling boy, the daughter of one of Titania's votaries. Here Barber gives the speech of Titania's refusal to give up the boy entire, with her marvelous retrospective narrative of the boy's pregnant mother:

> Set your heart at rest;
> The fairy land buys not the child of me.
> His mother was a vot'ress of my order,
> And in the spiced Indian air, by night,
> Full often hath she gossip'd by my side,
> And sat with me on Neptune's yellow sands,
> Marking th' embarked traders on the flood;
> When we have laugh'd to see the sails conceive
> And grow big-bellied with the wanton wind;
> Which she, with pretty and with swimming gait,
> Following (her womb then rich with my young squire)
> Would imitate, and sail upon the land
> To fetch me trifles, and return again,
> As from a voyage, rich with merchandise.
> But she, being mortal, of that boy did die,
> And for her sake do I rear up her boy;
> And for her sake I will not part with him. (2.1.121–37)

Barber explicates the speech, which is not about love and sexuality, note, but achieved pregnancy and parturition. The woman's joy and playacting as a merchant ship—"rich with merchandise," "rich with my young squire"—made their impression on Titania, served to commemorate the woman's mortality, and moved the fairy queen to adopt the child. This indeed is the tragicomedy of generation, when a mother dies in childbirth. Barber calls it "one of the most beautiful bravura speeches" of the *Dream*, and so it is.[21] Not surprisingly, given the influence of Barber's contribution, as Frye continued to lecture and write about Shakespearean comedy the terms *festive* and *festivity* became increasingly prominent.

The title of Frye's single most comprehensive lecture, "The Triumph of Time," patently reflects comedy's role in coming to terms with mortality, but in it Frye generalizes about the plot of comedy as challenging and resolving individual or group identities. The typical structure of the play in Shakespeare comes in three phases. First there are "anticomic" circumstances to contend with. These can be social, such as a harsh law or tyrannical power or parental differences—all those fathers with ideas of their own—or even the entrapment of sheer melancholy. The second phase, characterized by much confusion and potential sexual encounters, is that of "temporarily lost identity" usually accompanied by a "stock device of impenetrable disguise." The last phase constitutes what Frye calls the discovery of identity: "The identity at the end of a comedy may be social, the new group to which most of the characters are attached, or individual, the enlightenment that changes the mind or purpose of one character; or, as usually happens in Shakespeare, both." And then there is "the identity of two lovers who are finally united," often stretched to include several marriages in the end. In *As You Like It* and *Twelfth Night* heroines step aside at this point to change their male garments back to female. Shakespeare exploits the chances of seafaring as early as *The Comedy of Errors*, and Frye does not fail to take note of the presence of the sea in the last romances. "The mythical backbone of all literature is the cycle of nature," he claims, "which rolls from birth to death and back again to rebirth."[22]

What Frye refers to as lost identity and impenetrable disguise in the second phase of Shakespearean comedy is carried to the extreme by the so-called bed tricks of *All's Well That Ends Well* and *Measure for Measure*, plays that dramatize male resistance to marriage and parenthood. In both a young man has sexual intercourse with a young virgin who knows what she is doing but whom he imagines to be someone else. The bed trick was performed in the source of *All's Well*, a tale from Boccaccio, but then Shakespeare added it to the action of *Measure for Measure*: in the first play it consummates the marriage of Bertram to Helena against his will, in the second it seals the broken engagement of Angelo to Mariana. The act of sex—the women's role might coarsely be called the penetrable disguise—brings about the comedic love match, but initially against the men's will. One can understand why these plays were called problem comedies and formerly attributed to Shakespeare's dark mood, evidenced by his satiric take on the Homeric matter of *Troilus and Cressida* and the great tragedies to follow, beginning with *Othello*. At bottom the two problem comedies are about the facts of life: not having sex, but sexual reproduction and the survival of the species, with emphasis on the younger generation of males' acceptance of the facts.

All's Well That Ends Well begins with the extraordinary statement of the Countess of Rossillion, "In delivering my son from me, I bury a second husband" (1.1.1–2).[23] In order to underscore her sense of loss the countess compares the departure of her son Bertram for the court of France to the departure of her late husband to his death; the words "delivering my son" convey a second comparison between the departure of her son and his birth; and the two comparisons imply a third between the son's birth and husband's death that corresponds to the facts about generation. Sexuality has constrained the father to give life to the son, but when he married he also acceded to the passing of his generation and his own death. The comedy introduces the question of whether Bertram (young count, son, and "second husband") will acknowledge his biological and social role in turn. Instead, he refuses to consummate his marriage to Helena (a marriage commanded by the king). He defies time and nature by absurdly vowing, as if this were a fairy tale, that he will never sexually embrace Helena unless she first has a child by him. Thus Bertram dares the heroine to accomplish her desire, to make him a father, to accompany him in the passage from one generation to the next, to persuade him to face death even—if she can do so without his voluntarily consenting to any of these acts. By means of the bed trick in act 4 she succeeds.

Bertram is eager to seduce one Diana, the other virgin in the case: "He fleshes his will in the spoil of her honor," according to one of the French lords, "and thinks himself made in the unchaste composition"

(4.3.16–18). The importance of virginity before marriage is usually attributed to the assurance of heritage and property, but pornography and prostitution and seduction each attach a value to virginity independent of such considerations. Most obviously, the male seducer or purchaser values a virgin because she surrenders everything—her reputation and her future, "the spoil of her honor"—and thereby flatters him more than a bride can. Moreover, the possession of a virgin is *like* a marriage. Sex with that virgin occurs just once. If it is deliberate, it is a dedicated act, timeless in the sense that it has no duration. The apparent timelessness buoys the lover beyond death, while he turns his back on the purposeful implication of death in marriage and generation. The beauty of making love with a virgin is that it is like marriage and yet unlike. No wonder Bertram "thinks himself made in the unchaste composition"—thinks, that is, not only that his reputation as a gallant is made but that he has magically escaped from the generations of time and become his own maker. The betrayed virgin has no future, and the betrayer is committed to none. Similar desires underlie Angelo's attempted extortion of the virgin and novice Isabella in *Measure for Measure*. As Parolles tries to explain to the king in the denouement of *All's Well*, Bertram loved Diana "as a gentleman loves a woman. . . . He lov'd her, sir, and lov'd her not" (5.3.246–48). The virgin bride, on the other hand, has both a past and a future. She has been raised by a family for the consummation of marriage. In Helena's case she has been adopted by her husband's family. The wife is devoted by her society and her family and very much by herself, in this instance, to the future. Helena is determined, with the full authority of the king, to have children by the count, who is also to be devoted to the future and made responsible for the biological end of his existence, on the comedic principle that all is well that ends well. Bertram speciously employs the facts of ongoing generation when attempting to seduce the unwed Diana: "you should be as your mother was / When your sweet self was got" (4.2.9–10). This twisting of the truth that offspring are the biological means of extending life was undoubtedly learned from Parolles, the man of words, who lectures Helena in the first scene that "'tis against the rule of nature. To speak on the part of virginity is to accuse your mothers" (1.1.135–37).

Sex with a virgin is great sport and a miracle of self-generation, in sum, but a wife should be avoided at all costs. Lavatch the clown makes explicit Bertram's marital cowardice when the latter runs off to the wars, as well as the acknowledgment of his mortality that he shuns at home:

> CLOWN. Nay, there is some comfort in the news, some comfort.
>   Your son will not be kill'd so soon as I thought he would.
> COUNTESS. Why should he be kill'd?
> CLOWN. So say I, madam, if he run away, as I hear he does. The
>   danger is in standing to't; that's the loss of men, though it
>   be the getting of children. (3.2.36–43)

This problem comedy takes seriously jokes about "standing to't" in love and war. At the very least it registers that courage is expected in both fields; and since the French nobility participate in the military action only for personal glory, the marital action is the young count's primary responsibility. At least the older generation in *All's Well* are ready to stand by the law set forth in Deuteronomy 24:5 that stated, "When a man is newly married, he shall not go out with the army or be charged with any business; he shall be free at home one year, to be happy with his wife whom he has taken."

Much as in *All's Well That Ends Well* rather bewildering questions of honor are finally abandoned for marriage and a new generation to come, in *Measure for Measure* unresolved questions of government fall by the wayside when both Angelo the deputy and Vincentio the Duke of Vienna prepare to marry. The case of the duke, earlier disguised as a friar, and Isabella, the would-be nun who says not a word to his sudden proposal in the last scene, seems especially portentous because of his sudden about-face and her silence. Angelo and the duke fall in with the example of Claudio, Isabella's brother, earlier condemned to death for getting Juliet with child. To marry and procreate, the clown in *All's Well* has pointed out, is to concede one's death. Frye characterizes some proud words of Claudio in the prison scene—that is, before Isabella tells of her refusal of Angelo's attempt to bed *her*—as "a grotesque anticipation of the bed trick" that Mariana, Angelo's own betrothed, consents to: "If I must die, / I will encounter darkness as a bride, / And hug it in mine arms" (3.1.82–84).[24] These two plays, with forced final scenes that many critics object to, *are* comedies, but Shakespeare was indeed playing uncommon games with the facts of life.

The atmosphere begins to clear with the later tragicomedies, *Pericles*, *The Winter's Tale*, and *The Tempest*, also known as romances. These plays feature troubled but widely different fathers, each with a daughter at the time of her coming of age. It is as if, once the father has bowed to the inevitable passing of his own generation, he is reconciled to his fate by the prospect of having grandchildren. But until a lost generation has been recovered, the action unfolds as tragic. They are called romances partly because of absence and recovery reminiscent of Greek romance. Or because the final coming together is so unusual and transforming that story is mere myth—not a myth about the gods, but about humans. Jonathan Bate has shown how richly the playwright benefits from Ovid's *Metamorphoses* in his high comedies and then triumphantly transposes myth as stage drama in the romances.[25] Shakespeare's genius is such that he not only represents the father–daughter relations onstage but also at key points helps to elucidate their significance.

Pericles, Prince of Tyre was first performed about 1607 and was published two years later in a quarto with Shakespeare's name on it; but it did not appear in the first folio, and there is little evidence of his hand in the writing except for the last two acts. Nevertheless *Pericles* abounds in storms at sea and sole survivors, provides a virtual tour of Near Eastern principalities, and blesses no fewer than three fathers with attractive daughters: Antiochus with an unnamed sexually compelling beauty whom he beds; Simonides of Pentapolis with his daughter Thaisa; and Pericles with Marina, born at sea to Thaisa, whom he has married. The time span of the action is thus more typical of Greek romance than of drama. The hero perceives that "Time's the king of men, / He's both their parent, and he is their grave" (2.3.45–46). The action represented is of classical antiquity; the gods invoked are plural except for Diana, who appears in a dream to Pericles in act 5, as if to assure him of Marina's virginity, and advises him to visit her temple in Ephesus to discover more. Both the incest—more than a hint—of Antiochus and *his* daughter and the travails of Marina amid a prostitution ring are reminiscent of ancient New Comedy.

A youthful, adventurous Pericles travels on his own to Antioch, where he is confident he can solve the riddle pronounced by the king's daughter and win her for himself, though the penalty for not solving it is death. Neither the hero nor the audience, especially given the prologues to each act of the play spoken by Gower as chorus, could conceivably have much trouble with the riddle, which runs in part like this: "I sought a husband, in which labor / I found that kindness in a father. / He's father, son, and husband mild; / I mother, wife—and yet his child" (1.1.66–69). Pericles understands what is going on and gets the hell out of there as soon as he can. Incest messes with the orderly succession of generations, as the riddle itself makes clear: the Antioch couple are father and child biologically, husband and wife by copulation, and son and mother by substitution. In act 4, after she has been sold by pirates to the prostitution ring in Mytilene, Marina manages to save her chastity by shaming the necessarily well-to-do buyers of virginity who visit the brothel. In her own words about her experience to Pericles, on shipboard again but before their recognition of one another, "I am a maid, / My lord, that ne'er before invited eyes, / But have been gaz'd on like a comet." Pericles has been searching for his daughter in the seaports of the East but despairing of finding her. Now he puts together what he has been told with the young woman he sees before him and exclaims, "O, come hither, / Thou that beget'st him that did thee beget; / Thou that was born at sea, buried at Tharsus, / And found at sea again." Metaphorically therefore, at this moment of discovery, father and daughter do have more than one family relationship, because Pericles feels born again. Marina now answers to her name and declares, "Thaisa was my mother, who did end / The minute I began" (5.1.84–86, 194–97, 211–12). Or so they both believe.

The reason for dwelling on this partly Shakespearean creation is that it so evidently anticipated and inspired the double denouement of *The Winter's Tale*, in which the recovery of the protagonist's wife, again assumed to be deceased, also coincides with the recovery of the daughter. In *Pericles* father and daughter proceed to Ephesus as advised by Diana in the father's dream and find there Thaisa, serving in Diana's temple. She did not die in childbirth, was too hastily bestowed in a coffin at sea, and was found alive when the coffin was pried open ashore. "O, come," Pericles now exclaims to Thaisa, "be buried / A second time within these arms" (5.3.43–44). That metaphor reverses the brave sentiment of Claudio in *Measure for Measure* of encountering death like a bride in his arms and possibly, if Frye is right, reflects on the gist of the bed tricks in the problem comedies: accession to the passing of generations in the act of sexual reproduction. In *The Winter's Tale* Leontes would undo the whole action of the tragicomedy if he could, yet the lessons learned are similarly worthwhile.

"A sad tale's best for winter," according to Leontes' son Mamillius (2.1.25). Two generations are onstage in nearly every scene or, if not, then on the speakers' minds; and the seasons of the year become a prominent pastoral image for the ages of man. The play begins with the royal visitation of two childhood friends, King Polixenes of Bohemia having voyaged to Sicilia to stay with King Leontes and his queen, Hermione. The latter would like to share in their youthful bonding before she knew either man and prompts Polixenes to speak of it thus: "We were, fair queen, / Two lads that thought there was no more behind / But such a day to-morrow as to-day, / And to be boy eternal." The action quickly becomes fraught with the consciousness of passing time and the awareness of middle age. Leontes recalls for Hermione their own three-month courtship before she gave him her hand and declared, "I am yours for ever" (1.2.62–65, 105). Seconds later he is stricken with jealousy, even though—or because—he has urged her to make friends with Polixenes: a midlife crisis, as it might be called today. Parturition is already an issue, since Hermione is visibly big with child, as two of the ladies in her entourage remark; and suddenly Leontes is persuaded, and charges in public, that she is big with Polixenes' child. (Bohemia's visit has now lasted nine months owing to Sicilia's renewed invitations and urging of his wife to second these.) Not a single one of the king's followers agrees that he has any grounds for jealousy, and his chaste, innocent wife is both dignified and eloquent in defending herself. Speaking of fathers and daughters, note how one of the lords, Antigonus, defends Hermione to Leontes' face:

> Be she honor-flaw'd,
> I have three daughters: the eldest is eleven;
> The second and third, nine, and some five;
> If this prove true, they'll pay for't. By mine honor,
> I'll geld 'em all; fourteen they shall not see
> To bring false generations. They are co-heirs,
> And I had rather glib [castrate] myself than they
> Should not produce fair issue. (2.1.143–50)

Citing the ages of the three daughters adds a realist touch, and the theme is generation again. But Antigonus will exit in act 3 pursued by a bear. He is one of two named fatalities in this sad tale. The other is young Mamillius, male heir to the throne of Sicilia.

When Antigonus runs off and a shepherd enters on the shores of Bohemia in the midst of act 3, blank verse gives way to prose, but the matter spoken remains much the same. The shepherd's first words to himself, before he stumbles upon the infant daughter of Sicilia and Hermione, whom Antigonus has deposited there, are these: "I would there were no age between ten and three-and-twenty, or that youth would sleep out the rest; for there is nothing in the between but getting wenches with child, wronging the ancientry, stealing, fighting." Then his son enters, narrating what he has witnessed, the savaging of a man by a bear and shipwreck offshore, to which the shepherd famously replies, "Heavy matters, heavy matters! But look thee here, boy. Now bless thyself: thou met'st with things dying, I with things new-born" (3.3.59–63, 112–14). These two Bohemians are identified in the dramatis personae simply as Shepherd and Clown. But their dialogue also insists that two generations are onstage. The shepherd addresses his son as "boy," and the clown refers to his father as "old man" and questions if the sins of the old man's youth have been forgiven him. Shakespeare then enlists the figure of Time as a chorus to address the audience. Time therewith informs the audience that sixteen years have passed, that the name of the foundling child being raised as the shepherd's daughter is Perdita and that of the prince of Bohemia, Florizel: "A shepherd's daughter, / And what to her adheres, which follows after, / Is th' argument of Time. Of this allow, / If ever you have spent time worse ere now; / If never, yet that Time himself doth say, / He wishes earnestly you never may" (4.1.27–32).

Time certainly keeps his promise when delivering the wonderful pastoral interlude of the sheepshearing festival, enriched by the more licentious music of Autolycus and kept in suspense by the dramatic irony of the presence of Polixenes and Camillo in disguise. Perdita and Florizel are also playacting, she decked out in flowers and he in disguise lest his identity as the son of Polixenes be made known. Perdita worries over that deception even as she enters into the festive spirit of the occasion, but Florizel is so bold as to invoke the example of the gods themselves. (As in *Pericles* the action of *The Winter's Tale* is set in classical times.) Florizel cites escapades of Jupiter, Neptune, and golden Apollo, whose "transformations / Were never for a piece of beauty rarer" than Perdita, "Nor in a way so chaste, since my desires / Run not before mine honor." In short, he wholeheartedly accepts his role as the young protagonist of New

Comedy: "Or I'll be thine, my fair, / Or not my father's; for I cannot be / Mine own, nor any thing to any, if / I be not thine" (4.4.31–34, 42–45). Perdita clearly returns this love but knows that, as a shepherd's daughter, it will never be permitted her. She does not fail to express her feelings for Florizel indirectly in the talk of flowers that next engages the company.

As the pastoral scene initially unfolds, Perdita is at the center, equipped with flowers and knowledgeable about still other flowers. Pastoral life is seasonal and renews itself year after year. So now, with two generations of a royal family present in disguise, allusions to their respective ages appeal metaphorically to the seasons. Perdita welcomes the strangers Polixenes and Camillo to her circle with rosemary and rue, since "these keep / Seeming and savor all the winter long." This is the audience's as well as the king's first introduction to Perdita now come of age. He replies, graciously enough, "Shepherdess . . . well you fit our ages / With flow'rs of winter." Still more kindly, she subsequently offers them "flow'rs / Of middle summer" that she finds appropriate "to men of middle age" (4.4.74–79, 106–8). Right there, however, she and Polixenes manage to disagree about art and nature. Perdita disdains the art of cross-breeding flowers and will have none of that in her garden. Polixenes objects that it's all nature:

> POLIXENES.   You see, sweet maid, we marry
>   A gentler scion to the wildest stock,
>   And make conceive a bark of baser kind
>   By bud of nobler race. This is an art
>   Which does mend Nature—change it rather; but
>   The art itself is Nature.
> PERDITA.   So it is.
> POLIXENES. Then make [your] garden rich in gillyvors,
>   And do not call them bastards.
> PERDITA.   I'll not put
>   The dibble in earth to set one slip of them;
>   No more than were I painted I would wish
>   This youth should say 'twere well, and only therefore
>   Desire to breed by me. (4.4.92–103)

By "this youth" she indicates the disguised Florizel. The debate about art and nature is deeply ironic given their differences about the possible domestications of the prince. If Polixenes is right about nature, as he

seems to be, there would be no harm in his noble son mating with a shepherdess. Perdita's dissent on cross-breeding flowers plays right into the
hands of Polixenes' determination that his son not marry her, though her
dignity and straightforwardness in the cause of nature could well be
inherited from her mother Hermione. Perdita in this scene can also be
said to be disguised but without knowing it. Indeed her marriage will not
take place until her identity as the royal daughter of Leontes is restored.
The audience knows who she is, however, and the dramatic irony promises a happy ending to the comedy. Meanwhile Perdita hands out flowers
of spring, both to other shepherdesses nearby and to "my sweet friend."
She could wish to cover that sweet friend with flowers, she says. "What?
like a corse?" Florizel protests; and she responds, "No, like a bank, for love
to lie and play on; / Not like a corse; or if—not to be buried, / But quick
and in mine arms" (4.4.129–32). Both young people adopt a pastoral
license to render the sexual side of their love explicit. The figure seized
upon—to be buried like corpses—wholeheartedly accepts the passing of
their own generation.

Autolycus enters again, singing and playing the peddler. Conceivably
Polixenes may be enjoying the song and dance, since it takes him so long
to throw off his disguise and confront his son and Perdita. He does
confront them, with a "Mark your divorce, young sir," and a threat to kill
this "fresh piece / Of excellent witchcraft"; but he takes no immediate
action and stalks off. Perdita claims she was not frightened by this
outbreak but rather tempted "to speak and tell him plainly / The self-
same sun that shines upon his court / Hides not his visage from our
cottage, but / Looks on all alike. . . . Being now awake, I'll queen it no
inch farther, / But milk my ewes, and weep" (4.4.417, 422–23, 443–50).
Florizel pledges, "What I was, I am," and swears his constancy with an
oath that also testifies to comedy's embrace of nature and succeeding
generation. If he breaks faith, "Let nature crush the sides o' th' earth
together, / And mar the seeds within!" (4.4.464, 478–79). Significantly,
when Polixenes goes off, Camillo remains onstage nearly to the end of
this extraordinarily long scene. Camillo may be a lord—he originally
served Leontes in Sicilia—but he fulfills the role of the clever slave in New
Comedy. Florizel, as the young lover, has no fixed idea of what he shall do
except depart from Bohemia by sea with Perdita. Camillo, on the other
hand, in act 1 helped Polixenes escape from Sicilia instead of murdering

the man as ordered to, and since then has served in Bohemia. He achieved the right end, one can say, but deviously. Now he has an idea of how he may help Florizel and also return to Sicilia himself. But he is not straight-forward with his protégé; he advises him to indulge in half-truths and deceives him about what he intends to do himself. Now Camillo goes so far as to enlist Autolycus's help, just as the clever slave sometimes sides with rogues to assist him.

The last act returns the action to Sicilia. When Florizel and Perdita walk on, Leontes' thoughts go back to his childhood with Polixenes, much as they did in act 1: "What might I have been, / Might I a son and daughter now have look'd on, / Such goodly things as you?" (5.1.176–78). The dramatic irony overrides suspense. So many happy but highly improbable resolutions of the plot are in store that Shakespeare treats this like a prose romance: the climactic recognitions are narrated by three breathless gentlemen rather than staged directly in front of the audience. As it occurs to one of the gentlemen, "This news, which is call'd true, is so like an old tale, that the verity of it is in strong suspicion" (5.2.27–29). Art and nature are again at issue in the last scene, but in the last analysis all is natural. The art of sculpture gives way to the art of drama again, one can say, after Paulina has Hermione pose as the statue of herself. But Paulina has not resorted to magic; she has merely cared for Leontes' queen and Perdita's mother for sixteen years and kept her out of sight.

In *The Tempest* the character who takes on such responsibility for others' lives does resort to magic. Not only is the bookish Prospero deep into magic, the occult, and uncanny foreknowledge of events but, as in *A Midsummer Night's Dream*, Shakespeare introduces supernatural spirits and their performances onstage. Without question this tragicomedy features a father–daughter relation, but the relation is emphatically singular: one father, Prospero, and his daughter Miranda, who has never seen another man besides her father and the monstrous Caliban until the shipwreck that commences the action deposits Ferdinand, son to the king of Naples, on the enchanted isle. Time for the younger generation to come of age is a factor again, but this is not the time of the represented action onstage. *The Tempest* is one play by Shakespeare notable for its unity of time and place: the represented action occupies merely the daylight hours after the tempest has calmed. But it has been twelve years since Prospero was exiled from Milan by his usurping brother Antonio.

Miranda was three at that time and has no memories except her life on the island and homeschooling at the hands of her father. Caliban, who has been schooled to the degree he is capable of by Prospero, can only threaten to rape her. When Ferdinand arrives, Prospero assumes the role of the blocking character in comedy, but he is one of those parents who has foreseen and approves his daughter's choice and puts on a gruff act to slow things down—or perhaps simply to fulfill the comic part. He keeps fretting over virginity and worries over the chastity of Ferdinand and Miranda before marriage but concocts for them a festive wedding masque all the same. *The Tempest* takes place in the Mediterranean but has the atmosphere of the new world about it, with a touch of colonialism in the way Prospero has dealt with the prior inhabitants. He is far more occupied, however, with bringing to justice his former enemies from Milan and Naples, whom he has now managed to gather all in one place. Unlike *Pericles* and *The Winter's Tale* with their glances at the gods, except for the wedding masque this comedy plays out in early modern Christian times, more or less contemporaneous with its first performance. Yet the spirits that hover about the isle are not angels; there are no prayers or churches to attend. Perhaps Christianity is most readily apparent in the forgiveness Prospero exercises instead of taking revenge on his political hostages.

The Tempest makes wonderful theater but is harder to situate in the Shakespeare canon than *The Winter's Tale*. The brute Caliban sometimes makes beautiful poetry in describing the island. Prospero speaks unforgettable lines even when thoughts of Caliban intrude and he calls a halt to the masque:

> Our revels now are ended. These our actors
> (As I foretold you) were all spirits, and
> Are melted into air, into thin air,
> And like the baseless fabric of this vision,
> The cloud capp'd tow'rs, the gorgeous palaces,
> The solemn temples, the great globe itself,
> Yea, all which it inherit, shall dissolve,
> And like this insubstantial pageant faded
> Leave not a rack behind. We are such stuff
> As dreams are made on; and our little life
> Is rounded with a sleep. (4.1.148–58)

Marriage and death again, one may conclude: our *little* life with respect to the age of the universe, but *rounded*, completed rather than abruptly cut off. Prospero does not win the unexpected happiness of renewed marriage experienced by Pericles and Leontes, however, whose lost wives come back to life.

Miranda too is wonderful, wondering at this brave new world and therein reminding one that there is much in the world to be thankful for. But Miranda does not have the stature and independence of Hermione, Paulina, or, in her own generation, Perdita in *The Winter's Tale*. The queen of Sicilia in particular ranks among the relatively few surviving mothers in Western literature and has obviously set a standard for her coeval and her daughter. (It is appropriate, too, that Paulina marry Camillo, as Leontes urges in the lines that end that play.) Also, the conspirators in *The Tempest*, Antonio and Sebastian, are rather one-dimensional as well as ineffective; Gonzalo represents a better sort of nobility, if only there were more of him; the clowns, Trinculo and Stephano, are entertaining but no more than that. Unlike those comedians, Autolycus in *The Winter's Tale* is wicked and conniving but unpredictable and a vaudeville show in his own right. However Autolycus happens to have materialized in Bohemia, he is the namesake of a son of Hermes in Greek myth who was the maternal grandfather of Odysseus and "surpassed all men / in thievery and the art of the oath."[26] By fathering a bastard child Hermes–Mercury has helped out Shakespeare with this pastoral comedy too.

Robert Miola details ways in which New Comedy contributed to *The Tempest* and also to *Hamlet* and *King Lear*.[27] He is not entirely persuasive in claiming that the shipwreck and treasure in Plautus's *Rudens* influenced the tragicomedy, but the case of the two tragedies is different. Both of those major works incorporate impressive interludes of comedy; both dramatize conflict between two generations of a royal family. King Lear notoriously attempts to divide his kingdom among his three daughters, and the exile and return of his favorite, Cordelia, play out in such a way that Shakespeareans have often associated this tragedy with the subsequent romances. *King Lear* itself had one of the strangest fates of any tragedy in the history of the London stage. After the closing of the theaters in the early seventeenth century it was not performed as anything like the play Shakespeare wrote until the early nineteenth century.

2. UNFAILING IMPERSONATIONS BY MOLIÈRE

The comedic routines adopted by Plautus, Shakespeare, Molière, and other distinguished talents over the centuries bear importantly on social life and positively demonstrate the usefulness of role playing. It would be hard to exaggerate the part that impersonation plays in humanity's life at large, let alone the theater. Frye was surely right to feature disguise and confusion of identity as typical of the second phase in the structure of New Comedy, and the actor onstage representing a character pretending to be someone else is doubling his or her act of disguise. Putting on a mask, dressing up, imitating a friend or enemy, or an animal for that matter, are practices unquestionably older than any conventional stage. People are not necessarily content to be what they are; young ones expect to grow up and come of age; older folk look back and study counterfactually who they might have been. Many have occasion for hoping their bodies only temporarily mask their souls.

Hobbes, with his determination to define words carefully, proves an excellent authority to consult on the subject of impersonation within and without the theater, though in the seventeenth century he called it *personation*. The words *personate* and *personation* can still be found in English language dictionaries today but have largely been replaced by *impersonate* and *impersonation*, which have the same meaning. Hobbes's brief but quite extraordinary chapter 16, "Of Persons, Authors, and Things Personated," served as a necessary transition between part 1, "Of Man," and part 2, "Of Commonwealth," in the *Leviathan* and began as follows:

> A person is he *whose words or actions are considered either as his own, or as representing the words or actions of another man, or of any other thing to whom they are attributed, whether truly or by fiction.*
>
> When they are considered as his own, then he is called a *natural person;* and when they are considered as representing the words and actions of another, then is he a *feigned* or *artificial person.*
>
> The word Person is Latin . . . as *persona* in Latin signifies the *disguise* or *outward appearance* of a man, counterfeited on the

stage, and sometimes more particularly that part of it which
disguiseth the face (as a mask or vizard); and from the stage
hath been translated to any representer of speech and action, as
well in tribunals as theatres. So that a *person* is the same that an
actor is, both on the stage and in common conversation; and to
personate is to *act*, or *represent*, himself or another; and he that
acteth another is said to bear his person, or act in his name . . .
(as a *representer*, or *representative*, a *lieutenant*, a *vicar*, an
attorney, a *deputy*, a *procurator*, an *actor*, and the like).

In Latin *persona* did originally denote a stage mask; before there were
persons in our cognate meaning of the word there were masks; and in
this passage, whether theater or tribunal it seems all the world's a stage.
Hobbes carries on in this searching, honest, etymological vein because he
needs to connect bodies we are acquainted with at first hand to the body
politic, individuals to the commonwealth. Personation is about empowerment, whether it be of an actor, a representative, or a monarch; personation extends authority over time as well as space. Thus it becomes a way
of necessary hedging against mortality in the political sphere. Hobbes's
inclusion of acting is a good reminder of how individual characters,
whether fictional or historical—such as the monarchs in Shakespeare's
history plays—live over and over again on the stage. In chapter 16 Hobbes
was also preparing for parts 3 and 4 of *Leviathan* on true and false
Christianity. He carefully distinguishes between the true God and mere
idols, "gods of the heathen," who had no authority in themselves and
therefore could not properly be personated unless governments bestowed
authority upon them. Nevertheless,

the true God may be personated. As he was, first by *Moses*, who
governed the Israelites (that were not his, but God's people) not
in his own name (with *hoc dicit Moses*), but in God's name (with
hoc dicit Dominus). Secondly, by the Son of man, his own Son,
our blessed Saviour *Jesus Christ*, that came to reduce the Jews,
and induce all Nations into the kingdom of his father, not as of
himself, but as sent from his father. And thirdly, by the Holy
Ghost, or Comforter, speaking and working in the Apostles;
which Holy Ghost was a Comforter that came not of himself,
but was sent and proceeded from them both.[28]

Many Protestants, obviously, dispute one or two of these personations of God, and even on his own terms Hobbes would have to concede that the Holy Ghost must be a *"feigned* or *artificial person"* rather than a natural one.

In early modern times the heritage of New Comedy first manifested itself in commedia dell'arte, or a styled and easily repeatable comedy of improvisation. It is no accident that four of Shakespeare's early comedies were set in Italy. The Italian troupes traveled far and wide, but of course we do not have scripts for most of their acts, and much of the show was mimed as well as spoken. For an illustration of the comic empowerment latent in disguise and impersonation, however, one can hardly do better than turn to a work of another writer known primarily for his political acumen: Niccolò Machiavelli's comedy *La Mandragola*, or *The Mandrake*, composed about 1518. The *inamorato* of the plot, Callimaco, was sent off to Paris by his guardians when he was ten years old and made a life for himself there ever since: that is, until another Florentine gentleman boasted of the beauty of one Lucrezia back home, and now Callimaco has returned to Florence to see for himself. Lucrezia proves to be even more beautiful than reputed; she is married to Nicia, a wealthy doctor of laws but ignorant, a fool and pantaloon. His wife is forbiddingly chaste and so morally strict that most people are afraid of her. Callimaco is now help-lessly in love with her very image; he at once despairs and can think of nothing else; but he has struck up an acquaintance with a parasite, Ligurio, who promises to help. True to form, the young lover initiates none of the action; Ligurio, a practiced cheat, takes over. He already knows Nicia because Nicia is well-to-do. The old man above all wants to have a child, and so far his marriage with Lucrezia has been barren. Ligurio promises to help him also, and in act 2 he brings his two clients together by means of the comedy's first impersonation. Callimaco is to pose as a distinguished medical doctor whose practice is in Paris. The parasite proceeds to coach Callimaco and argues that it's easy to pass oneself off as a doctor simply by speaking a little Latin—or seeming to speak Latin.

Callimaco plays his part well. He even points out that it might just be the husband who is impotent. In any case, he informs Nicia that his wife need not go out of town to distant health spas in order to become preg-nant. A potion can be made from mandrake root that will render her fertile, a potion she can drink this very evening. If it were not for mandrake root, he confides, the queen of France would be childless. There is a catch however: the first man to have sex with her after she takes the potion will die within a week. Nicia protests, of course. But Callimaco and Ligurio answer that they will search the streets and back alleys of Florence this night for a young drunk who can be thrust into bed with Lucrezia and told what to do. The plot thickens: now Nicia concurs in deception and manslaughter; he is clearly the fool and laughingstock of the comedy. He does point out that his chaste wife will have to agree to go along with the plan, but Ligurio is prepared for this. They shall bribe her father-confessor to advise her accordingly and enlist her mother, Sostrata, on the husband's side as well. To the extent that Machiavelli indulged in satire in *The Mandrake*, the friar Timoteo is the object in the last three acts. It is taken for granted that almost any friar may be corrupted, and Ligurio intends to bribe this friar with Nicia's money. Lucrezia reluctantly agrees to consult Timoteo about the scarcely believable plan, and he responds quite rationally:

> Here we have a certain good: you will get pregnant, you will provide another soul for the good Lord up there. The uncertain evil is that the man who sleeps with you after the potion may die; but there are always those who don't die. However, since there is some question, it is better for Messer Nicia not to run that risk. As for the act itself, it is only an old wives' tale that it is a sin, for the will is what commits sin, not the body. The real sin is going against a husband's wishes, and here you are following his wishes; or taking pleasure in it, and here you are filled with displeasure. Besides that, we must always consider whether the end justifies the means. Your end is to fill a seat in Heaven and to make your husband happy. The Bible tells us that the daughters of Lot, thinking they were the last women on earth, consorted with their father; and because their intentions were pure, they did not commit a sin.

Thus, with Timoteo's rhetorical skills in play, Machiavelli does fulfill his prologue's promise to stage a foursome of comic types: "A wretched swain will weep and whine, / A doltish man of law will bumble, / A venal monk will help him stumble, / A most ingenious parasite / Will guide them all, for your delight."[29]

The secret plan is for Callimaco to be thrust into bed with Lucrezia after she has taken the potion (which, needless to say, need not be mandrake but any unfamiliar tasting drink). So now Ligurio has to improvise again, since Nicia expects Callimaco in his Parisian doctor role to join them in waylaying some young lout to sacrifice for that purpose, and the lout is also to be impersonated by Callimaco. The solution is to disguise Timoteo as Callimaco the doctor and have Callimaco the lout distort his features and wear a false nose. The disguises work, everything works. As Callimaco tells Ligurio the next morning, halfway through the night he confessed the entire plot to Lucrezia and won her over. She sighed and said to him, "Since your cleverness, my husband's stupidity, my mother's silliness, and my confessor's guile have led me to do what I would never have done by myself, I have to judge that this comes from a divine providence that willed it so. I am not capable of refusing what heaven itself wants me to accept." No doubt Callimaco's performance and his being in love helped to make up her mind. There in bed Lucrezia joined in the deception and suggested a more lasting relationship to her lover: "What my husband willed for this one night, he shall have for good and ever. You must therefore become his close friend. Come to church with us this morning, and then return to have lunch at our house."[30] A couple of brief scenes with all the principals before church that morning assure the spectators that these arrangements will be lasting and everyone a winner. Thus impersonation and disguise give people power over their lives. Given Callimaco's and Lucrezia's readiness, it seems very likely they can also fulfill New Comedy's promise of a new generation.

Machiavelli's earlier play *The Woman of Andros* was a straightforward adaptation of Terence's *Andria*, and his last, *Clizia*, an adaptation of Plautus's *Casina*. So his indebtedness to the Roman comedians is scarcely in doubt. In these less original comedies also, more than one senile gentleman gives way in the end to youthful lovers. In *Clizia*, as in *Casina*, father and son are in love with the same young woman. So little does this comic tradition care for the character of the bride that neither eponymous heroine ever appears onstage; they are not of the dramatis personae. Machiavelli's account of Lucrezia's point of view, though hearsay, does seem something of an improvement. But New Comedy, its Italian spin-offs and Italian players, with their often scarcely believable deceptions and impersonations, fed directly into the theater of Molière.

At the height of his career as actor and playwright, in 1668 Molière produced a play copied directly from Plautus's *Amphitruo*. Modern audiences obviously need not put much stock in the mythic denouement—Alcmena giving birth to the child Hercules—to delight in the impersonations in this play. There is always the awkwardness that Alcmena, the perfect and loving wife, has innocently slept with Jupiter. In the seventeenth century merely the represented fact is an affront to love and honor both. Molière's *Amphitryon*, however, begins with a charming exchange between Mercury and the goddess of Night instead of the long prologue spoken by Mercury in Plautus, and Sosie, played by Molière himself, has the last word as the curtain falls. Best of all is the frustrating awareness of Molière's Jupiter that he can scarcely take credit for seducing the chaste Alcmena when he has used his divine powers to appear exactly like her husband. Twice this false Amphitryon tries to hint to Alcmena that she should think of him as a lover as well as her husband. His frustration is a wry comment on Jupiter's powers of seduction that seems not to have occurred to Plautus—or to the god himself before now. Dryden's *Amphitryon*, the funniest and raunchiest of his plays, commences with a dialogue featuring Mercury and Phoebus (that is, Apollo) talking back to their sire Jupiter, in a scene that could easily be interpreted as both sacrilegious and politically rambunctious in Britain of the 1690s. Mercury has been wondering "into what form your Almightyship wou'd be pleas'd to transform your self to night. Whether you wou'd fornicate in the Shape of a Bull, or a Ram, or an Eagle, or a Swan . . . or in short, whether you wou'd recreate your self in Feathers, or in Leather?" But Dryden, having introduced one or two subplots to his version of the play, has Mercury himself fall for a lovely friend of Alcmena named Phaedra. Because Mercury is all the while impersonating Sosia, her seduction is not likely; but the factual counterfactual that the god next poses encounters another difficulty:

MERCURY. Suppose I were a God, and shou'd make Love to you?
PHAEDRA. I wou'd first be satisfi'd, whether you were a poor
    God or a rich God.
MERCURY. Suppose I were *Mercury*, the God of Merchandise?
PHAEDRA. What, the God of small Wares, and Fripperies, of
    Pedlars and Pilferers? . . . I had rather you were *Plutus* the

God of Money, or *Jupiter* in a Golden Shower: there was a
God for us Women! He had the Art of making Love.[31]

This Phaedra, the bedfellow of Alcmena when Amphitryon is away at the
wars, is the object of every male gaze, to be sure, but has other desires.
Whereas Jupiter laments that Alcmena cannot appreciate that he is not
her husband, Mercury apparently could not get far even if he were playing
himself.

Deliberate impersonation and much deeper self-deception are on
show everywhere in Molière's comedies. Molière was influenced by the
Italian theater independently of the practice and playscripts of Elizabethan
and Jacobean theater in England. His own astounding routines would
echo from the stage and films of four centuries to come. Four wonderful
doctor plays deliver both the epitome and the nadir of impersonation.
Doctors are supposed to help keep body and soul together, but to impersonate a doctor in commedia dell'arte actors performed half the part
simply by walking on in a black gown and a floppy hat. The costume may
well have symbolized for Molière how readily learned professions could
be put on and off, for his plays are mainly full of doctors merely pretending
to be doctors. In Le Médecin volant the so-called flying doctor is a servant
named Sganarelle. This was the first of seven comedies, from one- to
five-act duration, in which Sganarelle appeared, always a different character with the same name and always played by Molière. This practice,
adopted by Charlie Chaplin and others in silent film, itself challenges the
conviction that each person among us has a distinct and irreplaceable
being. The in-your-face brashness of the role playing when the celebrated
actor appears onstage redoubles the effect of familiarly typed characters.

Part of the fun in this brief debut of Sganarelle is the speed with which
the action unfolds in Le Médecin volant. One Lucile is pretending to be ill in
order to put off her father Gorgibus's plan to marry her off to a wealthy
suitor. She is in love with Valère and cannot very well pretend to be ill
indefinitely. The deception to be carried out next is proposed to Valère by
Lucile's cousin in the first speech of the play. Valère needs to find someone
to play doctor and recommend fresh air for the patient; then she can be
moved to a pavilion at the far end of the garden, from which the couple can
elope. The only available candidate is Valère's clownish servant Sganarelle,
and all he will require is ten pistoles and that doctor's gown. Naturally we

side with the young lovers against the mercenary father and *his* servant
Gros-René, but dramatic irony is also at work again, empowering the audience by letting us in on these deceptions of which Gorgibus and Gros-
René are unaware—as yet. One of the ways in which Callimaco establishes
his credentials as a doctor in *La Mandragola* is to demand of Nicia a urine
sample from his wife. The supposed doctor Sganarelle *drinks* a sample of
his patient's urine as a fresh and superior means of testing it, although the
audience sees through the upstairs window that the sample has been
poured from a wine bottle. (One cannot exactly call this a tasteless joke, but
what is it?) Sganarelle succeeds so well in impressing the gullible Gorgibus
with doctor talk and persuading him to dispatch his daughter to the
summer pavilion that he prematurely casts aside the black gown.

Suddenly now there are two of him: caught in his ordinary clothes,
Sganarelle hastily reintroduces himself to the puzzled and increasingly
suspicious Gorgibus as one Narcisse, the doctor's estranged and self-
depreciating twin. Pleased with his daughter's new doctor, Gorgibus
decides to bring the supposed brothers together and reconcile them.
Amid the rapidly accelerating impersonations and duplicities, Sganarelle
hastily throws off and on the gown and flies in and out of the house
window as Gorgibus runs out and back through the door. Sganarelle even
conducts an angry dialogue with himself in the window opening, by
turning first one profile and then the other to the onlookers. In the 1650s
Molière apparently had athletic skills approaching those of Buster Keaton.
The audience knows the game is up, that the disguises and lies are falling
apart, but roots for Sganarelle all the same. In the nick of time Lucile and
Valère return—married—and beg their father's forgiveness. Sganarelle
goes free and takes credit for his performance.

In 1666, in addition to *Le Misanthrope*, Molière produced a three-act
play *Le Médecin malgré lui*. Here Sganarelle again passes as a doctor, but the
doctor in spite of himself is a different character in different circumstances
from the Sganarelle of *Le Médecin volant*. He is again of low station and low
esteem but déclassé rather than a servant: he is married, with no fewer than
four children, but drinks and will not work at anything more complicated
than faggot gathering: that is, not even wood cutting but tying brush into
bundles to be sold for firewood. In a saying that has become proverbial he
boasts, "Il y a fagots et fagots" (2:17 and n).[32] The comedy gets under way
with a vigorous quarrel between Sganarelle and his wife, Martine, she

abusing him in the familiar *tu* and he holding forth in the polite *vous*. Sganarelle starts beating her, but when a neighbor tries to intervene Martine tells him to mind his own business. A husband and wife will go through the very same routine for Keaton's benefit in *Our Hospitality* (1923).

Again we have the standard New Comedy plot. Sganarelle's impersonation of a doctor is compelled by a serendipitous encounter between two servants of Géronte, another stereotypical father, and Martine. This time the daughter, Lucinde, has contrived to lose her voice in order to forestall her father's wishes, and the servants are in search of a doctor who can get her to talk. Martine is seeking revenge for that morning's beating from Sganarelle. She tells the men they will find a fabulous doctor out in the woods, one who will protest that he is not a doctor and do anything to avoid offering his services. When he is in that mood, she says, there is nothing that can be done but to beat him until he obliges. The servants accept this dubious story and easily track Sganarelle down, with results as Martine has foretold. The bullying husband of the first scene turns out to be an arrant coward: "Ah! ah! ah! Messieurs, je suis tout ce qu'il vous plaira" (2:19). He will be anything they wish. Géronte's people want him to be a doctor, and Sganarelle begins to think maybe he just *is* a doctor. He makes a pretty good show of it, too, as we might guess from his citing of Aristotle and Cicero when quarreling with his wife that morning. How can an audience fail to sympathize with a man who becomes an impostor under duress? He talks Latin gibberish—after making certain Géronte doesn't understand a word of that tongue—and he makes a few slips, such as remarking that the heart is located on the right side of the body. When Géronte counters that the heart is on the left side, Sganarelle famously replies that it used to be so, but doctors have changed all that now: "Nous avons changé tout cela, et nous faisons maintenant la médecine d'une méthode toute nouvelle" (2:32). In the Marx brothers' film *A Day at the Races* (1937), the wealthy hypochondriac played by Margaret Dumont will announce, "Dr. Hackenbush [Groucho] tells me I have high blood pressure on my right side and low blood pressure on my left side." And there *is* something grotesque about the asymmetry of our guts hidden within the lovely symmetry of our outer selves.

The previous year still another Sganarelle had appeared in *L'Amour médecin*, a *comédie-ballet*, or sort of musical that Molière helped invent and performed for royalty. The composer was Jean-Baptiste Lully. No fewer than five doctors appear onstage with, needless to say, differing opinions about Lucinde's melancholia. That's right, the daughter's name is again Lucinde, and so are the circumstances and basic plot familiar, but in this entertainment Sganarelle is the gullible father. Lisette, a maid, is the driving force behind the action and quickly has the audience on her side because she speaks out and speaks common sense to the household, much like Dorine in *Le Tartuffe*. What his daughter needs, Lisette tells Sganarelle, is a husband. She arranges to have Lucinde's lover, Clitandre, put on one of those black outfits and present himself as a new doctor, for love is the doctor and the cure for all such illnesses. Clitandre enters and explains that he does not believe in emetics, bloodletting, or drugs: he uses words and concentrates on the patient's mind (and indeed he proposes to Lucinde onstage but out of Sganarelle's hearing): "Comme l'esprit a grand empire sur le corps, et que c'est de lui bien souvent que procèdent les maladies, ma coutume est de courir à guérir les esprits, avant que de venir au corps" (1:805). His practice is to address the mind before attending to the body: these words addressed to the father are intended for Lucinde's ears as well, and the erotic double-talk continues.

Clitandre next dares to tell Sganarelle that the reason his daughter is looking better already is that he has told her he has come to ask for her hand in marriage—even though he personally thinks those who desire marriage are ridiculous—and suggests they keep up this pretense for a few days. Now our physician is in a position to profess his love for Lucinde openly and openly confess that his doctor's habit is a "pur prétexte inventé," which he has adopted simply to obtain his desire. Sganarelle is now being deceived by the exact truth, and the redoubled dramatic irony is delicious. Clitandre even persuades him to sign a marriage contract, by introducing a notary who he claims is really only his apothecary. He has also brought along the comédie-ballet team, whose harmony can help such "troubles de l'esprit." In the end Comedy, Dance, and Music sing a refrain in unison. These are the true physicians of the soul, without whom humanity would indeed suffer:

> Sans nous tous les hommes
> Deviendroient mal sains,
> Et c'est nous qui sommes
> Leurs grands médecins. (1:805–8)

This musical not only stages the classic duping of the old man by a slave—in this seventeenth-century instance the maid Lisette—allied with the younger generation, but begins to toy with that commonest of personations, the idea that we have souls as well as bodies. Clitandre declares that he works with spirit or mind, but he's a supposed doctor rather than a priest. Call him a pretended psychiatrist if you like; the patient this time, remember, is suffering from melancholia, a mental condition. Lucinde is not said to be faking her melancholy, in the way the other Lucinde is faking her aphasia and Lucile was stalling and pretending to be ill. *L'Amour médecin* therefore has more of a psychological bent than the other two plays. The erotic equivalent of the extrapolation from body to soul is the capping of sexual desire with love. The amorous subtext of Clitandre's declaration asks for Lucinde's love as well as sex. At the very least, these plays treat of people's alterable moods. Martine and her Sganarelle are reconciled in the end: the vengeful practical joke has worked out not so badly. The fathers in the plays almost all come around to accepting their children's marriages. Sometimes they almost cheerfully accept that the older generation is passing.

In *Le Malade imaginaire*, finally, the psychological case resides with the eponymous hypochondriac. There is no Sganarelle in the cast; but Molière played a father again, the hypochondriac Argan. Self-deception is a given in this comédie-ballet. If a man imagines he is ill, he is not quite who he thinks he is. It's a case of needing to become well but refusing to do so. One can argue that Argan's doctor, M. Purgon, assists with the deception, and another doctor, M. Diafoirus, and his son hope to profit from it too. Argan also has a second wife, a younger woman who is counting on him to die. And finally, a marriage plot is still at work here: Argan's daughter Angélique returns the love of one Cléante, but her father wants her to marry some doctor who will help care for him. The candidate is Diafoirus's son, a young man so stupid that he cannot even speak his part without coaching from *his* father. The glory of *Le Malade imaginaire* is the coordination of the action with the song and dancing. Molière had broken with Lully and this time collaborated with Marc-Antoine Charpentier. A cure of the *malade* is effected by the end, and it as if the refrain that concluded *L'Amour médecin* were true: Comedy, Dance, and Music really are the grand doctors of the soul.

How should Argan be cured of his hypochondria? What can suffice to counter such self-deception and its pampering? Fortunately this household includes another descendant of those fast-thinking, fast-talking Plautine slaves: the servant named Toinette. After a pastoral prologue with music and dances honoring Louis XIV, *Le Malade imaginaire* opens with a long soliloquy from Argan as he goes over his doctor and apothecary bills, detailing the treatments and drugs he has had for the last month. Then he rings the call bell for Toinette and rings repeatedly, more and more angrily. He's a sick man, and she doesn't come! When she enters, she is already putting on an act, pretending she has hurt her head and howling with pain every time the hypochondriac opens his mouth. From another fast-moving scene—Argan and his daughter speaking at complete cross-purposes—we learn of the marriage plot. This prepares for an even longer, angry confrontation with Toinette in Angélique's presence. Toinette says she won't allow Angélique to marry some doctor she has never met, when she loves another perfectly eligible young man. This outspoken servant is also quite capable of flattering her master and deceiving him. She is acquainted with Cléante and complicit when that young man, like Hortensio in *The Taming of the Shrew*, calls on Angélique and her father in act 2 disguised as a music master.

Between each of the acts there is an interlude of song and dance. Just before the second of these Molière introduces a new character, Béralde, a brother of Argan, who functions very much like the brother-in-law of Orgon in *Le Tartuffe* or the friend Philinte in *Le Misanthrope*: someone of sound judgment who is tactful and kind to the self-deceived central character played by the author and a voice of sanity that helps the audience keep its bearings amid all the craziness and contrived deception. After the interlude, which he gracefully compliments, and after a quick word or two with Toinette, Béralde sits down with Argan to talk about his health and about the medical profession. Béralde suggests that his brother must be in good health or he would have died by now from all that medicine he has swallowed. The two obviously differ on this subject. With another, more tendentious metatheatrical gambit, Béralde suggests that one of Molière's doctor plays would help divert Argan and put him straight about medicine. That really starts them arguing. "Si j'étois que des médecins," Argan says, "je me vengerois de son impertinence; et quand il sera malade, je le laisserois mourir sans secours" (2:826). If he were a doctor, he would take his revenge and let Molière die. And he continues under the proviso of this conditional to curse the author and actor of this play, who happens to be himself. (The metatheatrics presumably drew great laughter for three performances but were destined to pose a wretched irony for theater history: Molière collapsed during the fourth public performance of *Le Malade imaginaire* and died later the same night.)

This argument with his brother seems to give Argan pause, however, for when an apothecary comes in with an injection to take, he waves him aside; and that brings on M. Purgon, the doctor, who gives his patient a terrific scolding and walks out on him. Toinette then seizes her opportunity: she announces that still another doctor has called to see the master. She doesn't know who this new doctor is, but she and he are as alike as two drops of water, she says. In other words, we are about to witness her own impersonation of a doctor, and Toinette performs this double role hilariously. Not content to go offstage and return cross-dressed as the doctor, she comes on first as one and then as the other in rapid succession. It's that black gown again that makes it easy, and as for a doctor's manner, she simply parodies M. Purgon's. She prescribes all kinds of nonsense, far outdoing Sganarelle in *Le Médecin malgré lui*. Sganarelle forgot what side of the body the heart was on; Toinette questions why Argan needs two arms and advises amputation of one. Excising his right eye, she claims, would likewise strengthen the left. Argan is impressed because Toinette has told him that he/she is ninety years old. The doctor leaves, comes back as herself, and complains that the former made a pass at her when he was going out the door. Argan is beginning to share her doubts about this doctor.

Béralde takes this moment to put in another word for Angélique and question the sincerity of Argan's wife, Béline, who has urged that Angélique be placed in a convent. Not so, protests Toinette. Would they like her to *prove* how dearly Béline loves her husband? Just pretend you have died there in your chair, she tells Argan, for here comes your wife now. Toinette gives out a wail and exclaims to Béline that her husband is dead. The wife, however, is charmed by the act: Heaven be praised, she says, what can Toinette be crying about? Then the same experiment is conducted with Angélique, who breaks into tears and expressions of sorrow at her father's apparent demise. Notice that our hypochondriac himself has suddenly become rather deeply invested in this game. He fakes his own death. The one who was self-deceived accepts the crucial role in deliberately deceiving others. Two female relations have averred their loyalty to Argan; critically these asseverations have concerned his well-being and possible death; and the women's reaction to the latter can be tested in present time only by performing a lie. They say it takes a thief to catch a thief. Likewise, an impostor to expose an impostor, n'est ce-pas?

Cléante is also moved by this supposed death of Argan. He and Angélique beg her father to approve their marriage, and at last Argan gives in, *if* Cléante will become a doctor! And now Béralde has a thought—possibly a subliminal recollection of his brother saying what he would do if he were a doctor and Molière needed his help: why shouldn't Argan himself become a doctor? Yes, Toinette chimes in, then he would always have a doctor close at hand. Argan is obviously intrigued but doubtful. He's too old to study, he says. Wouldn't he have to learn Latin and the cures for various ailments? Not at all, his brother assures him; that will all come to him when he accepts "la robe et le bonnet de médecin." Moreover, the ceremony can be performed right here at home. Argan goes offstage to change, and Béralde explains to the others that he has a troupe of comedians outside prepared to perform the ceremony with music and dancing. And so the play ends, with an elaborate parody of installations conducted at the time by the Faculty of Medicine (2:845, 941–43n). Argan has progressed from hypochondriac to this celebratory impersonation of a doctor, and the satirist Molière who plays him to this cheerful accommodation. There is a common expression, Today I feel like a different person. It follows that on some days I would rather be someone else. If we ourselves are such impostors, we should have no difficulty appreciating New Comedy.

Someone is bound to protest that if the point is to demonstrate Molière's true opinion of impersonation, why not place in evidence *Le Tartuffe* instead of these doctor plays? The subtitle appended to *Le Tartuffe* was *L'Imposteur*, after all, and the officer of the king who arrests Tartuffe at the end declares, "Nous vivons sous un prince ennemi de la fraude" (1:704). Molière himself did not play the eponymous impostor but his victim Orgon, another gullible paterfamilias: every other character in the play except Orgon and his mother sees through the pious mask to the hypocrite Tartuffe is, and the melodramatic denouement exposes him as an out-and-out villain. It is still worth noting that it takes a deliberate counter-deceit on the part of Orgon's young wife to disenchant her husband and expose the hypocrite: in act 4 Elmire instructs Orgon to hide while Tartuffe imagines he is alone with her, and the husband thereby witnesses piety's sexual ambitions and his own betrayal.

The deeply troubling lesson of this play was surely unintended: after the first public performance in 1667 Le Tartuffe was closed down by the authorities, largely because the comedy was offensive to the church. Tartuffe is no priest, however; Molière was not satirizing the clergy, and if he had been there were precedents quite as familiar as the satirizing of lawyers and doctors. What disturbed people most was the foolishness of Orgon. He's a clown for sure, and his remarkable infatuation with Tartuffe's pretensions has made him another man: a born-again Christian. The represented action as a whole sets him against his family, and more than once he articulates this theme with complacency (as does Tartuffe):

> Il m'enseigne à n'avoir affection pour rien,
> De toutes amitiés il détache mon âme;
> Et je verrois mourir frère, enfants, mère et femme,
> Que je m'en soucierois autant que de cela. (1:646)

Tartuffe has taught him, in other words, to care not for this world, to detach his soul from all friendships, to care not even if his mother and brother, wife and children should die. Though this sounds very callous, it unmistakably recalls Jesus's teaching: "If any one comes to me and does not hate his own father and mother and wife and children and brothers and sisters, yes, and even his own life, he cannot be my disciple" (Luke 14:26).

One would assume, as Molière undoubtedly assumed, that an attack on hypocrisy in the person of Tartuffe was both justified and unmistakable. The play also provided an example of enlightened Christianity in the person of Orgon's brother-in-law, Cléante. But Orgon has become converted, changed to a new person apparently. As we have seen, there are in the teachings of Jesus commands that leave mere stage acting far behind: "He who finds his life will lose it, and he who loses his life for my sake will find it" (Matthew 10:39). In Le Tartuffe Molière was treading too close to the ingrained foolishness of Christianity, as treated at the beginning of the modern era by Erasmus with all seriousness in the peroration of his Praise of Folly:

To sum up (or I shall be pursuing the infinite), it is quite clear that the Christian religion has a kind of kinship with folly in some form. . . . the biggest fools of all appear to be those who have once been wholly possessed by zeal for Christian piety. They squander their possessions, ignore insults, submit to being cheated, make no distinction between friends and enemies, shun pleasure, sustain themselves on fasting, vigils, tears, toil, and humiliations, scorn life, and desire only death— in short, they seem to be dead to any normal feelings, as if their spirit dwelt elsewhere than in their body.[33]

Even absent the liberties allowed to drama and literature, pretending to be someone else—let's call it borrowing an identity—is not always wrong or punishable by law. What the costume department is to the theater, the fashion industry is to everyday life. Genesis 3:7 notwithstanding, clothes were probably not first adopted with foreboding and a burst of modesty. Man is an animal who readily imagines she or he can be different any day or night of the week. Sometimes impersonation beckons invitingly: life insists on art. Clothes apart, there is always that problem of how to become somebody. A good part of life *is* performance, if one believes Erving Goffman's *The Presentation of the Self in Everyday Life* and subsequent books.[34]

One universal experience of becoming a different person and entering on a new career is simply that of growing up. Every child sets his or her sights on becoming a full-size human *sapiens*. We do not by any means emerge from the womb as grown-ups; it takes at least a year to walk and talk, another fifteen or twenty to gain full stature. Some people never grow up, they say, and what could that mean? The truth is that one does not have to be born again to achieve this new life: just don't be such a child. Regardless and inevitably the generations succeed one another. In comedies since Greek and Roman times, slaves—and others with nothing much to lose—side with the younger generation coming into its own; their very clownishness results in unexpected moves and serves as cover. The routines of New Comedy kept being applauded in motion pictures of the twentieth century and beyond.

The typical role that Buster Keaton created for himself combined that of clown and male adolescent, with an ingénue playing along and one or both fathers playing opposite. It's the familiar love plot again, but with the lover so young that he has trouble standing upright on his feet and so naïve that he sometimes hasn't heard about the facts of life. The most comprehensive of such Keaton films is *Steamboat Bill Jr.* of 1928. Junior arrives on the train from Boston (and from what college might that be?) to the unnamed river port, where Bill senior, the skipper and owner of the *Stonewall Jackson*, is losing business to the owner of a much newer, grander riverboat called, after himself, the *King*. It's the class thing again, with a screwball political resonance thrown in. The film opens at the railway station with the old routine of recognition—which is he? who's this? Senior is appalled when he finally recognizes his son. (Keaton is about half as tall as Ernest Torrence, the actor playing his father.) A change of costume for the young man is immediately called for, and Keaton's classic poker-faced resistance is first evident in a struggle with his father over a cap he has been wearing. Kitty, his young lady acquaintance from the East, also arrives in town and proves to be the daughter of that hated King. Senior can no more teach Buster how to use his fists, however, than how to run the machinery of his steamboat. There ensues much embarrassment over inept handling of the boat and falling into the river. Junior has some success in tricking his father and connecting up with Kitty, but it takes a natural disaster to turn this disaster of a son into a man: first the wind, with near misses from falling buildings that single out the hero as blessed by providence; then the raging flood, from which in a dazzling five-minute burst of competence— easily outflying the *médecin volant*—he saves from drowning one after another his father, Kitty, and her father. It is plain to see now that Bill Jr. will likely become heir to the Kingdom on the river. As in a comedy by Plautus, the young are never quite as hopeless or helpless as they are hapless.

3. ADAPTATION OF THE TRAGICOMEDY BY NOVELISTS

Property handed down from generation to generation has the virtue of outlasting the individual owners, thereby providing a crutch to the biological facts of life. There is something about the inheritance of property, however, that seems to call for narrative rather than theater. Certainly this was a theme very much at home in the long nineteenth century, when the novel dominated fresh literary endeavors. Inheritance is another signal of the passing generations, and marriages figure here too, though mostly in favor of the gentlemen in question.

Henry Fielding, a contemporary of Hume who also sought to make his mark at a very young age, wrote first for the stage. His farce dubbed *Tom Thumb*, a tragedy of tragedies, was supposedly a newly discovered Elizabethan script. Two of his comedies, *Mock Doctor* and *The Miser*, were adaptations of Molière. But with *Joseph Andrews*, an extended parody of Samuel Richardson's *Pamela* "written in imitation of the manner of Cervantes," Fielding turned to the novel and began to win his modern-day reputation. In 1749 he published his epic in prose called *The History of Tom Jones, a Foundling*, composed with great care in eighteen books. This is comedy on the road, involving a cross-section of the population of England and a variety of sexual escapades well told, as Tom Jones comes to manhood and undeniably learns a few things about life. There are two fathers to contend with, the hero's foster father, Allworthy, and Squire Western, father of the unspoiled and needless to say, very attractive Sophia Western. Once the difficulties are cleared up and the identity of Tom Jones certain, he and Sophia marry and will inherit the adjoining country estates of Squires Allworthy *and* Western.

The novels of Walter Scott, beginning anonymously with *Waverley* in 1814 and thereafter certified to be "by the author of *Waverley*," regularly, happily, and properly concluded with both marriage and the inheritance of property in land. Properly—politically correct, one might say—because Scott was a conservative thinker in an era in which the right to landed property was celebrated as the basis of the stability of society by such as Edmund Burke. A nation of landed gentlemen, with a parliament personating them, is also the best defense against revolution. As Burke pointed out, "The power of perpetuating our property in our families is one of the most valuable and interesting circumstances belonging to it, and that which tends the most to the perpetuation of society itself. It makes our weakness subservient to our virtue; it grafts benevolence even upon avarice."[35] Families need not necessarily reassemble in heaven therefore, since a substantial estate on earth could be handed down in perpetuity. Scott's novels, of which he wrote about two a year until his death in 1832, were immensely popular and widely imitated throughout the nineteenth century—and not only in Great Britain. As all-time literary exports go, they rival Shakespeare's plays.

Scott was a contemporary of Jane Austen and admired her novels, which also owed a good deal to Shakespeare. As in Shakespeare's high comedies, her heroines come to understand themselves better by the end.[36] Fathers are tolerated but tend to be laughable and to get in the way; marriage for love in the denouement is enhanced by the inheritance of property. *Persuasion* may be an exception, since Captain Wentworth's fortune comes from prize money won at sea with the navy; but there is nothing to prevent him from purchasing a country estate, a practice followed by successful industrialists, merchants, bankers, and conquistadors to this day. *Pride and Prejudice* and *Mansfield Park* devote considerable space to the possession and care of landed property. Scott and Austen would both say, if one asked them, that human nature was the same in all ages; but Scott was a historical novelist who set his novels in various time frames and actually helped westerners to become more conscious of historical time.[37] The Scottish novels set in the seventeenth and eighteenth centuries are his best written and best informed; *Ivanhoe*, a medieval tale, may be the best known today. Scott did not invent the historical novel, but his success with the genre insured that it would be undertaken by others. Without his example, it's hard to imagine Tolstoy undertaking *War and Peace*. The growing awareness of history thus became increasingly secular. Widespread literacy competed with concern about the ways of Providence.

In the art of the novel, as Georg Lukács spelled it out, "the historical novel transforms the social novel into a genuine history of the present."[38] Lukács had particularly in mind the achievement of Balzac, who himself paid tribute to Scott in the preface to the *Comédie humaine*. History keeps right on unfolding, however; it doesn't come to an end like the pages of a book. This awareness of history makes the customary narrative closure of comedy appear arbitrary. Thus Thackeray, a follower of Scott and Fielding both, observed to readers in the midst of *Vanity Fair*, "As his hero and heroine pass the matrimonial barrier, the novelist generally drops the curtain, as if the drama were over then: the doubts and struggles of life ended: as if, once landed in the marriage country, all were green and pleasant there. . . . But our little Amelia was just on the bank of her new country, and was already looking anxiously back towards the sad friendly figures waving farewell to her across the stream, from the other distant shore."[39] That's just a fiction, Thackeray reminds his reader, much like crossing the river Styx in the underworld. But then the rites of passage of real life may as well be fictions too, since history keeps rushing along and going about its business, like nature in the Epicurean universe depicted by Lucretius.

Scott's historical novels were not only vested with heritable real estate; they were profoundly committed to a secular fiction of the social contract. The author himself noted that his heroes hesitated to act independently, and so did some of his shrewder critics. Retrospectively he tended to make fun of those young men, the first of whom he had suggestively named Waverley. But when these heroes find themselves in a tight spot, their first instinct is to seek out the authorities, in Waverley's case literally to place himself under arrest.[40] "One of the first motives to civil society, and which becomes one of its fundamental rules," according to Burke, "is, *that no man should be judge in his own cause*. By this each person has at once divested himself of the first fundamental right of uncovenanted man, that is, to judge for himself, and to assert his own cause."[41] Nonetheless, virtually all Scott's novels were crafted as comedies, in many of which one may be sure that fathers perform their part. As Robert Gordon has noted, "One cannot help being amazed at the amount of sheer narrative energy and motivation that Scott finds in the impercipience of fathers."[42]

Without question Scott was inspired by Shakespeare's history plays, yet it is almost forgotten today how intimately he was familiar with earlier dramatists other than Shakespeare. There may have been little live theater in the neighborhood of Edinburgh, but Scott was another voracious reader. Moreover, he worked directly on the plays of Beaumont and Fletcher; likewise, the plays of Dryden, for publication in a multivolume edition that remained the best available text for a century and more to come. Scott's own first publication was a rough translation of *Götz von Berlichingen*, one of Goethe's early historical dramas. It's almost embarrassing that Erich Auerbach never devoted a chapter of *Mimesis* to Scott's realism. Auerbach wrote brilliantly of the mixture of styles in Shakespeare by explicating a scene from 2 *Henry IV*, but one of his principal criteria for realism in the nineteenth-century novel was consistency of style such as one might find in Flaubert. Scott took to the mixture of styles in Shakespeare—typically couched in blank verse spoken among the high characters and prose among the low—and adopted it for his own purposes. In the Scottish novels, officers and gentlemen, heroes and heroines, speak standard English, whereas servants, retainers, and locals likely speak in dialect. Jokes play better in the low style; and, as in the tradition of New Comedy generally, retainers like clever slaves have more freedom of action than their masters. Shakespeare also demonstrated, in *Henry IV* especially, how the contrast of high and low styles could represent in short space, without harping on the matter, the wide range of occupation and opinion that make up a nation. Scott adopted the same procedure and instructed George Eliot, Thomas Hardy, and William Faulkner among others how realism might be enhanced by a mixture of styles.

Charles Dickens, still admired for his comic masterpieces in prose, was thoroughly acquainted with dramatic comedy and tragedy. He both frequented the London theater and habitually worked off steam after the demanding absorption of composing a serialized novel by performing as amateur actor, producer, and director in his own right. It became almost routine for Dickens to fill in a break between novels by energetically staging a play among his friends and acquaintances; and there is broad agreement that he brought on his death by touring about with dramatic readings from his novels and stories. The actor and director William Charles Macready was an older friend, and without question Macready's *King Lear* of 1838 made a deep impression on the young novelist. The first evidence of this was Dickens's *The Old Curiosity Shop* of 1840–41, a more or less spontaneous serial that narrated the death of Little Nell and sealed the author's reputation for sentimental fiction. A more deliberate and carefully planned use of *Lear* followed with *Dombey and Son* of 1846–48, in which the firm of Dombey and Son proved to be a daughter after all. And among Dickens's later novels, *Little Dorrit* owed even more to Shakespeare's play. All three novels, note, focused on the Cordelia figure rather than the bourgeois stand-ins for King Lear himself: but such in general was the nineteenth century's shaping of Shakespeare's extraordinary work. Except for Little Nell, the daughters in Dickens live to marry happily after, but modestly and selflessly, especially the eponymous Little Dorrit.[43]

It seems perverse to associate comedy in the hands of Dickens with Shakespeare's most harrowing tragedy. A clue to some of the play's nineteenth-century redactions was its relation to Shakespeare's late tragicomedies: the focus on a new generation by fathers confronting a daughter. But then, recovery from an illness and total loss of consciousness was often the turning point in old or new romance (think of Esther Summerson, the daughter in search of a parent in *Bleak House*). In the scene with Kent and the doctor, Lear awakes—to music—in the presence of Cordelia: "You are a spirit, I know; [when] did you die?" and "Do not laugh at me, / For (as I am a man) I think this lady / To be my child Cordelia" (4.7.48, 67–69). In Shakespeare's principal source, the anonymous play *King Leir*, the pair of them do survive as in a comedy; so also in Nahum Tate's version of 1681. In Shakespeare, however, father and child remain alive and reunited for just one more scene, that of their capture by the forces of Goneril, Regan, and Edmund. In the final moments of the tragedy Lear enters with the slain Cordelia in his arms. Albany, Kent, and Edgar compare these moments to the end of time; but critics who try to elevate Cordelia to a Christ figure are too hasty. Lear's own desperate hope is that if "she *lives* . . . It is a chance which does redeem all sorrows / That ever I have felt" (5.3.266–68; emphasis added). Her continuing to live would make up for all the foregoing unbearable suffering. Although the source play *King Leir* was set in Christian times, moreover, Shakespeare sets *King Lear* in pre-Christian times, and its gods are plural.

Still, Shakespeare's play is very much about the coming of death. Lear would have liked to spend the rest of his days with his favorite daughter, but he lost that chance along with his temper in that first scene. In the grim subplot Gloucester is also an old man and very much mistaken. Yet unlike Shakespeare's other tragedies—or almost any tragedy—both Lear and Gloucester die natural deaths. Gloucester's heart "burst smilingly," according to his son Edgar (5.3.200); and Lear dies onstage desperately trying to believe that his daughter still breathes. All three of Lear's children predecease him. In the tragic manner, they are respectively stabbed, poisoned, and hanged. But the two natural as opposed to violent deaths accord with the normal passing of generations: that is, with an inevitability shared by the comedy of generation.

In an essay primarily devoted to the riddle of Portia's three caskets in *The Merchant of Venice*, Freud argued that Cordelia represents death itself: "She is the Death-goddess who, like the Valkyrie in German mythology, carries away the dead hero from the battlefield."[44] Moreover, Freud, who was born in 1856 and whose favorite Dickens novel was *David Copperfield*, understood from nineteenth-century literature how easily heroines coalesced with angels and goddesses of death. In a century notable for the advance of knowledge on many fronts and with new respect for science, this strictly gendered phenomenon is hard to explain. Possibly increased secularism of the culture was responsible: it became more believable to bring angels down to earth and install them in the home. Freud was hardly the only one to single out or to deify Shakespeare's Cordelia. Victor Hugo went so far as to say that the character Lear was but the occasion for the daughter and cited a precedent for daughters breast-feeding fathers. That is to say, the play was crafted to commemorate the youngest of the three sisters: "That admirable human creature Lear acts in a supporting role to this ineffable divine creation, Cordelia. All the chaotic tragedy of crimes, vices, madness, and miseries has its reason for being in this splendid vision of virtue."[45] Compare the role of Jean Valjean's adopted child Cosette in *Les Misérables*. The long historical novel, which Hugo worked on for twenty years before it was published in 1862, concluded with the death of Valjean, the hero whose misfortunes famously began with his theft of a loaf of bread. The last words in the novel are four lines of verse that an anonymous hand has inscribed in pencil on the otherwise unmarked tombstone:

> He sleeps. Although his lot was a strange one,
> He lived. He died when he no longer had his angel;
> The thing came of itself, simply,
> As the night forms while the day fades away.[46]

Cosette has not died, however. Jean Valjean simply loses his angel when she marries her young man Marius Pontmercy, who is more like one of the proper heroes of Scott. Hugo would resort to a similar contretemps for the denouement of *Les Travailleurs de la mer*.

Told in the first person and consciously autobiographical, *David Copperfield* is not one of Dickens's novels directly shaped by *King Lear*, but the narrator regularly refers to the heroine Agnes Wickfield as an angel. Soon after David first meets her he associates Agnes with church windows. Dora, his highly inadequate "child-wife," meets the angel through David and, on her deathbed, asks to be alone with her. Agnes thus is in a position to announce his first wife's death by pointing upward, and thereafter David thinks of Agnes and speaks to her as his angel. "You remember, when you came down to me in our little room—pointing upward, Agnes? . . . Until I die, my dearest sister, I shall see you always before me, pointing upward!" In Victorian novels addressing a young woman as "sister" frequently anticipated a warmer relationship. This comedy ends with *their* marriage, and his narrative with a silent prayer: "Oh Agnes, oh my soul, so may thy face be by me when I close my life indeed; so may I, when realities are melting from me like the shadows which I now dismiss, still find thee near me, pointing upward!"[47] His angel's gesture of pointing upward (in the iconography of Western art the posture of John the Baptist), while promising, does not do away with the fact of death. The first time Agnes points upward, she might just be pointing to what happened upstairs before she descended to "our little room," the sitting room of David and his child bride. Agnes does have a father, whom she watches over until his death, while Uriah Heep (more like a grotesque double for the hero than an independent agent) lusts after her and Mr. Wickfield's business. But this is a common role of hero-ines in New Comedy: their care for the male parent attests to their future care of a husband. Mothers, such as Agnes and other heroines are destined to become, are either missing altogether, the butt of comedy, or else wicked. As Austen quipped on the first page of *Northanger Abbey*, the first drafted of her published novels, "instead of dying in bringing [Catherine Morland] into the world, as any body might expect," the hero-ine's mother "still lived on—lived to have six children more—to see them growing up around her, and to enjoy excellent health herself."[48] Herein Austen is at once mocking and violating the general rule. The culture takes for granted—from a male point of view, of course—that a female devotes herself to generation, then passes on. But parturition seldom occurs in the foreground of a novel, unless perhaps the mother should die in childbirth, as she does in the very first pages of *Dombey and Son*.

Before the birth of little Paul, Mr. Dombey resents his six-year-old daughter Florence simply because she is a girl. After ten years of marriage he still has no male heir to take over the banking business. Now the widower Dombey has what he has wanted so badly; but the child is frail and thoughtful, unlike his father and with an unworldly, almost saintly air. Famously, in a quiet moment together, little Paul breaks the silence thus: "Papa! what's money?" Mr. Dombey is staggered and at a loss for words but recovers, pats his child's head reassuringly, and says, "Money,

Paul, can do anything." Then (to make this quite marvelous conversation short) the child puts a question that resonates throughout the novel: "Why didn't money save me my Mama?" With a triumph of Dickensian sentimentality in the fifth monthly number of the novel, little Paul dies peacefully facing out to sea, and the child's passing prefigures the tragicomic denouement of *Dombey and Son*. At the end of the fifteenth number, by thrusting his Cordelia out into the London streets Mr. Dombey could be said to outdo King Lear at his worst. The impact of Shakespeare's tragedy is unmistakable at a good many points, and in the next-to-last number, when father and daughter come together again, she will ask his forgiveness: "Papa! Dearest Papa! Pardon me, forgive me! I have come back to ask forgiveness on my knees. I never can be happy more, without it." By then Florence has married Walter Gay, a young man of modest means unexpectedly returned from a long sea voyage, and they have already had their first child, a boy whose name is Paul. In this tale of generations Dickens seems also to have been influenced by Shakespeare's late romances: "My little child was born at sea, Papa."[49]

A decade later *Little Dorrit*, with its more mature, marriageable protagonist who happens also to be back from a long sea voyage after years in the Far East, comes closer to interpreting and enlarging upon the scope of *King Lear*. Most of the novel, especially the first half, is narrated from Arthur Clennam's perspective. But it is as if Dickens took the idea for this plot from Lear's exchange with Cordelia after they are taken prisoners:

> CORDELIA.   We are not the first
>   Who with best meaning have incurr'd the worst.
>   For thee, oppressed king, I am cast down,
>   Myself could else out-frown false Fortune's frown.
>   Shall we not see these daughters and these sisters?
> LEAR. No, no, no, no! Come let's away to prison:
>   We two alone shall sing like birds i' th' cage;
>   When thou dost ask me blessing, I'll kneel down
>   And ask of thee forgiveness. So we'll live,
>   And pray, and sing, and tell old tales, and laugh
>   At gilded butterflies, and hear poor rogues
>   Talk of court news; and we'll talk with them too—

> Who loses and who wins; who's in, who's out—
> And take upon's the mystery of things
> As if we were God's spies; and we'll wear out,
> In a wall'd prison, packs and sects of great ones,
> That ebb and flow by th' moon. (5.3.3–19)

Dickens adopts this spirit of survival against the odds and creates a comedy from this prospect of imprisonment. His Cordelia will be idealized and attractively developed; whereas his Lear is outwardly proud, inwardly ashamed, manifestly helpless, and therein a butt of the comedy. Again there will be some fanciful autobiographical touches, coloring the experience of his middle-aged protagonist. The prison proves to be the Marshalsea, the debtors' prison near the south bank of the Thames, where Dickens's father was incarcerated and where, as was possible in those days, his mother accompanied her husband while the twelve-year-old Charles was put out to work in a shoe-blacking warehouse. In the novel, William Dorrit has earned the title of "the Father of the Marshalsea" from the other prisoners, and he is cared for by his daughter Amy—"born there"—except in the daytime, when *she* goes about earning what little they have to eat.

The walls of the Marshalsea prison keep the world outside in perspective, just as Lear imagined. *Little Dorrit* has a great deal to say about who's in, who's out, and packs and sects of great ones. Dickens reduces the government of England to the Circumlocution Office with its bureaucracy and toadyism. But the sweep of his satire is much broader than that. He divided the novel precisely in half, ten equal monthly installments in the first half titled "Poverty" and ten in the second called "Riches." Thus midway through readers can anticipate an excursion into Christian ethics—and toward judgment day, as it were. A clownlike character named Pancks researches the history of William Dorrit's finances and comes up with a surprising inheritance, and the Dorrit family marches triumphantly out the gate of the Marshalsea. Amy has two older siblings much like Cordelia's, except that one is a woman and the other, little better than a boy. Both frown on Little Dorrit's selflessness and are not often on the scene in the chapters devoted to poverty; and both are now prepared to live it up in the fashionable world, as is the sometime Father of the Marshalsea. Arthur Clennam assists by going back into the prison and carrying forth in his arms their sister—she who was born there and has fainted, reluctant to surrender her days of forgiving and caring for the Father of the place and his followers. Besides, despite her small stature and contentment at being called Little Dorrit, Amy is in love with Arthur, the hero back from China and estranged from his mother and family business in the city.

Amy's family seeks to get as far as possible from London and the Marshalsea: that is, as far as possible from their past and people who have known them. They set off on a grand tour across the Alps and into Italy. At a dinner entertainment for his new fashionable acquaintances, William Dorrit has a stroke, speaks aloud as if he were back within the prison walls, and thereby betrays his past; Little Dorrit comes to her father's side and stays there through his last days. Meanwhile in London the shady scheme of the financier named Merdle (from the French *merde*) falls to pieces, but not before Clennam has invested his own, his partner Daniel Doyce's, and other people's money. When the bubble bursts, the hero finds himself a debtor imprisoned in the same room formerly occupied by the Father of the Marshalsea, where Little Dorrit comes to him and makes her love known. Their love story contributes another dimension to the lessons of the novel, since the protagonist now is condemned to the life of impoverished confinement that he has only witnessed before and is morally responsible for the plight of others as well. Nor will he accept what amounts to Little Dorrit's proposal of marriage until he learns she has lost her fortune too. Yet, "looking back upon his own poor story, she was its vanishing point. Every thing in its perspective led to her innocent figure. He had traveled thousands of miles towards it; previous unquiet hopes and doubts had worked themselves out before it; it was the centre of the interest of his life; it was the termination of every thing that was good and pleasant in it; beyond there was nothing but mere waste and darkened sky."[50] Here Clennam imagines time as a drawing in perspective. But that vanishing point and termination of everything, beyond which there was nothing but waste and darkened sky, identifies their marriage with the end of life. For all his hopes and doubts and previous misunderstandings (he is also shadowed throughout the novel by a nasty criminal double variously named Rigaud, Blandois, or Lagnier), the younger man is certainly an improvement on the Father of the Marshalsea, who inhabited the very room where these thoughts occur to him. *Little*

Dorrit is emphatically a story of the passing of generations, for Arthur has taken Amy's weak and troublesome father's place. No thoughts could more soberly express the tragicomedy of generation.[51]

These daughters in Dickens no doubt pose a special case, just as surely as they record their author's responsiveness to Shakespeare's exceptional use of Cordelia in *King Lear* and of Marina, Perdita, and Miranda in his tragicomic romances. Those stage plays and these novels are obviously not the only way to run with the plot of New Comedy. But from the male point of view of the artists and dominant view in the culture daughters are emphatically fine depositaries of a younger generation—if the older generation is to pass with a smile. Gender matters, not because of some secret incestuous desire but because a child of the same gender can more readily be seen as a rival or be envied as one who outlives the parent. Youth matters because otherwise there would be no representatives to survive the passing generation. Mothers are by definition members of the older generation and, much like fathers, if you will, may become butts of laughter: no use crying over their passing. But then, quite apart from the culture in question, there is this biological fact about women for men to reckon with. The females of the species demonstrably bear and give birth to children. The males consequently downplay this female role and exaggerate their assumed leadership because inwardly they have to acknowledge that their bodies are divorced from the business of parturition for nine months and more. So let us hand it to Shakespeare and Dickens for featuring special out-of-the-way plots that occupy a full generation of time and celebrate the tragicomic facts of life.[52]

The ground rules of New Comedy could be traced in novel after novel of the long nineteenth century, but surveying modern literary history is not practical here. The tragicomedy of generation repeats itself over and over, and there need not every time be new incarnations of Cordelia or angels pointing upward. Much the same thing could be said of opera in the long nineteenth century. True, Wagner gave major singing parts to an angel Elisabeth as well as to the goddess Venus in *Tannhäuser*, and Freud was not wrong to have *Die Walküre* in mind when associating lead caskets with angels of death. Wagner also scripted and composed according to rule *Die Meistersinger von Nürnberg*, however, one of the great New Comedies of all time (and for some devotees his greatest opera). The role of Hans Sachs, as one who also loves Eva and generously gives way to the younger Walther whom she loves, puts music to a grander theme, but this does not diminish or detract from the more conventional roles of her foolish father, the goldsmith Pogner, and the ostensible would-be husband Beckmeister. *Der Rosenkavalier* by Richard Strauss and Hugo von Hofmannsthal is another tragicomedy, following the same pattern. Another wealthy merchant is bent on marrying into the nobility, by offering up his daughter Sophia to Baron Ochs; and this time the female lead, the Marschallin, will surrender her young lover. Cross-dressing is part of the game from the moment the curtain rises; disguises and imper-sonations succeed like magic, as if almost anyone can be gulled so; and the knight of the rose Octavian, now in love with Sophia at first sight, enlists a couple of amoral go-betweens of the type to be found in classical theater in order to fool and deflate Ochs altogether in act three of this comedy set to music. When the London theater began to revive and pick up momentum again in the 1890s, all four of Oscar Wilde's plays took up the cause of New Comedy. The last of these, *The Importance of Being Earnest*, had only Lady Bracknell to represent the older generation, yet the deception and impersonations carried out by the young men were worthy of Plautus, commedia dell'arte, and Molière. George Bernard Shaw crafted comedies that were far more ideologically driven, but they still typically came to a close with marriage and prospective generations in view. That would seem to be part of the message. Shaw dwelt on genera-tion in *Man and Superman* especially, and there quite blatantly repre-sented what he called the "Life-Force" in the shape of a woman.

Something of the life force should be allowed to novels written by the increasingly driven ideologue D. H. Lawrence (who, for his time, also exhibited in his fiction a remarkable recall for the Bible). *Aaron's Rod* signaled the novelist's new direction with its deliberately contrived alter-native to Jesus named Lily, and this book was followed by the far more elaborate and doctrinaire works *Kangaroo* and *The Plumed Serpent*. The author's opinion of Christianity was unquestionably influenced by Friedrich Nietzsche, though he was always careful to distinguish his will to *life* from Nietzsche's will to power. Lawrence's last novel, *Lady Chatterley's Lover*, written in 1928, was more like his earlier work but proved most difficult of all to get published, no doubt because of its embrace of nongenerative anal sex as well as some prohibited vocabulary. This tragicomedy began with the announcement, "Ours is essentially a tragic age, so we refuse to take it tragically."[53] The novel closes with the gamekeeper Mellors awaiting a divorce so that he can live with Connie, also waiting apart and pregnant with his child. She knows better than to go back to Chatterley, who would spitefully take the child from the adulterers and claim it as his own. Lawrence preached of this present life and a monogamous relation between a man and woman irrespective of civil law or religious sacrament. He did not believe that women were anywhere near equals of men, but at least Connie and her child will not have to live apart from the gamekeeper. Lawrence's posthumously published *Apocalypse*, which posed as an extended commentary on the book of Revelation, summarized his religion of the will to life and opposition to Christianity. According to Lawrence, readers of Revelation worshipped Christ mainly as the guarantor of an afterlife, and indeed "the Son of God, the Jesus of John's vision . . . holds the keys that unlock death and Hades. He is Lord of the Underworld. He is Hermes, the guide of souls through the death-world, over the hellish stream."[54]

So much for Hermes—or for Jesus Christ, conflated with Hermes and deflated accordingly. Yet in "The Man Who Died," a better-known, two-part story also written in the last years of his life, Lawrence humanized Jesus according to his own lights. The man in question is never named and in fact did not die. The narrative assumes he was taken down from the cross and was put away prematurely. Now he emerges from the tomb, rejects the advances of one Madeleine, and boards with a local farmer while recovering from his wounds. In part 2 he sets forth and next encounters a priestess of the Egyptian cult of Isis. The priestess and the man who died come together and lose their mutual virginity. In Lawrence's parable Jesus thus acquires the secular afterlife available to cocks and hens (featured in part 1) as well as to men and women: namely, one generation following after another.

Still another modernist novel with a difference is *To the Lighthouse*, completed at the height of Virginia Woolf's literary powers and with a daughter's moving secular take on marriage and death. The work was autobiographical to a degree, Mr. and Mrs. Ramsay stand-ins for Leslie and Julia Stephen, and Mr. Ramsay still devoted to the novels of Walter Scott. In a diary entry in which Woolf pondered the new project she wrote, "I am making up 'To the Lighthouse'—the sea is to be heard all through it. I have an idea that I will invent a new name for my books to supplant 'novel'. . . . But what? Elegy?"[55] *To the Lighthouse* is scarcely a tragedy; Mrs. Ramsay has passed on before the end, but she has borne eight children and is aware of her passing as that of others before her. After ten years Mr. Ramsay finally agrees to venture forth with their two youngest, a teenage son and daughter, by crossing the sea to the lighthouse. The result is a sad as well as affectionate narrative: an elegy, one might say, for nineteenth-century tragicomedy.

Historically New Comedy has renewed itself over and over again, regardless of the personal or ideological purposes to which it is put. Stage and film have clearly not yet seen the last of it; and though some modernist literature of the early twentieth century may seem to have deserted the cause of generation, plentiful more widely read novels and popular plays have carried right on. New Comedy has essentially always been tragicomedy, having a laugh at acquiring one or more secular identities and then losing all, with hope for the generation that follows.

4. JESUS VS. GOD IN SARAMAGO'S NOVEL

Fast forward to the last decade of the twentieth century, and a novel that is both saturated with the life-and-death theme of New Comedy and itself a daring essay in humanist comedy. It may also be recognizable as a historical novel, one of thousands of such drawing on the contribution of Scott to modern historicism. Just possibly, in *The Gospel According to Jesus Christ* (1991), José Saramago was influenced by Lawrence's "The Man Who Died." Saramago's postmodernist novel begins in the present tense with a description of what appears to be one of countless paintings of the crucifixion, the narrator remarking the source of light and duly identifying the figures surrounding Christ on the cross. This beginning consists of a single paragraph of about twenty-two hundred words. There are no named or numbered chapters in the novel; however, breaks in narrative time are typically marked by the start of a new page. Thus the next portion introduces the reader to young Joseph the carpenter awakening before dawn, whispering his customary prayer of thanks to God, and going outside to urinate, where the only other creature stirring is his donkey.

In the translation by Giovanni Pontiero, Joseph then "praised God who in His infinite wisdom had endowed mankind with the essential orifices and vessels to live, for if any one of them should fail to close or open as required, the result would be death." (Note the wry application of a vocabulary not likely to be the character's own, typical of Saramago's irony.) Dawn approaches with such clouds and light as Joseph has never seen, and he is for a moment terrified, mindful of old tales of signs from heaven. But when he reenters the house Mary is awake "listening, staring into space, as if waiting," and they make love. "God, who is omnipresent, was there but, pure spirit that He is, was unable to see how Joseph's flesh touched Mary's, how his flesh penetrated her flesh as had been ordained. . . . Out in the yard, God could hear neither the gasp that escaped Joseph's lips as he came nor the low moan Mary was unable to suppress" (11–13).[56]

The first third of *The Gospel According to Jesus Christ* is essentially told from Joseph's point of view, but all of the novel adopts the human point of view—more particularly a male view, for one historical observation that Saramago makes early on and repeatedly demonstrates is the subordination of women in this culture. Mary has her own intimations of divine (or devilish) goings-on but keeps them to herself; and the notion of a virgin mother is nowhere admitted. Joseph, by then a father of at least six children by Mary, will himself be crucified by Roman soldiers at the age of thirty-three. After that, the point of view becomes mainly that of Jesus but returns several times to that of the family he leaves behind. A novel that commences graphically with the crucifixion and holds to that action in the end nonetheless reads like a comedy because of a distancing in the vocabulary employed, the matter-of-fact dialogues of human and divine voices, the cross-examination by Jesus of God's motives, the value attributed to *this* life, including intimate sexual companionship, and the encompassing irony of this *Gospel* compared with those of the canonical evangelists, from which Saramago borrows most of his supernatural effects. That it is a tragicomedy goes without saying.

Indeed it would be hard to imagine a novel more dedicated to New Comedy's theme of the passing generations. The affirmation of this life is punctuated by the emphasis on mortality throughout. Even the tall beggar (angel or devil) who comes to the door in Nazareth when Mary is alone and performs the annunciation, makes the point: "Earth to earth, ashes to ashes, dust to dust, nothing begins without coming to an end, every beginning comes from an ending. . . . Good woman, you have a child in your womb and that is man's only destiny, to begin and end, to end and begin." Or the narrator will begin a new chapter, "Since the world began, for every person who is born another dies." The mortal protagonists a number of times pass by Rachel's tomb near Jerusalem (Genesis 35:20)—Rachel, the mother of Joseph and Benjamin, who looks out for the children of generations to come. When Joseph the carpenter comes this way, he reflects that "children die because their fathers beget them and their mothers bring them into the world, and he took pity on his own son, who was condemned to die although innocent" (17, 60, 66–67). By this account the child Jesus is everychild. Even so, the vitality and promise of humanity inhere in children.

When Joseph's own time has come round, he too is innocent. He has traveled with that donkey in search of one of his neighbors who has joined a group of Jewish insurgents determined to oppose the avaricious Roman rule of Galilee. The Roman soldiers have been merciless, crucifying every armed opponent they can put their hands on. Our carpenter is swept up along with the insurgents, even though they testify that he is not one of them. A rebel who befriends Joseph to this extent stoically remarks that none of them is likely to escape the same fate. "God will save you," Joseph ventures; and the rebel responds, "Surely you're forgetting that God saves souls rather than bodies" (129). That kind of repartee and the whole notion that a normally stay-at-home Joseph should suffer the same fate as his eldest son Jesus will suffer set the tone of *The Gospel*, which reads like a parable or set of parables. Death indeed awaits every animal and human being; as the end of life, death is the worst thing that will happen to the individual being in question; theoretically God might alter the how, when, and where of the death, but he does not intervene, according to this historical novel, except when it is in his interest to do so.

As in the synoptic gospels, Jesus is born in Bethlehem and laid in a manger, but here the birth takes place in a nearby cave. Joseph, who has found casual employment in Jerusalem, happens to overhear talk among soldiers of Herod's order to slay all the male children in Bethlehem up to the age of two (Matthew 2:16). He runs all the way to the cave and tells Mary that they must flee, though in the event they remain safely hidden in the cave while cries of horror and grief are heard from Bethlehem, before making off at dawn over untraveled ways toward Nazareth. This episode leaves Joseph troubled for the remainder of his life by a dream of killing his own son, so guiltily aware has he become that he never stopped to warn the parents of other infant boys in Bethlehem. When young Jesus eventually hears of his father's endless guilt feelings, he adopts them as his own and soon suffers a correspondent nightmare of his father bent on killing him to make up for his sin. This is the singular sin attributed to Joseph and Jesus in the novel, and after all it is a sin of forgetfulness rather than a deliberate act. Their persistent feelings of guilt do reflect a moral awareness of doing to others as we would have them do to us (Matthew 7:12; Luke 6:31). The dreams are uncanny and, like so many things in the novel, open to interpretation. Violence between father and son is the stuff of Western tragedy, but the filicide in the dreams of these two has most likely been displaced and denotes God's intended use of Jesus.

When Joseph the father does not return on that fatal day he went to look for his missing neighbor, the boy Jesus, as the eldest son, accompanies Mary his mother, runs ahead and locates Joseph's broken corpse, the last of forty who have been crucified by the Roman soldiers. Mary and Jesus are understandably overcome with grief and bafflement—and the nightmare. She now confides that "your father dreamt he was a soldier marching with other soldiers on their way to kill you," and he exclaims, "But that's my dream" (149–50). Two days after this, despite his mother's protests, Jesus leaves home and carpenter's shop to his brothers and sisters in order to work out his guilt and remorse by traveling to his birthplace, the cave near Bethlehem where Joseph first experienced the dream. He encounters one Salome, the midwife who helped deliver him, and they talk of the children who had to die when "the angel of death, disguised as Herod's soldiers, descended into Bethlehem and slew them." It was the will of God, she tells him. But Jesus "hardly heard Salome's words, because it suddenly dawned on him that man is a mere toy in the hands of God and forever subject to His will, whether he imagines himself to be obeying or disobeying Him" (180–81).

Saramago's novel becomes a sort of bildungsroman as Jesus comes of age and learns from the world nearby. Left alone in the cave, he falls asleep and dreams of mothers with dead infants in their arms but is awakened by a lightning flash and the presence of a tall figure like the one who first appeared to Mary as a beggar. Now this anthropoid is dressed as a shepherd—"call me Pastor"—who claims he has known Jesus since he was born. Eventually the reader ascertains that he is neither beggar nor shepherd but the devil. Meanwhile Jesus, who has no means of supporting himself, offers to help tend the flock and is accepted: "I was waiting for you to ask," says Pastor (187). The next four years would seem to correspond to Jesus's forty days in the wilderness and temptation by Satan (Matthew 4:1–11; Luke 4:1–13). Even in the Bible it has to be said that the relation of God and the devil is somewhat mysterious. Here, at least, the savior-to-be learns a good deal about caring for an extraordinarily large flock of sheep.

A turning point comes when Jesus decides to celebrate Passover in Jerusalem for the first time without his family. Pastor doesn't mind, though he himself never prays (and is not Jewish). Instead, he tempts Jesus by saying he may take one of their clean lambs along for sacrifice if he likes. But Jesus becomes wary and is not prepared to sacrifice one of the lambs he has helped care for in any case. Whatever lamb he sacrifices, this devil points out, someone will have cared for it. Without the customary lamb or the money to purchase one, Jesus stoops to begging with his hand held out before he enters the Temple. An elderly, well-to-do patriarch tells his family to give Jesus one of the lambs they are bringing to sacrifice. But when his benefactors move out of sight, "Jesus pressed his lamb to his breast, unable to fathom why God could not be appeased with a cup of milk poured over His altar, that sap of life which passes from one being to another, or with a handful of wheat, the basic substance of immortal bread." Moreover, "then Jesus decided, in defiance of the law of the synagogue and the word of God, that this lamb would not die, that what he had received to deliver to the altar would continue to live and that he would leave Jerusalem a greater sinner than when he arrived" (208–9). With a shock he next sees coming along the road his brothers James, Joseph, and Judas, his sister Lisa, and his mother Mary, who bursts into tears. He has to tell them he is not going to the Temple and the lamb will not be sacrificed. He gets into an argument with Mary, who has heard from and glimpsed that tall creature from a distance more than once and calls him a demon. She may be right, but this episode does not end until Jesus has returned to Pastor, tended the sheep again for a while, and met God in the desert while searching for the very sheep whose life he saved. Or rather, on that day he comes upon God in a column of smoke, hears the voice of God.

Terrifying as this first encounter must be, the staccato dialogue that follows might be staged by clowns: "You brought me here, what do You want with me. For the moment nothing, but the day will come when I will want everything. What is everything. Your life. You are the Lord, You always take from us the life you gave us. There is no other way, I cannot allow the world to become overcrowded." Jesus will know all in good time; in exchange for that life "I will give you power and glory." But Jesus pesters God with more questions: "Can I save my sheep. So that's what's bothering you. Yes, that's all, may I. No. Why not. Because you must offer it in sacrifice to Me to seal our covenant. You mean this sheep. Yes. Let me choose another from the flock, I'll be right back. You heard Me, I want this one." Jesus has not even a knife on him, but "a brand-new cleaver" suddenly appears at his feet. "The cleaver went up, took aim, and came down as swiftly as an executioner's ax or the guillotine, which has not yet been invented. The sheep did not even whimper. All one could hear was, Ah, as God gave a deep sigh of satisfaction" (220–22).[57]

Afterward, when Pastor asks him why he sacrificed the sheep, Jesus replies, "Because God was there and I had no choice." Pastor takes his crook, carves a line on the ground, and replies, "You've learned nothing, begone with you" (222; in Matthew 4:10 Jesus tells Satan to be gone). Arguably, Jesus has refused the devilish temptation to defy God and save his favorite sheep—and perhaps that is what his four years in the wilderness are all about. Shepherds do not sacrifice their sheep, especially in this vague pasturage that is by no means conducted as a business. Saramago offers it as a zoological parable, the brief chance to live that sheep and humans share. The boy in Jesus has almost come of age, though after this parting he dreams that the last words of Pastor might have been spoken by his father. Reviewing his life so far, he asks himself, "Why should a lamb rescued from death eventually die as a sheep, an absurd question if ever there was one, it might make more sense if rephrased as follows, No salvation lasts, and damnation is final" (225).

Without quite deciding to return to Nazareth, Jesus turns northward along the banks of the Jordan. While resting and cooling his torn feet, he hears a woman singing, imagines that she is naked, and feels the blood rush to his genitals, just as it does with all animals. He takes pleasure in watching the fishermen at work in the Sea of Galilee for a couple of days and actually goes out on the lake with two brothers named Simon and Andrew. Before they come back to shore empty-handed, Jesus asks them to cast their nets again, with the result that their catch is now full. But the immediate turn in the life of Jesus will not yet be that of his ministry and miracle making, but of coming of age as a man by making love with a woman. Pacing painfully west toward Nazareth and his family, he finds one foot bleeding so badly that he calls for help at a house near a town called Magdala. Behold, this is the house of prostitution operated by Mary Magdalene, with not just a mat on the floor but a real bed. She takes Jesus in, tends to his foot, falls directly in love, and makes a man of him. "While you live with me, I will not be a whore, I stopped being one the moment you came into this house." Jesus remarks in turn, "It took me eighteen years to get here" (238). Mary teaches him the art of love; Jesus responds both physically and by murmuring verses from the Song of Solomon as if he understood them for the first time. She puts the sign up on the gate to indicate that she is occupied, and he stays with her a week before going on to seek his family in Nazareth.

In classical New Comedy at least it was not uncommon for a young man and a prostitute to fall in love and for the two to marry in the end. During that week Jesus confides in Mary Magdalene and tells her of the persistent dream of his father coming to kill him as a child. The four years since he left home commenced with the death of that father, crucified for something he never did or thought of doing, though possessed of a conscience riven by guilt for not having tried to save other infant boys in Bethlehem from Herod's cowardly slaughter. After this week of sleeping with Mary Magdalene, Jesus will no longer experience the dream. Sexual bonding is the joyous way to anticipate the passing of each generation. Contrast God's Scrooge-like purpose of decreasing the surplus population.

Jesus's reunion with his family in Nazareth is even more uncomfortable than his encounter with five of them in Jerusalem. Neither his mother nor his brothers believe he has seen God. He abruptly returns to the house in Magdala and the other Mary, who is older than Jesus but expressly not old enough to be his mother, and proclaims to her, "I have seen God," before spending the rest of the night telling her his story: a gospel memoir within *The Gospel According to Jesus Christ*. Mary's rejoinder to this story: "You have to be a woman to know what it means to live with God's contempt, and now you'll have to be more than a man to live and die as one of His chosen" (259–60). They live together in Magdala for several weeks before they move out, leaving the mocking neighbors behind and the house of prostitution in flames. In another far stretch from the synoptic gospels, Jesus and Mary Magdalene not only make love but remain together until the end. Mary stays with Jesus as disciples gather, miracles occur, and the mission expands. They sleep together, she comforts him and advises him to the best of her ability. She is the only person to whom he tells everything. An angel meanwhile appears to the other Mary to inform her that she was mistaken not to believe Jesus and that God wants her to be near when her son dies.

At the wedding in Cana the two Marys embrace, but Jesus denies his mother: "Woman, what have I to do with you" (291; compare John 2:4). It is hard to imagine God wanting Mary Magdalene present at the crucifixion, however. She has her own opinions about what Jesus has confided to her: "Frankly, ever since you came into my life, I never felt I was lying with the son of a god. You mean of God. If only you weren't" (347). Jesus speaks good-naturedly here, but there is an edge to Mary's voice, and sadness. She is the frank spokesperson for humanity and a bit cynical: "The one thing God cannot do is not love Himself." In this *Gospel* without question death confronts every living human or animal being, and for Mary that's the worst thing. So she interferes, successfully, with the raising of Lazarus from the dead because that will mean Lazarus has to die all over again. All Jesus has to say is, "Lazarus, arise, and Lazarus will rise from the dead, because it is the will of God, but at the very last moment Mary Magdalene placed a hand on Jesus' shoulder and said, No one has committed so much sin in his life that he deserves to die twice, and dropping his arms, Jesus went outside to weep" (341, 362). Because Saramago conflates Mary Magdalene with the Mary of Mary and Martha (Luke 10:38–42; John 11:1–44), Martha is her sister and Lazarus her brother.

In Saramago's historical novel two outstanding differences from the synoptic gospels are the crucifixion of Joseph the carpenter and the role of Mary Magdalene. Joseph's crucifixion is obviously harder to interpret than Mary's role. The Bible does not record Joseph's destiny; crucifixion is a bit much. Saramago stresses not only the inevitable death of each generation but also the murderous cruelty of mankind. The Roman soldiery never hesitates to torture and to kill. Their means need not have been invented by God, except in the sense that God has created the whole shebang. Men are capable of cruelty uncharacteristic of most of the animal kingdom. On the other hand, men and women, as in the life of Jesus and Mary Magdalene imagined here, are capable of bonding both sexually and trustfully, socially and intimately, more so than other creatures. The couple share thoughts as well as nature's calls for sexual reproduction, eating, and sleeping. But these two innovations are not the only surprises in Saramago's gospel *segundo*.

The Gospel According to Jesus Christ includes a lengthy face-to-face meeting between God and Jesus. This is God's way of preparing Jesus for his destined role and Jesus's chance to cross-examine God about his plan and the future. The dramatic dialogue calls for Saramago's most able humanist gamesmanship, calculated to amuse his readers even while conceding their mortality. Following a discussion with the disciples (here designated simply the "friends" of Jesus and Mary) about whether he is the son of God or perhaps the Messiah, and after the not-so-simple miracle of the loaves and fishes ("we know what he did, but will never know how he managed it"), Jesus goes out alone on the Sea of Galilee one unseasonably misty morning, when he "sees that this is the day he has been waiting for" (300–4, 305). As he rows along he is totally surrounded by fog until suddenly there comes a light, and he sees God sitting athwart the stern of the boat. This time God appears as a tall man, elderly and dressed as a well-to-do Jew. Jesus speaks first: "Here I am. . . . I've come to find out who I am and what I must do henceforth to fulfill my part of the covenant." As they converse God seems to become increasingly anthropomorphic because of the give-and-take and the colloquial, matter-of-fact language. Jesus is emphatically a man, a human mortal being, part of the point of The Gospel throughout. He wants to know what the devil meant by telling him he was the son of God. God slowly nods his agreement. "But how can a man be the son of God. If you're the son of God, you are not a man. But I am a man, I breathe, I eat, I sleep, and I love like a man, therefore I am a man and will die as a man. In your case I wouldn't be too sure." Jesus next hears the sound of someone swimming and sees God smiling. This proves to be Pastor, a second "creature with human form." Pastor is not a good swimmer. God introduces him as the devil, and he spends the rest of the dialogue in the water clinging to one side of the boat with his arm and occasionally contributing a few words. "Jesus looked from one to the other and saw that without God's beard they could have passed for twins, although the devil was younger and less wrinkled" (307–10). In the event, God does admit that the two work together.

The mismatch of styles and subject matter can scarcely fail to make the dialogue entertaining. God speaks with congenial seniority, the mature Jesus with lawyerlike insistence and irony, and Satan with the familiarity of old. The subject is nothing less than God's illimitable power and his immediate plans for deploying it. Under questioning from Jesus he explains his motives for having a son who shall be crucified, his desire to establish a catholic church, and something of what the next couple of millennia have in store for humanity. God explains that, after 4004 years with the Jews—the last four evidently coinciding with Jesus's years with Pastor—he wants help "to spread My word, to help Me become the god of more people. . . . And what is this part You have reserved for me in Your plan. That of martyr, My son, that of victim, which is the best role of all for propagating any faith and stirring up fervor." His son recalls the promise of power and glory sounded from the column of smoke in the desert, but now face to face in this small boat he goes right to the point. "What good will it do for me to have power and glory when I'm dead. Well, you won't be dead in the absolute sense of the word, for as My son you'll be with Me, or in Me, I still haven't decided." But under further questioning it seems God *has* decided on crucifixion because "a martyr's death should be painful and, if possible, ignominious, that the believers may be moved to greater devotion." That seems questionable, except perhaps with believers who themselves feel deprived, demeaned, or ashamed of themselves. Jesus immediately thinks of his father; but now God has clearly chosen him, and he begins to protest: "I want to end our covenant, to have nothing more to do with You, I want to live like any other man" (311–12). But, as he once again is informed, everything prescribed by God must come to pass.

Completely disillusioned, Jesus tells God and the devil to get lost, so to speak—to go back by air or sea the way they came, while he makes his own way home. When neither of them stirs or speaks, the designated savior jeers, "Then you prefer to go by boat, better still, I'll row you ashore myself so that everyone can see how alike God and the devil are and how well they get on together." But try as he might, straining on the oars, he cannot make the boat head toward shore. Sitting in the stern is the power that rules the universe, who now speaks poetically, "You are the lamb of

God, My son, which God himself will carry to the altar we are preparing here" (313, 315). From this time on Jesus essentially submits to his fate, without ceding that God has the better argument or forgetting their differences when it comes to sacrificial lambs. God is pleased, and at his adopted son's request tells him—reluctantly—more of his intentions and the times ahead.

A church will be established by those who follow Jesus Christ "as their spiritual leader." God cautions his chosen son, however, that even this "will last no more than several thousand years, for I was here before you and will continue to be here after you cease to be what you are and what you will be." Historical time will thus extend beyond the time of writing of this novel, and God's omniscience has no limit either, though he can be distracted or forgetful in his account of the future. Jesus wants to know if his followers will be happier than at present. "Not in the true sense of the word," is the answer, "but they will have the hope of achieving happiness up in heaven, where I reign for all eternity and where they hope to live eternally with Me" (319). God confirms that only angels accompany him in heaven at present and once again indicates that any similar accommodation for human beings awaits the upcoming crucifixion—a reminder that sends an inward shudder through his questioner.

How much suffering of others, how much suffering altogether will the founding of a Christian church require? "You insist on knowing. I do. Very well then, the church I mentioned will be established, but its foundation, in order to be truly solid, will be dug in flesh, its walls made from the cement of renunciation, tears, agony, anguish, every conceivable form of death." And Saramago scripts, for God's part in the dialogue no less, one of the longest and surely the darkest of satiric catalogues in Western literature. "Let's start with someone you know and love"—the cruel deaths of the disciples, one after the other. Go on, Jesus insists. "God sighed, and in the monotonous tone of one who chooses to suppress compassion He began a litany, in alphabetical order so as not to hurt any feelings about precedence and importance" (320–21), a list of the names and manner of death of approximately 170 saints and martyrs.

That slight rhetorical trick is a favorite with Saramago: he takes an idiom like "in alphabetical order" that most readers recognize and then spells out its commonplace meaning in alternative language, in this case, "so as not to hurt any feelings about precedence and importance." That much is the narrator's voice, not God's direct discourse. Throughout *The Gospel According to Jesus Christ* intrusions of this voice, sometimes ironically concerned with the implicit inadequacies of any given vocabulary, help prevent the gospel story from being wholly satiric *or* tragic. In the present case, isn't the novelist slyly suggesting that either he or God must have taken the names of the saints and martyrs from an existing alphabetical index in the first place? Let us run through Saramago's catalogue of gruesome deaths faster by omitting the names altogether, since they provide no historical or truly relevant order. Here is what shall happen— and it is God who now speaks as if he might be reading aloud—to those martyrs whose names begin with the first three letters of the alphabet:

> put to death with a seven-pronged pikestaff . . . hammered to death over an anvil . . . burned at the stake . . . burned at the stake hanging by his feet . . . disemboweled . . . crucified and impaled on nails . . . stabbed six times . . . beaten to death with the shinbone of an ox . . . burned at the stake and her breasts cut off . . . strung up on the gallows and decapitated . . . his entrails ripped out . . . drawn and quartered . . . stoned and burned alive . . . clubbed to death . . . burned at the stake after her teeth had been knocked out . . . decapitated and burned at the stake . . . drowned with a millstone around her neck . . . bled to death by being forced onto a chair covered with nails . . . shot with arrows . . . decapitated . . . likewise . . . stoned and burned at the stake . . . strangled . . . speared to death . . . thrown onto iron spikes . . . gored by a savage bull . . . put to death with a millstone around his neck . . . stabbed with a dagger by his disciples . . . buried alive . . . decapitated . . . beheaded . . . tortured repeatedly with millstones tongs, arrows, and snakes . . . decapitated . . . likewise . . . drowned with an anchor around his neck . . . both decapitated . . . disemboweled . . . beheaded . . . killed by a judge who knocked his head against the stairs of the tribunal, and on reaching the end of the letter C, God said, And so on, it's all much the same, with a few variations and an occasional refinement which would take forever to explain, so let's leave it at that.

But Jesus insists that he continue; and God reluctantly obliges still more cursorily through letter R before he pauses again: "Have you had enough, God asked Jesus, who retorted, That's something You should ask Yourself, go on" (321–22, 324). With two such brief interludes Saramago maintains the drama of a catalogue at once stupefying and stultifying.

After his alphabetized account of martyrdom is complete, God casually refers to self-inflicted torments of the flesh that will be practiced by some followers of Jesus, mortifications of the body by which to repent their sins and to pray for their souls. That draws Jesus's attention also. It seems there will not only be those who wear hair shirts and flagellate themselves but also others who perch on pillars or retreat to the desert to live solitary lives. The narrator adds that as "His voice fell and died away, God was now contemplating an endless procession of people, thousands upon thousands of men and women throughout the world entering convents and monasteries, some buildings rustic, many palatial." These are the same religious that Erasmus looked askance at; here God seems almost as skeptical, or bored, when he continues, "They will call themselves Benedictines, Cistercians, Carthusians, Augustinians, Gilbertines, Trinitarians, Franciscans, Dominicans, Capuchins, Carmelites, Jesuits." Without much prompting he goes on to mention that there will be wars and massacres, wars fought in the name of another god yet to appear (presumably referring to Allah and the Muslim religion), plus the Crusades and internecine religious wars to follow. And then there's the Inquisition—what is that? God is tired, doesn't really wish to go into this; but the Inquisition is a kind of police force and tribunal, he says, directed against heresies and perversions identified with such as "Lutherans and Calvinists, Molinists and Judaizers, sodomites and sorcerers." The Inquisition sentences heretics to prison, exile, or the stake. "Did You say the stake. Yes, in days to come, thousands upon thousands of men and women will be burned at the stake." Jesus is puzzled because earlier God has dwelt upon and even catalogued so many followers, martyrs to the new faith, who are also destined to be burned or otherwise tortured to death. The plaintiff has been fairly sharp throughout at cross-examining the defendant. Now God himself, the strategic planner of events to come, blandly utters the most self-damning anomaly in his design: "They will be burned alive because they believe in you, others because they doubt you" (326, 329–30).

Almost any reader's instinct must be to laugh at this capsule summary of early Christianity, if only from surprise. Such an incongruous conjunction of tortures has never likely occurred to most people. Other readers will immediately see that there is a problem and laugh uneasily since laughter brings relief. Even silent readers do not like to feel themselves alone, so it is better to laugh in any case when no answer immediately comes to mind. Given time, theologians or ecclesiastics shall work the problem round to resolve the anomaly of believers and unbelievers alike being burned alive, but laughing is one way to gain time. Actually, Saramago's devil has already ventured an observation similar to God's, though less succinctly delivered. The devil's part in this long dialogue amid the mist covering the Sea of Galilee is mostly passive. When he does put in a word, he seems to empathize with mortals. No doubt that's why he's called the devil: men, women, and children are often said to be devilish—or sometimes just sorry devils—and he has to get close in order to tempt them. This devil also gets the last word on his master's offhand summaries of future Christians' experience: "One has to be God to countenance so much blood," he remarks (330).

The issue of repentance arises in the dialogue when Jesus asks God what kind of ministry is expected of him. What should he say to the people? Well, there is one thing all men, "whatever their race, color, creed, or philosophy," have in common: they are all sinners. Hence "the only word no man can say does not apply to him is repentance, because all have succumbed to temptation, entertained an evil thought, broken a rule, committed some crime, serious or minor, spurned a soul in need, neglected a duty, offended religion and its ministers, or turned away from God, to all such men you need only say, Repent, repent, repent." Jesus protests that it shouldn't be necessary to sacrifice his life for this purpose: another prophet or two should do the trick. God argues that the time for prophets has passed; nowadays something stronger is needed: "Such as a son of God hanging from a cross. Yes, why not. And what else am I supposed to say to these people, besides urging them to repent." It is Jesus who calls repentance into question, even though he and his earthly father before him mourned and regretted so deeply the deaths of the male children of Bethlehem, which Joseph might have prevented. But so might God have saved those children. God agrees that people may get tired of hearing about repentance, but Jesus should be able to think of other lines to take: "Look at the cunning way you avoided sacrificing your lamb. That was easy enough, the animal had nothing to repent" (316–17). Saramago plays with the gospel of repentance as another means of recruitment: repent and in the end you'll go places, beyond the grave, maybe to heaven. As for punishments, whether for believers or unbelievers, that is an issue over which the devil also interrupts the conversation: "I don't recall having invented sin and punishment or the terror they inspire. Be quiet, God snapped, sin and the devil are one and the same thing. What thing is that, asked Jesus. My absence" (325–26). Who instigated repentance then, if not humanity?

With its insistence on death Saramago's novel has New Comedy's affirmation of life, coupled, to be sure, with a humanist agenda. The action includes the passing of two male generations: Joseph's wrongful crucifixion coincides with Jesus's puberty; Mary and Mary Magdalene outlive Jesus's own crucifixion. *The Gospel According to Jesus Christ* comes down firmly and confidently on the side of human mortality. At the same time it conducts recognizable humanist games with the deity's extraordinary powers and anthropomorphic emotions and especially his good intentions—the old puzzle of how an omnipotent and omniscient God could ever want to be in charge of this world he has created. Saramago cheerfully puts the question to the reader whether the Christian faith has brought more happiness into the world than unhappiness, not to say violence and mayhem historically committed in its name. Like humanists of early modern times, he doesn't try to resolve such questions or force his readers to choose.

Appropriately, some of the setups employed by those humanists are also invoked in this retake, including the polytheism of classical times. Jesus wonders whether people will accept his newly attained divinity, and the question produces this exchange with God: "Isn't it permitted to doubt me. No. Yet we're allowed to doubt that the Jupiter of the Romans is god. I am the one and only Lord God, and you are My son" (330). Or there is a longer exchange between this divine father and son that brings out Jesus's instinctive preference (honed by Mary Magdalene) for life on earth. Again, how do we know people will believe in me: "Take the Gentiles and Romans, for example, who worship other gods, You don't expect me to believe they will give them up just like that to worship me. Not to worship you but to worship Me." Their divine give-and-take concludes, "Men have always died for gods, even for false and lying gods. Can gods lie. They can. And You are the one and only true god among them. Yes, the one and only true god. Yet You are unable to prevent men from dying for You when they should have been born to live for You on earth rather than in heaven, where You have none of life's joys to offer them. Those joys too are false, for they come from original sin, ask your friend Pastor, he'll explain what happened" (319–20).

If it seems strange for the one and only God to speak familiarly of other gods at large, consider another passage in the dialogue when God solemnly claims to respect a formal treaty among the gods. This time Jesus is arguing that, instead of staging the crucifixion of his son with the aim of increasing his own following among the peoples of the world, "wouldn't it be simpler and more honest for You to go out and conquer those other countries and races Yourself." God answers—and surely he has to be kidding—"Alas, I cannot, it is forbidden by the binding agreement between the gods ever to interfere directly, can you imagine Me in a public square, surrounded by Gentiles and pagans, trying to persuade them that their god is false while I am their real God, this is not something one god does to another." Rather, as usual man is the best tool at hand. With a sensibility recalling that of Epicurus and Lucretius, thoughtfulness like that of Montaigne, and certainty anticipating the anthropology of Ludwig Feuerbach, God graciously adds, "Man generally speaking is the best thing that ever happened to the gods" (313). But such gestures toward polytheism are aberrations in this dialogue. It is basically God and the designated savior one-on-one.[58]

The fog covering the sea begins to lift, and suddenly their dramatic confrontation is at an end: "Jesus looked around, but God was no longer there . . . no sign of the devil in the water, no sign of God in the air." He rows toward shore and when he looks over his shoulder sees his disciples and others launching boats to meet him halfway. Jesus imagines he has been at sea for a day and a night at most, but Simon corrects him: "Forty days, shouted Simon, then lowering his voice, You've been on the lake forty days" (332–33). By such means Saramago keeps the reader guessing, both as to the supposed facts of the representation and the significance of forty days. Another parable of temptation by the devil? or recalling Moses's forty days and nights with God laying down the law on the mountain (Exodus 24:18)? For the remaining days of his ministry, however,

Jesus himself seems resigned to the excruciating end that awaits him. We are told little of his thoughts other than what can be deduced from his words and motions. That does not exclude some wry observations along the way, as when a soldier apologetically whispers in his ear that he has to obey orders, and Jesus replies, "A king does not arrest another king, a god does not kill another god, and that is why ordinary men were created, so that arrests and killings could be left to them" (370). On that last day Mary Magdalene comes forth from their tent weeping at his side. To Pontius Pilate, and over the objections of the High Priest, Jesus insists on being crucified for posing as King of the Jews rather than claiming to be the Son of God. The former title will do the business, and he has no desire to oblige his heavenly father with the latter. Saramago does not mince words when his protagonist's hands are nailed to the transom of the cross and hoisted up, the entire weight of his body suspended from the hands until his legs are driven against the post, for Jesus "feels the pain as his father felt it before him" (376).

Jesus is dying, dying when the heavens above open and God the father appears, "and His words resound throughout the earth, This is My beloved son, in whom I am well pleased." But the man Jesus, not the immortal God, gets the last word: "Remembering the river of blood and suffering that would flow from his side and flood the globe, he called out to the open sky, where God could be seen smiling, Men, forgive Him, for He knows not what He has done" (376–77). The message parodies Luke 23:34, "Father, forgive them"—the men who have crucified him—"for they know not what they do." Just so Saramago's novel serves as another tragicomedy of the passing generations. Jesus innocently suffers a torturous death, as his innocent father has before him, but he has learned to value this life and intimacy with Mary Magdalene. He dies but not before getting the best of the argument in the case of Jesus vs. God. The summary of future events that cross-examination elicits from God himself provides the test of history still to come. At least a humanist *viewpoint* is the one to prevail here. Such is *The Gospel According to Jesus Christ* according to José Saramago.

In his *Anatomy of Criticism*, Northrop Frye traced the several broad categories of narrative and plays—comedy, romance, tragedy, and irony— to four *mythoi*, or myths respectively associated with the seasons—spring, summer, autumn (familiarly known as the fall), and winter. Few would deny that New Comedy often mounts a tragic crescendo before persisting with its happy end. Frye pulls way back in his overview of the *mythoi*, or pre-generic plots, and states it this way: "The ritual pattern behind the catharsis of comedy is the resurrection that follows the death, the epiphany or manifestation of the risen hero." As elsewhere in the *Anatomy* he has in mind the Bible and religious convictions as well as the vast scope of classical, medieval, and modern literature: "Christianity, too, sees tragedy as an episode in the divine comedy, the larger scheme of redemption and resurrection. The sense of tragedy as a prelude to comedy seems almost inseparable from anything explicitly Christian."[59] It would seem that not only are tragedy and comedy inseparable but that comedy dominates in an apocalyptic plot when the seasons, along with time, come to a stop.

Whether one smiles or is troubled by reading Saramago's historical novel, Frye's conclusion is worth bearing in mind. It is hard to imagine a work in which tragedy and comedy become more terrifically mixed. Saramago confirms the pairing of the two genres, for sure, but *The Gospel According to Jesus Christ* turns the received plot on its head. Had Frye lived longer, he must have delegated Saramago's novel to the *mythos* of winter— that is, Irony, dragging out the darkness between autumnal tragedy and springtime comedy.[60] Jesus dies; all of his fellow human beings die. It is God who goes on living—more or less happily ever after. The future course of history that the immortal one grudgingly reveals to his adopted son is grim, to say the least. Deaths with torture piled on. For two millennia now. You have to laugh.

NOTES

ACT ONE. LAUGHTER AT THE GODS IN CLASSICAL TIMES

1. Stephen Halliwell, *Greek Laughter: A Study of Cultural Psychology from Homer to Early Christianity* (Cambridge: Cambridge University Press, 2008), 3. Halliwell's thoroughgoing study is devoted to a history of laughter, on the principle that the immediate cultural context tends to determine what is laughable or not.

2. *The Homeric Hymns*, trans. Michael Crudden (New York: Oxford University Press, 2001). Line numbers in parentheses.

3. Norman O. Brown, *Hermes the Thief: The Evolution of a Myth* (Madison: University of Wisconsin Press, 1947), 71–72, 127–28.

4. Erich Auerbach, *Mimesis: The Representation of Reality in Western Literature*, trans. Willard R. Trask (Princeton: Princeton University Press, 1983), 3–23.

5. Cedric H. Whitman, *Aristophanes and the Comic Hero*, Martin Classical Lectures 19 (Cambridge: Harvard University Press, 1964). Whitman did not list Cario. *Wealth* has been thought to anticipate the New Comedy of the fourth century, and Cario is not formally the protagonist.

6. All quotations are from *Aristophanes*, ed. and trans. Jeffrey Henderson, 4 vols., Loeb Classical Library (Cambridge: Harvard University Press, 1998–2002). Line numbers in parentheses.

7. M. S. Silk, *Aristophanes and the Definition of Comedy* (Oxford: Oxford University Press, 2000), 221–43, treats such characters as "recreative" in a number of senses.

8. Aristophanes was disappointed that his earlier version of *Clouds* received third prize, so possibly he added this speech in revision. In the parabasis the chorus leader speaks undisguisedly for the playwright (518–62).

9. See Francis Cornford, *The Origin of Attic Comedy* (1913; rpt. Ann Arbor: University of Michigan Press, 1993).

10. Stephen Greenblatt, another fan in a long line of humanists, has championed Lucretius in *The Swerve: How the World Became Modern* (New York: Norton, 2011). Greenblatt also details how the enterprising Florentine collector Poggio Bracciolini first recovered a copy of *De rerum natura* in the early fifteenth century.

11. Lucretius, *De rerum natura*, trans. W. H. D. Rouse, rev. Martin Ferguson Smith, Loeb Classical Library (Cambridge: Harvard University Press, 1992). Book and line numbers in parentheses.

12. See Stephen Jay Gould, *Ontogeny and Phylogeny* (Cambridge: Harvard University Press, 1977).

13. Accounts of his influence from the Middle Ages to the twentieth century can be found in *The Cambridge Companion to Lucretius*, ed. Stuart Gillespie and Philip Hardie (Cambridge: Cambridge University Press, 2007), chaps. 12–19. See also Alison Brown, *The Return of Lucretius to Rennaisance Florence* (Cambridge: Harvard University Press, 2010).

14. Cicero's writings occupy twenty-eight volumes of the Loeb Classical Library, translated and revised by various scholars throughout the twentieth century. *Academica*, along with *De natura deorum*, can be found in vol. 19.

15. Cicero, *De oratore*, trans. E. W. Sutton and R. Rackham, Loeb Classical Library (1942; rpt. Cambridge: Harvard University Press, 1988), bk. 2, sect. 217, 230.

16. *De divinatione*, trans. William Armistead Falconer (1923; rpt. Cambridge: Harvard University Press, n.d.). The dialogue shares vol. 20 of the Loeb Cicero with *De senectute* and *De amicitia*. Book and section numbers in parentheses.

17. Cicero, *De natura deorum*, trans. H. Rackham, Loeb Classical Library (1933; rpt. Cambridge: Harvard University Press, 1979). Book and section numbers in parentheses.

18. The passage, in Latin, can be found in *Die Chronik des Hieronymous*, ed. Rudolf Helm (Berlin: Akademie-Verlag, 1956), 7:149. Jerome was translating from the Greek an already fragmented *Chronicle* of Eusebius but filled in passages of his own. For a sixteenth-century critique of Jerome's freewheeling translation, see Anthony Grafton's *Joseph Scaliger: A Study in the History of Classical Scholarship* (Oxford: Clarendon, 1993), 2:569–81.

19. Lucian, *Chattering Courtesans and Other Sardonic Sketches*, trans. Keith Sidwell (London: Penguin, 2004). Sidwell calls this dialogue "Two Charges of Literary Assault," but he appends a useful list of the varying titles of all the dialogues. Both Sidwell and Casson (note 20) provide paragraph numbering from M. D. Macleod's Oxford Classical Text of the Greek, and these numbers are given here in parentheses. Macleod was also one of the translators of the Loeb Classical Library *Lucian* (8 vols., 1913–67).

20. *Selected Satires of Lucian*, trans. Lionel Casson (New York: Norton, 1968). Between the two of them, Casson and Sidwell serve up a repast of highly readable translations from Lucian.

21. See David Marsh, *Lucian and the Latins: Humor and Humanism in the Early Renaissance* (Ann Arbor: University of Michigan Press, 1998); and Douglas Duncan, *Ben Jonson and the Lucianic Tradition* (Cambridge: Cambridge University Press, 1979).

22. Alberti's book was completed in 1450 but not printed until 1520. *Momus*, ed. and trans. Sarah Knight and Virginia Brown, I Tatti Renaissance Library (Cambridge: Harvard University Press, 2003), is the first English translation. Anthony Grafton, *Leon Battista Alberti: Master Builder of the Italian Renaissance* (New York: Farrar, Straus and Giroux, 2000), 305–11, sees the book as an allegory partly directed against Pope Nicholas V's penchant for papal palaces. But taken as a whole *Momus* might be read as a mock excursus in autobiographical fiction, Alberti the outsider in the character of the exiled and execrated god Momus. Lucian had not hesitated to portray himself in some of his dialogues.

23. In a book not to be missed, Peter Gay crafted five dialogues spoken by the ghosts of Lucian, Erasmus, and Voltaire: see *The Bridge of Criticism* (New York: Harper, 1970).

ACT TWO. HUMANIST GAMES IN CHRISTIAN TIMES

1. For classic treatments of parallel developments in the fine arts, see Erwin Panofsky, *Studies in Iconology: Humanistic Themes in the Art of the Renaissance* (New York: Oxford University Press, 1939); and Edgar Wind, *Pagan Mysteries in the Renaissance* (London: Faber and Faber, 1952).

2. Francis Bacon, *Essays, Advancement of Learning, New Atlantis, and Other Pieces* (New York: Odyssey Press, 1937), 8–9.

3. Ibid., 12.

4. See especially Auerbach's *Dante: Poet of the Secular World*, trans. Ralph Mannheim (Chicago: University of Chicago Press, 1961), 1–23.

5. For the design of this ironic project and its oratorical paradigm, see especially Walter Kaiser, *Praisers of Folly: Erasmus, Rabelais, Shakespeare* (London: Gollantz, 1964), 35–50; also David Marsh, *Lucian and the Latins: Humor and Humanism in the Early Renaissance* (Ann Arbor: University of Michigan Press, 1998), 148–80.

6. Erasmus, *Praise of Folly*, trans. Betty Radice (1971; rpt. London: Penguin, 1993). Page numbers in parentheses. Radice's translation is the same as that in the *Collected Works of Erasmus* (Toronto: University of Toronto Press, 1974–), vol. 27.

7. Erasmus's prefatory letter to More defends his stance; in turn, the inhabitants of Utopia "are very fond of fools. It is a great disgrace to treat them with insult, but there is no prohibition against deriving pleasure from their foolery. . . . If anyone is so stern and morose that he is not amused with anything they do or say, they do not entrust him with the care of a fool." St. Thomas More, *Utopia*, ed. Edward Surtz, S.J. (New Haven: Yale University Press, 1964), 113.

8. Except where noted, all quotations from the Bible are from the Revised Standard Version, specifically *The New Oxford Annotated Bible with the*

Apocrypha (New York: Oxford University Press, 1977). Obviously different translations of well-known passages like this may sound truer to some ears. Thus the Authorized or King James Bible writes "charity" for love here.

9. 1 Corinthians 2:9 in the King James version. Betty Radice quotes this but modernizes the verb forms.

10. *The Handbook of a Christian Soldier*, trans. Charles Fantazzi, *Collected Works of Erasmus*, 66:26.

11. Bacon, *Essays*, 8–9.

12. Erasmus, *Handbook of a Christian Soldier*, 86.

13. *The Complete works of Montaigne*, trans. Donald M. Frame (Stanford: Stanford University Press, 1957). Book, essay, and page numbers in parentheses, followed by page number of the Pléade edition, with its far more detailed annotation: Montaigne, *Oeuvres complètes*, ed. Albert Thibaudet and Maurice Rat (Paris: Gallimard, 1962). The letters A, B, C refer to portions of the text first published in 1580, 1588, and after 1588, respectively.

14. Richard H. Popkin, *The History of Scepticism: From Savonarola to Bayle*, rev. ed. (New York: Oxford University Press, 2003), 44–57. This is an expanded and updated version of the book first published in 1960. Popkin affords a detailed history of ideas surrounding the achievement of such as Montaigne, Descartes, Pascal, Hobbes, Spinoza, and Bayle.

15. See Peter Harrison, *"Religion" and the Religious in the English Enlightenment* (Cambridge: Cambridge University Press, 1990), 10–14.

16. Plutarch, *Moralia*, trans. Frank Cole Babbitt, Loeb Classical Library, 16 vols. (Cambridge: Harvard University Press, 1969), 5:384D–394C.

17. Seneca, *Naturales quaestiones*, trans. Thomas H. Corcoran, Loeb Classical Library (Cambridge: Harvard University Press, 1971), bk. 1, preface 5.

18. Hugo Friedrich, *Montaigne*, ed. Philippe Desan, trans. Dawn Eng (Berkeley: University of California Press, 1991), 104–5.

19. Thomas Hobbes, *Leviathan*, ed. Edwin Curley (Indianapolis: Hackett, 1994. References in parentheses to chapter and paragraph. This edition includes, in translation, selected variants from the Latin edition of 1668.

20. See Philip Pettit, *Made with Words: Hobbes on Language, Mind, and Politics* (Princeton: Princeton University Press, 2008).

21. See Quentin Skinner, "Hobbes on Representation," *European Journal of Philosophy* 13:2 (2005): 155–84; and Pettit, *Made with Words*, 55–69.

22. In a remarkable series of lectures Mark Lilla has argued that by this move Hobbes gave an irreversible turn to the standing and understanding of Christianity over time. See *The Stillborn God: Religion, Politics, and the Modern West* (New York: Knopf, 2007), 55–102.

23. Quentin Skinner, "Hobbes and the Classical Theory of Laughter," in his *Visions of Politics* (Cambridge: Cambridge University Press, 2002), 3:142–76.

24. Thomas Hobbes, *On the Citizen*, ed. and trans. Richard Tuck and Michael Silverthorne (Cambridge: Cambridge University Press, 1998). Parenthetical references to chapter and paragraph.

25. John Locke, *Two Treatises on Government* (London: Dent, 1988), Second Treatise, chap. 1. For an account of Locke's position on religious issues, including capital punishment, see Jeremy Waldron, *God, Locke, and Equality: Christian Foundations of Locke's Political Thought* (Cambridge: Cambridge University Press, 2002).

26. Benedict de Spinoza, *Theological-Political Treatise*, trans. Jonathan Israel and Michael Silverthorne (Cambridge: Cambridge University Press, 2007), 6. The reference to Hobbes is annotation 33. Chapter and paragraph numbers are in parentheses.

27. For an account of the excommunication, see Yirmiyahu Yovel, *Spinoza and Other Heretics*, vol. 1, *The Marrano of Reason* (Princeton: Princeton University Press, 1989), 3–13. Jonathan I. Israel, *Radical Enlightenment: Philosophy and the Making of Modernity, 1650–1750* (Oxford: Oxford University Press, 2001), 159–327, provides another detailed account of Spinoza's milieu and influence.

28. See Yovel, *The Marrano of Reason*, 128–52.

29. See J. Samuel Preus, *Spinoza and the Irrelevance of Biblical Authority* (Cambridge: Cambridge University Press, 2001), 162–66.

30. The Latin reads *res politicas*, but Israel and Silverthorne have preferred the amended text.

31. Quotations are from the text in *A Spinoza Reader: The "Ethics" and Other Works*, ed. and trans. Edwin Curley (Princeton: Princeton University Press, 1994). Curley is also the translator of Princeton's *Collected Works of Spinoza*, vol. 1 (1985), which I have consulted; but he has slightly revised his translation of *Ethics*, and the layout of the *Reader* text is much easier to follow. Curley's separate guide to the argument, *Behind the Geometrical Method: A Reading of Spinoza's "Ethics"* (Princeton: Princeton University Press, 1988), is also useful. Another lucid and straightforward assist is Steven B. Smith's *Spinoza's Book of Life: Freedom and Redemption in the "Ethics"* (New Haven: Yale University Press, 2003).

32. *The Philosophical Works of Descartes*, trans. Elizabeth S. Haldane and G. R. T. Ross, 2 vols. (Cambridge: Cambridge University Press, 1968), 1:165, 170. Descartes circulated his *Meditations* in manuscript and invited comments. Some of the most telling objections came from Hobbes and appear in this edition at 2:60–78.

33. A useful sorting out of proofs of the existence of God by Descartes and Spinoza respectively can still be consulted in Harry Austryn Wolfson, *The Philosophy of Spinoza: Unfolding the Latent Process of His Reasoning* (1934; rpt. 2 vols. in one, New York: Meridian, 1958), 1:176–213.

34. See Paul Oskar Kristeller, "Stoic and Neoplatonic Sources of Spinoza's *Ethics*," *History of European Ideas* 5 (1984): 1–15; Susan James, "Spinoza the Stoic," in *The Rise of Modern Philosophy*, ed. Tom Sorell (Oxford: Clarendon, 1993), 289–316; Jonathan I. Israel, *Enlightenment Contested: Philosophy, Modernity, and the Emancipation of Man, 1670–1752* (Oxford: Oxford University Press, 2006),

457–70; and Genevieve Lloyd, *Providence Lost* (Cambridge: Harvard University Press, 2008), 90–128, 129–234.

35. On Spinoza's third kind of knowledge, see Yovel, *The Marrano of Reason*, 154, 164–71.

36. The best introduction to this underground phenomenon is Silvia Berti, "The First Edition of the *Traité des trois imposteurs*, and Its Debt to Spinoza's *Ethics*," in *Atheism from the Reformation to the Enlightenment*, ed. Michael Hunter and David Wootton (Oxford: Clarendon, 1992), 183–220. See also Richard H. Popkin, *The Third Force in Seventeenth-Century Thought* (Leiden: Brill, 1992), 135–48; and Israel, *Radical Enlightenment*, 694–700. A translation of a French edition of 1777 is provided by Abraham Anderson, *The Treatise of the Three Impostors and the Problem of the Enlightenment* (Lanham, Penn.: Rowan and Littlefield, 1997).

37. Stuart Hampshire, *Spinoza and Spinozism* (Oxford: Clarendon, 2005), lv, xxiii.

38. Pierre Bayle, *Political Writings*, ed. and trans. Sally L. Jenkinson (Cambridge: Cambridge University Press, 2000), 263.

39. Pierre Bayle, *Historical and Critical Dictionary: Selections*, trans. Richard H. Popkin (1965; rpt. Indianapolis: Hackett, 1991), 51. There is little overlap between Popkin's and Jenkinson's selections from the *Dictionary*.

40. Ibid., 204 and n.

41. Elizabeth Labrousse, *Bayle*, trans. Denys Potts (Oxford: Oxford University Press, 1983), 87.

42. Pierre Bayle, *Various Thoughts on the Occasion of a Comet*, trans. Robert C. Bartlett (Albany: State University of New York Press, 2000). Section numbers in parentheses. The French text he uses is also readily available: *Pensées diverses sur la comète*, ed. A. Prat (Paris: Société des Textes Français Modernes, 1994).

43. "De superstitione" may be consulted in vol. 2 of the 16 vols. of Plutarch's *Moralia* in the Loeb Classical Library. This essay was the inspiration of a good many humanist reflections that atheism was scarcely as impious as superstitious, false religion.

44. Richard Popkin's selections from the *Dictionary*, 405. Bayle added four clarifications to the 1702 edition with the purpose of defending himself against his critics.

45. Ibid., 300, 295, 304.

46. Cf. Ovid, *Metamorphoses*, trans. Frank Justice Miller, rev. G. P. Gould, Loeb Classical Library (Cambridge: Harvard University Press, 1977), bk. 7, ll. 20–21: "video meliora proboque, / deteriora sequor."

47. For the former, see H. T. Mason, *Pierre Bayle and Voltaire* (Oxford: Oxford University Press, 1963).

48. David Hume, *A Treatise of Human Nature*, ed. L. A. Selby-Bigge (1888; rpt. Oxford: Clarendon, 1967), 413–15. Norman Kemp Smith, *The Philosophy of David Hume: A Critical Study of its Origins and Central Doctrines* (1941; rpt. London: Macmillan, 1966), stressed the influence of Bayle throughout. Moreover, Kemp Smith was persuaded that "Hume had . . . no knowledge of Spinoza's teaching, save what he derived from Bayle" (325).

49. David Hume, *An Enquiry concerning Human Understanding*, ed. Stephen Buckle (Cambridge: Cambridge University Press, 2007), chap.11.

50. Ibid.

51. Ibid., chap. 12.

52. David Hume, *Dialogues concerning Natural Religion*, ed. Dorothy Coleman (Cambridge: Cambridge University Press, 2007). Part and paragraph numbers in parentheses.

53. Cf. Bayle, "Paulicians," note E, in *Historical and Critical Dictionary: Selections*, ed. Richard Popkin, 169.

54. See Norman Kemp Smith's analysis of the argument, in his edition of *Dialogues concerning Natural Religion* (1947; rpt. Indianapolis: Library of Liberal Arts, n.d.), 57–75.

55. Dwight Culler, "The Darwinian Revolution and Literary Form," in *The Art of Victorian Prose*, ed. George Levine and William Madden (New York: Oxford University Press, 1968), 230.

56. Well after the publication of *Origin of Species* in 1859, however, Darwin professed to entertain the idea of God as the creator also. See his *Autobiography*, ed. Nora Barlow (1958; rpt. New York: Norton, 1969), 85–96.

57. References in parentheses are to volume and page in *The Complete Prose Works of Matthew Arnold*, ed. R. H. Super, 11 vols. (Ann Arbor: University of Michigan Press, 1960–77). The exhaustive annotation in this edition answers almost any question one has about the particulars in a given text. The best and most balanced assessment of the religious works is Ruth apRoberts, *Arnold and God* (Berkeley: University of California Press, 1983).

58. Arnold's turning to the question of personal immortality in his conclusion is rather like the move John Stuart Mill made at the end of his essay "Utility of Religion," published posthumously the year before in *Three Essays on Religion* (1874). See *The Collected Works of John Stuart Mill*, 33 vols. (Toronto: University of Toronto Press, 1963–91), 10:426–28. The most memorable of the three essays is "Nature."

59. In *St. Paul and Protestantism* (1869–70) Arnold proposed the *"stream of tendency by which all things seek to fulfill the law of their being"* as an idea of God that modern science might accommodate (6:10); and he defended the expression in *Literature and Dogma* (6:189). In his note to the first instance (6:423–24), R. H. Super displays the similarity of the language both to a line from Wordsworth's *Excursion* and to a passage from Spinoza's *Ethics*. But as it happens the latter refers simply to an individual person's being.

60. See U. C. Knoepflmacher, *Religious Humanism and the Victorian Novel: George Eliot, Walter Pater, and Samuel Butler* (Princeton: Princeton University Press, 1965), esp. 24–71.

61. Lionel Trilling, *Matthew Arnold* (1939; rpt. New York: Meridian, 1955), 304–5.

62. Ludwig Feuerbach, *The Essence of Christianity*, trans. George Eliot (1854; rpt. New York: Harper, 1957), 29–30, 184.

63. Peter L. Berger, *The Social Reality of Religion* (London: Faber, 1967), 28. Berger's book on comedy, thirty years on, also dwells on religion: *Redeeming Laughter: The Comic Dimension of Human Experience* (Berlin: de Gruyter, 1997).

64. *The Complete Poetical Works of Thomas Hardy*, ed. Samuel Hynes, (Oxford: Clarendon, 1984), 2:33–37.

65. In *The Art of Victorian Prose*, ed. Levine and Madden, 224–46.

66. August Wilhelm von Schlegel, *A Course of Lectures on Dramatic Art and Literature*, trans. John Black, rev. A. J. W. Morrison (London: Bohn, 1846), 176–78.

ACT THREE. LAUGHTER AT THE PASSING GENERATIONS

1. Quotations are from the five volumes of Plautus's plays in the Loeb Classical Library, newly reedited and translated by Wolfgang de Milo (Cambridge: Harvard University Press, 2011–13). Line numbers in parentheses.

2. Emrys Jones, *The Origins of Shakespeare* (Oxford: Clarendon, 1977), 13.

3. See especially Graham Bradshaw, *Shakespeare's Scepticism* (Ithaca: Cornell University Press, 1987); and A. D. Nuttall, *Shakespeare the Thinker* (New Haven: Yale University Press, 2007).

4. See Leonard Barkan, *The Gods Made Flesh: Metamorphosis and the Pursuit of Paganism* (New Haven: Yale University Press, 1986).

5. Jan M. Ziolkowski, "Juggling in the Middle Ages: The Reception of *Our Lady's Tumbler* and *Le Jongleur de Notre-Dame*," in *Studies in Medievalism* 15 (2006): 157–97.

6. See Alexander Welsh, *Reflections on the Hero as Quixote* (Princeton: Princeton University Press, 1981), 149–223.

7. See Alexander Welsh, *The City of Dickens* (1971; rpt. Cambridge: Harvard University Press, 1986), 213–28. Despite the title, this is a thematic and contextual study of Dickens's oeuvre, not topographical.

8. Postscript to *The Varieties of Religious Experience* (1902), in *The Writings of William James*, ed. John J. McDermott (New York: Modern Library, 1968), 785.

9. St. Augustine, *The City of God against the Pagans*, trans. Philip Levine, 7 vols., Loeb Classical Library (Cambridge; Harvard University Press, 1966), book 14, chap. 25.

10. *The Woman of Andros*, in *Terence*, ed. and trans. John Barsby, 2 vols., Loeb Classical Library (Cambridge: Harvard University Press, 2001). Line numbers in parentheses.

11. Northrop Frye, *A Natural Perspective: The Development of Shakespearian Comedy and Romance* (New York: Columbia University Press, 1965), 72.

12. Quotations are from *The Riverside Shakespeare*, ed. G. Blakemore Evans et al., 2nd ed. (Boston: Houghton Mifflin, 1997). Act, scene, and line numbers in parentheses.

13. See Eduard Fraenkel, *Plautine Elements in Plautus* [1922], trans. Thomas Drevikovsky and Frances Muecke (Oxford: Oxford University Press, 2007), esp. 159–72.

14. See Allardyce Nicoll, *The World of Harlequin: A Critical Study of the Commedia dell'Arte* (Cambridge: Cambridge University Press, 1963), 40–74.

15. Influence on eight of Shakespeare's comedies is persuasively set forth in Robert S. Miola, *Shakespeare and Classical Comedy: The Influence of Plautus and Terence* (Oxford: Clarendon, 1994).

16. Frye, *A Natural Perspective*, 72.

17. Robert M. Torrance, *The Comic Hero* (Cambridge: Harvard University Press, 1978), 61, 69.

18. C. L. Barber, *Shakespeare's Festive Comedy: A Study of Dramatic Form in Relation to Social Custom* (1959; rpt. New York: Meridian Books, 1963), 4–5.

19. Ibid., 92.

20. See especially Alfred Harbage, *Shakespeare and the Rival Traditions* (1952; rpt. Bloomington: Indiana University Press, 1970), 222–58.

21. Barber, *Shakespeare's Festive Comedy*, 136–38.

22. Frye, *A Natural Perspective*, 73–78, 119.

23. The following three paragraphs are adapted from my article "The Loss of Men and Getting of Children: *All's Well That Ends Well* and *Measure for Measure*," *Modern Language Review* 73 (1978): 17–28. For some historical context and additional bibliography, see the original article.

24. Northrop Frye, *The Myth of Deliverance: Reflections on Shakespeare's Problem Comedies* (Toronto: University of Toronto Press, 1983), 27–28. In this set of lectures Frye makes a point of relating the problem comedies to Shakespeare's subsequent romances.

25. Jonathan Bate, *Shakespeare and Ovid* (Oxford: Clarendon, 1993), esp. 144–51, 157–62, 215–63.

26. See *The Odyssey of Homer*, trans. Richmond Lattimore (New York: Harper and Row, 1965), bk. 19, ll. 392–466.

27. Miola, *Shakespeare and Classical Comedy*, 155–69, 174–87, 187–201.

28. Thomas Hobbes, *Leviathan*, ed. Edwin Curley (Indianapolis: Hackett, 1994), 101, 103.

29. *The Mandrake*, trans. David Sices, act 3, scene 11; in *The Comedies of Machiavelli*, bilingual edition by David Sices and James B. Atkinson (Hanover: University Press of New England, 1985).

30. Ibid., act 5, scene 4.

31. *Amphitryon; or, The Two Sosia's*, in *The Works of John Dryden*, ed. Earl Miner and George Guffey (Los Angeles: University of California Press, 1976), 15:233, 260. The play was turned out in high and low styles, with music by Henry Purcell.

32. Molière, *Oeuvres complètes*, ed. Robert Jouanny, 2 vols. (Paris: Garnier, 1962). Volume and page numbers in parentheses. I have left Molière's verse and prose untranslated but tried to be sure the meaning is clear by ample paraphrasing. Splendid English translations have been turned out over the years by Richard Wilbur, but not of these particular plays.

33. Erasmus, *Praise of Folly*, trans. Betty Radice (London: Penguin, 1993), 128.

34. Erving Goffman, *The Presentation of Self in Everyday Life* (New York: Doubleday, 1959).

35. Edmund Burke, *Reflections on the Revolution in France*, ed. William B. Todd (New York: Holt, Rinehart and Winston, 1959), 60. See Alexander Welsh, *The Hero of the Waverley Novels, with New Essays on Scott* (Princeton: Princeton University Press, 1992), 63–85.

36. Stuart Tave compares *Pride and Prejudice* to Shakespearean comedy in *Lovers, Clowns, and Fairies: An Essay on Comedies* (Chicago: University of Chicago Press, 1993), 58–59. Scott's appreciative account of *Emma* and Austen's earlier novels appeared in the *Quarterly Review* in 1815.

37. For example, see Lionel Gossman, *Between History and Literature* (Cambridge: Harvard University Press, 1990), for Scott's influence on the French historians Augustin Thierry and Jules Michelet.

38. Georg Lukács, *The Historical Novel*, trans. Hannah Mitchell and Stanley Mitchell (London: Merlin, 1962), 169.

39. William Makepeace Thackeray, *Vanity Fair: A Novel without a Hero*, ed. Geoffrey Tillotson and Kathleen Tillotson (Boston: Houghton Mifflin, 1963), 250.

40. See Alexander Welsh, *Strong Representations: Narrative and Circumstantial Evidence in England* (Baltimore: Johns Hopkins University Press, 1992), 76–99.

41. Burke, *Reflections on the Revolution in France*, 71.

42. Robert C. Gordon, *Under Which King? A Study of the Scottish Waverley Novels* (Edinburgh: Oliver and Boyd, 1969), 161.

43. Alfred Harbage's studies of Shakespeare and the history of Elizabethan and Jacobean theater are well known; in his lecture published as *A Kind of Power: The Shakespeare–Dickens Analogy* (Philadelphia: American Philosophical Society, 1975) he sketched some remarkable parallels between the dramatist's career and the novelist's.

44. "The Theme of the Three Caskets" (1913), in *The Standard Edition of the Complete Psychological Works of Sigmund Freud*, ed. James Strachey, 24 vols. (London: Hogarth, 1953–74), 12:291–301.

45. Victor Hugo, *William Shakespeare*, ed. Dominique Peyrache-Leborgne (Paris: Flammarion, 2003), 223–26. This hurriedly composed book appeared in 1864 to mark the tercentennial of Shakespeare's birth and to coincide with the publication of Hugo's son's translation of the plays.

46. Victor Hugo, *Les Misérables*, ed. Maurice Allem (Paris: Gallimard, 1951).

47. Charles Dickens, *David Copperfield* (London: Oxford University Press, 1962), 843, 877.

48. *Northanger Abbey*, in *The Novels of Jane Austen*, 3rd ed., ed. R. W. Chapman, 5 vols. (London: Oxford University Press, 1933), 5:13.

49. Charles Dickens, *Dombey and Son* (London: Oxford University Press, 1960), 92–93, 843–44.

50. Charles Dickens, *Little Dorrit* (London: Oxford University Press, 1953), 733.

51. For more on *Dombey and Son* and Shakespeare, see Alexander Welsh, *From Copyright to Copperfield: The Identity of Dickens* (Cambridge: Harvard University

Press, 1987), 87–103; and for *Little Dorrit*, "A King Lear of the Debtor's Prison," *Social Research* 70 (Winter 2003): 1205–30.

52. Retrospectively Dickens's investment in *King Lear* seems prescient, since by the mid-twentieth century *Lear* overshadowed even *Hamlet* in thoughtful appraisals and responses to Shakespeare's plays. See R. A. Foakes, *Hamlet vs. Lear: Cultural Politics and Shakespeare's Art* (Cambridge: Cambridge University Press, 1993).

53. D. H. Lawrence, *The First and Second Lady Chatterley Novels*, ed. Dieter Mehl and Christa Jansohn (Cambridge: Cambridge University Press, 1999), 223. (The opening sentence of the second version of the novel; the first began with the same statement worded slightly different.)

54. D. H. Lawrence, *Apocalypse*, introduced by Richard Aldington (New York: Viking, 1932), 39.

55. *The Diary of Virginia Woolf*, ed. Anne Olivier Bell, 5 vols. (London: Hogarth, 1977–84), 3:34.

56. José Saramago, *The Gospel According to Jesus Christ*, trans. Giovanni Pontiero (New York: Harcourt, 1994). Page numbers in parentheses. The translation capitalizes pronouns, including possessive pronouns, referring to God. In the original *O Evangelho segundo Jesus Cristo*, *Deus* is capitalized but not so the pronouns.

57. Saramago's punctuation is minimal—no question marks, exclamation marks, colons, or dashes—and he doesn't always stop to supply the speakers' names in direct discourse. The dialogue moves back and forth, alternate voices separated by commas. In his English translation Pontiero renders such exchanges easier to follow by introducing periods instead of commas at the end of each character's part.

58. It is curious, however, how even Judaism and Christianity betray tendencies to populate heaven with heroes like King David or provide a sort of family for God, as in the Trinity. See Peter Schäfer, *The Jewish Jesus: How Judaism and Christianity Shaped Each Other* (Princeton: Princeton University Press, 2012).

59. Northrop Frye, *Anatomy of Criticism* (Princeton: Princeton University Press, 1957), 215. An earlier draft of the same approach, including the last sentence here, was published as "The Argument of Comedy," in *English Institute Essays, 1948*, ed. D. A. Robertson Jr. (New York: Columbia University Press, 1949), 66.

60. Northrop Frye died in 1991, the year *O Evangelho segundo Jesus Cristo* first saw the light. José Saramago, who was awarded the Nobel Prize in Literature for 1998, died in 2010.

INDEX

Academy, 3, 47, 51–52, 58, 143
Alberti, Leon Battista, 63
Alexander the Great, 134
Anderson, Abraham, 254*n*36
anthropology, 38, 92, 165–66, 176, 245
anthropomorphism, 12, 48, 55, 86, 91–92, 94, 99, 117–18, 141, 146, 149, 162, 238, 244
Aphrodite, 11. *See also* Venus
Apollo, 12–14, 26, 162, 194, 205
apRoberts, Ruth, 255*n*57
Aquinas, St. Thomas, 101
Ares, 11. *See also* Mars
Ariosto, Ludovico, *Orlando Furioso*, 112
Aristophanes, 3, 4, 15, 16, 33, 41, 55, 62, 71; *Acharnians*, 17; *Birds*, 23–32, 33, 56, 62–63; *Clouds*, 17–23, 28, 29, 33–34, 57; *Lysistrata*, 17; *Peace*, 31
Aristotle, 15, 69, 101, 107, 208
Arnauld, Antoine, 144
Arnold, Matthew, 3, 70, 155–68; *Culture and Anarchy*, 156–57, 159; "Function of Criticism," 159; *God and the Bible*, 161–64; *Literature and Dogma*, 156, 158–61, 168; *St. Paul and Protestantism*, 160
Arnold, Thomas, 156
atheism, 67, 68, 129, 130–33, 139, 254*n*43
Athena, 11, 59
Auerbach, Erich, 15–16, 69, 219, 251*n*4
Augustine, St.: *City of God*, 88, 176–77; *Confessions*, 176
Austen, Jane, 175; *Mansfield Park*, 218; *Northanger Abbey*, 223; *Persuasion*, 218; *Pride and Prejudice*, 218

Bacon, Francis, 68, 70, 112, 141; *Essays*, 68–69, 70, 86
Balzac, Honoré de, 1, 2, 218
Barber, C. L., 184–87
Barkan, Leonard, 256*n*4
Bartlett, Robert C., 125
Bate, Jonathan, 191
Bayle, Pierre, 3–4, 123–39, 140, 147, 148, 153, 154, 160; *Dictionnaire historique et critique*, 70, 122–25, 129, 131–32, 142; *Pensées diverses sur la comète*, 125–39

Berger, Peter L., 166
Berti, Silvia, 254n36
Bible, 88, 194–95, 110–15, 128, 135, 155, 157, 163–64, 251n8; 1 Corinthians, 76, 78, 79, 80, 82, 83, 84, 96–97, 113; 2 Corinthians, 75, 78, 83, 84, 87, 113; Deuteronomy, 114, 190; Ecclesiastes, 79, 113; Exodus, 86, 107, 114, 245; Genesis, 15, 163, 215, 232; Isaiah, 79, 96; Jeremiah, 157, 160; John, 69, 85, 163, 237; Judges, 97, 112; 2 Kings, 112; Luke, 80–81, 82, 185, 233, 234, 237, 246; Matthew, 81, 104, 106, 111, 185, 214, 232, 233, 234, 235; Proverbs, 79, 85, 113; Romans, 80, 105, 111, 185
Boccaccio, Giovanni, 188
Botticelli, Sandro, 35
Bradshaw, Graham, 256n3
Brown, Alison, 250n13
Brown, Norman O., 14–15
Burke, Edmund, 47, 217, 219

Carneades of Cyrene, 51–52
Casson, Lionel, 59, 63
Catholicism, 68, 98, 99–103, 106, 124, 129, 140
Cervantes, Miguel de, Don Quixote, 175
chance, 48–49, 119, 127–28, 167–68, 184, 187, 235
Chaplin, Charlie, 206
Charpentier, Marc-Antoine, 210
Cicero, Marcus Tullius, 3, 15, 41–55, 70, 88, 90–91, 95, 132, 143, 167, 208; Academica, 42; De divinatione, 41–47, 54, 126; De natura deorum, 41–42, 46–55, 61, 91, 92, 146, 153–54; De oratore, 42–44
Cicero, Quintus Tullius, 42–43
Cleanthes of Assos, 143
commedia dell'arte, 5, 69, 175, 179–80, 202

Commines, Philippe de, 134
Copernicus, Nicolaus, 138, 145
Cornford, Francis, 250n9
Crudden, Michael, 12
Culler, Dwight, 154–55, 167–68
Curley, Edwin, 253n31
Curtius, Georg, 161–62

Dante, 1, 2
Darwin, Charles, 36–37, 155, 255n56; Origin of Species, 157, 167
Darwinism, 38, 95, 168
deism, 49, 139, 144, 147, 149
Democritus, 69
Descartes, René, 115–17, 120, 123, 161–62; Meditations, 115–16
Diagoras, 132
Diana, 40, 191
Dickens, Charles, 5, 175, 220–27; Bleak House, 221; David Copperfield, 221, 222–23; Dombey and Son, 220, 223–24; Little Dorrit, 220, 224–27; The Old Curiosity Shop, 220
Dionysius of Syracuse, 51, 52–53
divination, 43–45, 49–50, 99, 126, 131
Donne, John, 67
dramatic irony, 61, 175, 178–79, 181, 194, 197, 207, 209
Dryden, John, 172, 219; Amphitryon, 205–6
Duncan, Douglas, 251n21

Eliot, George, 164–66, 167, 220
Elizabeth I, 103
Epicureanism, 34, 39, 48, 50
Epicurus, 32, 33, 35–36, 44–46, 52, 58, 69, 101, 119, 123, 133, 141–42, 145, 149, 245
Erasmus, Desiderius, 3, 63, 70–84, 87, 90, 138, 158, 173, 242; Handbook of the Christian Soldier, 84–87; Praise of Folly, 70–84, 185, 214–15
Euripides, 17, 61, 62, 173
Eusebius, 250n18

Faulkner, William, 220
Fawkes, Guy, 68–69
fear, 34–35, 39–40, 99, 105, 108, 120, 123
Feuerbach, Ludwig, 245; *Essence of Christianity*, 165–66
Fielding, Henry, 175, 218; *Joseph Andrews*, 217; *Tom Jones*, 217
Filmer, Robert, 108
Foakes, R. A., 259n52
Fraenkel, Eduard, 256n13
Frame, Donald, 90–91
France, Anatole, 174
François I, 129
Freud, Sigmund, 221–22, 227
Friedrich, Hugo, 97
Frye, Northrop, 178, 183–84, 187, 190, 192, 200, 246–47

Galileo, 138, 145–46
Gay, Peter, 251n23
generation, 4–5, 142, 147–48, 171–72, 174, 183, 187, 188–93, 196, 204, 210, 215, 221, 224, 227, 228, 229–30, 231–32
Goethe, Johann Wolfgang von, 159, 219
Goffman, Erving, 215
Gordon, Robert, 219
Gossman, Lionel, 258n37
Gould, Stephen Jay, 250n12
Grafton, Anthony, 250n18, 251n22
Greenblatt, Stephen, 250n10

Haeckel, Ernst, 37
Halliwell, Stephen, 11
Hampshire, Stuart, 122–23
Harbage, Alfred, 257n20, 258n43
Hardy, Thomas, 220; "God's Funeral," 166–67; "Plaint to Man," 166
Henderson, Jeffrey, 18
Henri II, 129
Henry VIII, 103
Hephaestus, 11. *See also* Vulcan

Heracles, 30–31, 60
Hermes, 12–15, 17, 18, 21–23, 31, 55–56, 57, 59–62, 134, 199. *See also* Mercury
higher criticism, 104, 113, 155–56, 163–64
Hobbes, Thomas, 3–4, 67, 68, 70, 98–111, 122, 138, 164; *De Cive*, 98, 106, 107–8; *Leviathan*, 98–107, 200–202
Homer, 11–12, 49, 60; *Iliad*, 11, 128; *Odyssey*, 3, 11, 14, 75, 130, 199
Hugo, Victor, 5, 222; *Les Misérables*, 222
Huguenots, 68, 129
Huizinga, Johan, 2, 5
Hume, David, 3, 67, 70, 139–55, 156, 160, 168; *Dialogues concerning Natural Religion*, 55, 139, 143–55; *An Enquiry concerning Human Understanding*, 140–42; *History of England*, 140; *The Natural History of Religion*, 142–43; *A Treatise of Human Nature*, 140–41
Hymn to Hermes, 12–15, 57

Ibn Ezra, Abraham, 111, 113
identity, 5, 172, 174–75, 182–83, 187–88, 196, 200, 215–16, 217
impersonation, 5, 171, 180–82, 200–202, 204, 206–8, 213–15, 228
Iphigenia, 40, 52, 68–69, 90, 97, 131
Iris, 28–29
Israel, Jonathan I., 253nn27,34

James, Susan, 253n34
Jepthah, 97, 107–8
Jerome, St., 53, 133, 163, 173, 250n18
Jesus, 69, 75, 76, 79, 80, 87, 109, 114, 155, 158, 159, 163–65, 228–29. *See also* Saramago, José
Jones, Emrys, 173
Jongleur of Notre Dame, 174–75
Jupiter, 34, 45, 53, 130, 172–73, 194, 205–6. *See also* Zeus

Kaiser, Walter, 251n5
Keaton, Buster, 207; *Our Hospitality*, 208; *Steamboat Bill Jr.*, 216
Kemp Smith, Norman, 254n48, 255n54
Knoepflmacher, U. C., 255n60
Kristeller, Paul Oskar, 253n34

Labrousse, Elizabeth, 125
Lawrence, D. H., 228–29; *Aaron's Rod*, 228; *Apocalypse*, 229; *Lady Chatterley's Lover*, 228–29; "The Man Who Died," 229, 230
Lewes, G. H., 167
Lilla, Mark, 252n23
Lloyd, Genevieve, 253n34
Locke, John, 108
Louis XI, 134
Lucian, 3, 15, 55–63, 70, 141; "Death of Peregrinus," 63; "Double Indictment," 56–59; "Eros and Zeus," 57; "Hermes and Maia," 57; "Philosophies for Sale," 59; "Praising of a Fly," 63; "Zeus Tragoedus," 59–62, 63, 130
Lucretius, 3, 15, 42, 45–46, 53, 70, 93, 101, 118, 119, 123, 141, 145, 155, 219, 245; *De rerum natura*, 32–41, 68–69, 90–91, 94–95, 131, 146, 177
Lukács, Georg, 218
Lully, Jean-Baptiste, 208, 210

Machiavelli, Niccolò, 5; *Clizia*, 204; *La Mandragola*, 202–4, 207; *The Woman of Andros*, 204
Macready, William Charles, 220
Maimonides, 111
marriage, 4–5, 101–2, 173–74, 175–76, 177, 183, 185–90, 199, 209–10, 216–17, 223, 226, 228
Mars, 130. *See also* Ares
Marsh, David, 251nn21,5
Marx Brothers, *A Day at the Races*, 208
Mason, H. T., 254n47
Massenet, Jules, 174

Menander, 16, 62, 173
Mercury, 172–73, 205–6. *See also* Hermes
metaphysics, 98, 132, 142, 161–62, 168
Mill, John Stuart, 255n58
Milton, John, 67–68; *Paradise Lost*, 148
Miola, Robert, 199, 257n15
Molière, 5, 19, 172, 175, 179, 205–15, 217; *L'Amour médecin*, 208–9; *Amphitryon*, 205; *Le Malade imaginaire*, 210–13; *Le Médecin malgré lui*, 207–8, 212; *Le Médecin volant*, 206–7; *Le Misanthrope*, 207, 221; *Le Tartuffe*, 209, 211, 213–14
Momus, 60
Montaigne, Michel de, 3–4, 70, 88–97, 105, 130, 146, 245; "Apology for Raymond Sebond," 89–97; "Of Custom," 88; "Of Experience," 88
More, Sir Thomas, 3, 63; *Utopia*, 74
Moses, 104, 107, 109, 114

nature, 32–37, 40–41, 44–45, 52, 67–69, 75, 95, 107, 111–12, 117–20, 129 139, 144–45, 146, 153, 187, 195–97, 255n58
New Comedy, 4–5, 167–68, 171–72, 177–79, 182–85, 191, 196, 200, 204, 208, 215–16, 220, 227–28, 230–32, 236, 244
Nicoll, Allardyce, 257n14
Nietzsche, Friedrich, 228
Nuttall, A. D., 256n3

Old Comedy, 15, 16–32, 57, 172, 178
Origen, 84
Ovid, 32, 186; *Metamorphoses*, 112, 136, 174, 191

Pan, 57–58
Panofsky, Erwin, 251n1
parturition, 186–87, 193, 223, 227
Paul, St., 75–76, 78–80, 83–85, 87, 105

Pentateuch, 104, 141
Pettit, Philip, 252n20
Philon of Larrisa, 143
Pirandello, Luigi, 172
Plato, 15, 19, 55, 69, 84, 85; *Republic*, 83
Plautus, Titus Maccius, 4, 5, 69, 71,
    173, 178–79, 216; *Amphitruo*, 172–73,
    205; *Casina*, 204; *Menaechmi*, 178;
    Mostellaria, 182–83; *Pseudolus*,
    182–83
Plutarch, 93–94, 129, 130–31
Pontiero, Giovanni, 230
Popkin, Richard, 88, 252n14
Poseidon, 21, 30–31, 60
Preus, J. Samuel, 253n29
Prometheus, 29–31, 62
Protestants, 89, 101, 124, 129, 140, 202

Renan, Ernest, *Life of Jesus*, 164–65,
    168
Romulus, 130

Saramago, José, 67, 259n60; *The
    Gospel According to Jesus Christ*, 5,
    67, 176, 230–47
satire, 15, 18, 34, 57, 73–77, 138, 149,
    161, 203, 225
satiric catalogue, 92, 99, 127, 240–42
Schäfer, Peter, 259n58
Schlegel, August Wilhelm von,
    167, 184
Sebond, Raymond, 89
Seneca, 93
Shakespeare, William, 5, 173–74, 175,
    180–99, 201, 218, 256n12; *All's Well
    That Ends Well*, 173–74, 187–90; *As
    You Like It*, 184, 187; *The Comedy of
    Errors*, 173, 178, 180, 182, 187;
    Hamlet, 174, 199; *Henry IV*, 219–20;
    King Lear, 174, 181–82, 199, 220–22,
    224–25, 227; *Love's Labor's Lost*,
    185–86; *Measure for Measure*, 173–74,
    187–88, 189, 190; *Pericles*, 174,
    190–92, 194, 199; *The Taming of the*

Shrew, 180–81, 182; *The Tempest*,
    174, 190–91, 197–99; *Troilus and
    Cressida*, 188; *Twelfth Night*, 184, 187;
    The Winter's Tale, 174, 190–91,
    192–97, 198, 199
Shaw, George Bernard, 228; *Man and
    Superman*, 228
Sidwell, Keith, 56
Silk, M. S., 249n7
Skinner, Quentin, 252nn21,23
Smith, Steven B., 253n31
Socinians, 119, 123
Socrates. *See* Aristophanes: *Clouds*
soul, 35, 38, 46, 79, 83–85, 90,
    100–101, 135, 142, 175, 206, 210,
    223, 229, 232, 242
Spinoza, Baruch, 3–4, 70, 108–21, 130,
    132, 138; *Ethics*, 115–22, 139, 165;
    Theological-Political Treatise, 108–15,
    122, 164
Stoicism, 43–45, 50, 119
Strauss, David Friedrich, *The Life of
    Jesus, Critically Examined*,
    164–65
Strauss, Richard, and Hugo von
    Hofmannsthal, *Der Rosenkavalier*,
    228
superstition, 36, 39, 43, 54, 67–68,
    100, 129–31, 140, 151–52, 156,
    254n43

Tave, Stuart, 258n36
Terence, 4, 69, 173, 178–79; *The
    Woman of Andros*, 177, 204
Thackeray, William Makepeace, *Vanity
    Fair*, 218–19
theologians, 75–76, 89, 125, 127, 138,
    153–54, 165
theology, 70, 114, 118, 123, 151, 158,
    162, 183
Tolstoy, Lev, *War and Peace*, 218
Torrance, Robert, 184
tragicomedy, 5, 172, 174, 187, 190, 192,
    216–30, 231, 246

Traité des trois imposteurs, 122
Trilling, Lionel, 166

Vanini, Giulio Cesare, 132
Venus, 35, 227. *See also* Aphrodite
Virgil, 32, 86
Voltaire, 139
Vulcan, 75–76. *See also* Hephaestus

Wagner, Richard: *Die Meistersinger von Nürnberg*, 227–28; *Tannhäuser*, 227; *Die Walküre*, 227
Waldron, Jeremy, 253*n*25

Whitman, Cedric, 17
Wilbur, Richard, 257*n*32
Wilde, Oscar, *The Importance of Being Earnest*, 228
Wind, Edgar, 251*n*1
Woolf, Virginia, *To the Lighthouse*, 229–30

Yovel, Yirmiyahu, 253*nn*27,28

Zeus, 12–14, 19–20, 21, 26–27, 29–31, 33–34, 56–57. *See also* Jupiter
Ziolkowski, Jan M., 256*n*5